Charles Henry Butcher

Armenosa of Egypt

A Romance of the Arab Conquest

Charles Henry Butcher

Armenosa of Egypt
A Romance of the Arab Conquest

ISBN/EAN: 9783744760799

Printed in Europe, USA, Canada, Australia, Japan

Cover: Foto ©ninafisch / pixelio.de

More available books at **www.hansebooks.com**

Armenosa of Egypt

A Romance

of

The Arab Conquest

BY

CHARLES HENRY BUTCHER

D.D., F.S.A.

CHAPLAIN AT CAIRO; FORMERLY DEAN OF THE
CATHEDRAL, SHANGHAI, CHINA

WILLIAM BLACKWOOD AND SONS
EDINBURGH AND LONDON
MDCCCXCVII

PREFATORY NOTE.

My warmest acknowledgments are due to Mr A. J. Butler, of Brasenose College, Oxford, for the help which his admirable work on the Coptic Churches of Egypt and his valuable suggestions have given me in writing this book.

CONTENTS.

CONTENTS.

NOTES.

CONTENTS.

CONTENTS.

NOTES.

INTRODUCTION.

THE seventh century offers generous opportunities to the writer of Romance. There is a background of authentic and important history, and there are figures moving on the borderland between fact and fiction which fulfil all the requirements of the story-teller. The sceptical historian of the school of Von Ranke and Weil is obliged to dismiss characters and incidents related by the Moslem Al Wakidi and the English Ockley, but we may well turn to those delightful authors for our plot and personages while we strive to be absolutely accurate in our picture of the period.

When this tale begins, the Emperor Heraclius had closed the last of the six campaigns which freed the world for ever from the dominion of Persia. Had he died in 629 he would have ranked with Alexander,

Hannibal, and Cæsar as one of the great world-conquerors. The victory over Chosroes and the deliverance of the East from the Zoroastrians was one of the many blessings which the great Byzantine sovereigns conferred on the world. But no sooner was Dastagerd, the treasure city of the Persians, taken than a cloud arose among the Arabs, like that which develops into a tremendous Genius in one of their own stories, and suddenly the forces of New Rome, wearied with a seven years' war, had to confront the fresh armies of fanatic Islam. Again the battle is between two races and two religions, and in Egypt, where our scene is laid, two remarkable champions were opposed to each other. The Arabs were led by Amru or Amr, called Amr-ibn-al-Asi; the representative Christian was the Copt George the Pagarch, called the Mukaukis.

Amr was one of the bravest warriors of Islam. After a brilliant campaign in Syria he obtained permission of Omar to invade Egypt with a force of five thousand men. He took Perenum or Farma and Belbeis, where he was opposed by the Egyptian militia, who were Copts; then he laid siege to Babylon, the fortress of which the remains are still visible in Old Cairo. Amr in many points anticipated the highly idealised figure of the Kurd Salâh-ad-Dîn, the virtuous Saladin of Dante, the hero of Scott's 'Talisman.' Thus in him Mohammedanism is seen at its best, while the foremost Christian of Egypt was a mysterious character whose action is difficult to explain and impossible to justify. So many and hard are the problems connected with George the son of Mennas that Von Ranke doubts whether such a person ever existed, and even writers of high authority still confuse his name and his title of honour. The Papyrus documents in the collection of the Archduke Rainer have yielded their secrets to the German archæologist Karabacek, and his monograph on the Mukaukis of Egypt has explained one of the hardest enigmas of the Islamite Conquest. It is impossible to understand the man and his unique position without first making an effort to comprehend the state of Egypt political and religious.

The key to the political situation was the ever-increasing exhaustion of the empire brought to a crisis by the life-and-death struggle with Persia. All through his reign Heraclius had been hampered by want of money. He was weighed down by the extravagance of his surroundings. To quote the historian Finlay: "The luxury of the Roman Court had during ages of unbounded wealth and unlimited power assembled round the Emperor an infinity of courtly offices and caused an enormous expenditure which it was extremely dangerous to suppress and impossible to continue." This had been so strongly felt that Heraclius had actually contemplated removing the seat of empire to Carthage. If this strain was felt before the Persian war, it was intensified during its continuance. Heraclius wanted money above all things. Chosroes had held Egypt, the granary of Rome, for nine years, and the man who had the financial control of Egypt and the task of collecting the revenues from its peasantry was George the son of Mennas, called the Pagarch, whose title of honour, $\mu\epsilon\gamma\alpha\nu\chi\acute{\eta}s$, "Your Excellency" or "Your Magnificence," has been perverted into a proper name by every English historian from Gibbon to Bury.

Though some of this man's acts bear a more favourable interpretation than is usually placed on them, ambition and perhaps avarice were strong motives with him. He had extraordinary opportunities of enriching himself, and during the Persian occupation he had a valid excuse for not remitting the

Egyptian tribute to Constantinople. A large portion of this tribute he has been accused of appropriating to himself. Certainly when the Emperor was firmly reseated on his throne the arrears were impatiently required. Dreading lest if he failed to meet these demands he would be superseded or disgraced, the Pagarch is believed to have trafficked with the Arabs, and in spite of Von Ranke, it seems possible that at an earlier day he had exchanged messages and gifts with the Prophet Mohammed. Still it is surprising that he did not lose the favour of Heraclius, though the existence of a story recording the betrothal of Armenosa and Constantine affords *prima facie* evidence for believing he retained that favour to the last.

Of this there are two explanations. First, he may by enormous efforts have actually sent large sums to Constantinople, though still retaining enough to maintain his splendid position in Egypt. Secondly, he may have pleased Heraclius by accepting as satisfactory his cherished scheme of religious comprehension—the Monothelite doctrine.

This leads us to note the situation of the two great religious parties whose differences were intertwined so closely with the politics of the day. The

Jacobites, or Monophysites, who had affirmed the one nature of Christ and had been condemned at the Council of Chalcedon or Constantinople, were strongest in Egypt, comprising in fact the native Egyptians; but the garrison and a large number of the officials were Melchites or Kingsmen. Thus there was constant danger of friction between the army of occupation and the populace. The legionaries of New Rome had just gained a series of victories, and freed Egypt from Chosroes; they were therefore disposed to look down on the natives, and were perhaps not sorry to have the term "heretic" to hurl at them. But experience proved that the Egyptian people were not to be browbeaten or oppressed with safety. The seafaring population of Alexandria had always been formidable. The wealthy citizens of Memphis had an organised militia force well equipped and disciplined, and the Jacobite priesthood had far-reaching influence. The Emperor longed to make peace between the contending parties. He hoped to do it by the adoption of the term Monothelite for Monophysite, thus affirming one will or "theandric energy" instead of one nature in Christ. It seems incredible that George, a native Egyptian, should have held the place he did had he been a Jacobite.

It is certain he was not a Melchite. All the discrepancies are cleared up if we believe him to have professed the faith of the Emperor. Thus he would have been enabled to preserve the position of intermediary between his nation and his sovereign, which he was maintaining with such marvellous tact when this story opens.

ARMENOSA OF EGYPT.

CHAPTER I.

HOW THE HOLY RELIC WAS BROUGHT TO MEMPHIS.

On a certain spring day, in the year of Christ 639, the people of Egypt were keeping a double holiday. First it was a day of great moment to the Church, when a holy relic sent by the Emperor Heraclius was to be carried in solemn pomp to the great cathedral of Memphis. It was also a popular festival, dating from time immemorial, and known as The Smelling of the Zephyr. The secular holiday corresponded to the spring festival in the old Roman calendar—the Feast of Flora, which reappears year by year in Europe, when young men and maidens, with the excuse of a saint's day to aid them, go

A

forth to celebrate the coming of May. It is the
festival of the opening spring, when everything in
nature tells of winter past and genial days to come,
when life and hope begin to burgeon once more in
the fields and gardens of the old, old world, when
fresh thoughts of quickening love pulse gladly in
the young man's heart, and touch the maiden's
cheek with the glowing hue of the rose.

In Egypt the winter has no biting rost or angry
storms, so the contrast of its seasons is not violent
as with us. But on this day the balm in the air
has a spell to invite city dwellers and villagers
to go afield, and blends, perhaps by some subtle tie
of blood, with the reminiscence of a happy primeval
worship that brightened men's lives before a temple
or a pyramid was raised by the religions of Fear.

Those who could not leave the city decorated
their houses and shops with palm branches and
rose wreaths, to make them look as much like the
country as possible. Every man who had a garden
invited his friends, and spread tables piled with
fruits wrapped in cool leaves. But the people
loved best to go beyond the city limits and wander
in the groves of palm and acacia and tamarisk,
dancing and singing to the pipe and the cymbals,

and stretching themselves on the ground in the pleasant shade.

The island of Rhoda was the favourite resort. Here the rose-gardens were crowded with the richer citizens, and tents of many colours were pitched, and men and maidens wandered in the groves of orange and myrtle, and their elders sat on carpets covering the steps of marble and alabaster that descended to the sacred river. The Nile itself was sparkling with a flotilla of skiffs and barges. Each boat was gay with waving streamers and merry with music. And ever and anon the laughter rang in silvery peals as one crew splashed another in passing with the spray of its gilded oars.

But in Memphis the ecclesiastical function dominated the popular feast. The city was in holiday dress; the streets, as well as the fields and gardens, were filled with an ever-moving crowd clad in the gayest colours; but, besides all this, the churches were festooned with flowers. Wooden arches were erected in the great thoroughfare. The ancient lake of Menes glittered with small pleasure-boats,—some shaped like birds, others like flowers, others resembling the Turkish caïque or the Venetian gondola. Here, as on the Nile, the water-parties waged mimic war, pelting each other with roses and sweatmeats ; and the passengers in the streets exchanged jokes and banter, laughing and clapping hands at every humorous incident, after the manner of good-natured crowds in all ages and countries.

But as the morning advanced, the noisier sports ceased. Processions of priests appeared with crosses and banners. Signs of some transaction unusual on a spring festival were visible. In the principal square scaffolds were erected to seat the great ones of the city; and since dawn workmen had been actively employed in putting up extra supports for the structures that were expected to be most crowded, and in covering the planks with silken carpets and embroidered drapery. Jugglers and showmen were performing in all the open spaces, and sherbet-sellers with their clinking cups and porous bottles were busy supplying the wants of the spectators, and inviting the thirsty to drink without fee or charge at the expense of the Most Excellent and Benevolent the Pagarch,[1] whose liberality flowed as the river.

Though the festivity was general, and the poorest lanes in the city and suburbs showed their few

[1] See Note A, The Pagarch.

strips of triangular scarlet cloth, and their lamps
ready to contribute a tiny gleam to the night's
illumination, the centre of the pageant was the
ancient church of St Gabriel the Harbinger, which
stood opposite the huge remains of the house of
Ptah, now known as the White Church. The
bronze doors of the sanctuary were wide open.
Urns steaming with fragrant incense were placed
in its porch and between the pillars of its long
colonnade. The steps were covered with carpets,
and acolytes and vergers were busy marshalling
those whose rank gave them the right of occupying
the scarlet chairs on the great dais. Precautions
were taken in case of riot; for though the people
were gay and good-humoured, there was always
danger in Egypt from the religious passions. Melchites and Jacobites were as little likely to mix as
oil and water, and at any moment the men now
laughing and jesting together might fly at each
other's throats. To guard against this danger, small
bodies of legionaries were placed at irregular intervals amongst the mass of sightseers, and, wherever
they could be masked by porch or parapet, larger
bodies were drawn up fully armed. A soldier's eye
would have detected that these troops were scientifi-

cally disposed, and that at any moment they could occupy every post of vantage and surround the great square.

The crowd had begun to collect at daylight. Now, as the day advanced, the discordant noises of the multitude settled into a low hum of anticipation. A pathway was cleared through the street from the Governor's palace to the Church of the Archangel, and the people began to question and discuss the object of their gathering together.

"They won't be long now—see, the lictors are clearing the way. Well done, lictors! clear out the Jacobite scum and let the Emperor's loyal and faithful lieges have the front benches to themselves. Who can enjoy the sight of the holy relic or reap the full benefit of His Beatitude's benediction if he is jostled by an unsavoury heretic and——"

The speaker, a corpulent critic, whose stained arms and hands showed the traces of the dyeing-vat he worked in, was interrupted by his neighbour, a sharp-faced druggist—

"Silence, Lampo! Is this the day to rip up sores and call ugly names? Is the divine Heraclius as orthodox as he should be? *I* don't know, nor you either; perhaps he is, perhaps he is not. The man

who has banged Chosroes and his sun-worshippers
out of Egypt and restored the true cross to
Jerusalem may think as he pleases, and when he
honours Memphis with a peculiar mark of his
favour, and the trusty and well-beloved Pagarch
spends a thousand pieces on olibanum to set the
censers asmoke, the best we can do is to thank the
saints and keep silence about dangerous questions."

"Right, friend," struck in a grim ruffian in a
leather apron. "I have seen tongues that cackled
too freely stuck through with a hissing hot skewer
before now, so take my advice and keep quiet."

"No offence, no offence; *upon my tongue a big ox
has trodden,* quoth the man in the play," said the
dyer, turning pale and fidgeting uneasily.

"You are more glib with heathen stage plays
than holy homilies, it seems, friend," said a tall
monk in a goatskin mantle.

"In for it again," muttered Lampo. "This
corner is getting too warm for me;" and the poor
fellow slunk off through an opening in the crowd,
and left his place to the druggist, who slipped into
it with a complaisant smile.

"I only came to Memphis from the Thebaid last
night," said the monk, "so I know not the cause

of this solemnity. Is it the consecration of a bishop?"

"The divine Emperor has presented an inestimable relic, even a fragment of the true cross, to the Church of St Gabriel the Harbinger. It has been set in a frame of gold and rubies, and is to be displayed at the celebration of the Adorable Mysteries this morning."

"Thrice blessed was the chance that brought me hither on an auspicious day. Thou needst not stoop, friend," to the druggist. "I could see easily over thy head were another cubit added to thy stature. Here they come."

The procession, which was long and splendid, now came in sight. First, to clear the way, appeared a troop of running footmen, selected for their speed and grace of limb. These men, who have been from the earliest days a feature in Egyptian pageants, were attired in jackets of gold embroidery, had their legs bare, and carried white wands. They were followed by two bands of music—one consisting of metallic, the other of stringed, instruments, which played alternately. The silver trumpets and clashing cymbals of the first were supposed to stir the pulses of the valiant Greeks, and the flutes and

citherns of the second gave undoubted pleasure to
the less martial Egyptians. After this a space was
interposed, and then the military part of the
pageant began. It was headed by Celadion, the
commandant of the imperial fortress of Babylon.

Before the Persian invasion, high commands in
the army were oftenest bestowed by favouritism.
The friend of a eunuch or a Court lady had the best
chance, unless the War Minister were a needy man,
when the posts were shamelessly sold. But in the
campaign against Chosroes these officers had been
weeded out. Some had disgraced themselves by
notorious proofs of incapacity. Others had wisely
retired from the service, to make way for men who
knew the trade of war. None knew it better than
Celadion. Trained at the camp at Issus, and distinguished at the Phasis and at Dastagerd, he was
at the close of the war appointed to Egypt; and
Heraclius never made a wiser choice. To-day he
looked a thorough soldier. His armour, of old
Roman fashion, was of frosted silver; his high crest
was surrounded with a laurel chaplet, his truncheon
crowned with a winged Victory, his cream-coloured
steed trapped and bridled with blue leather. The
legionaries marched behind him with the measured

tread, evenly sloped spears, and faultless line which
always impress undisciplined masses. A perfectly
ordered, highly polished, keenly bristling war-
machine, the long lines of men moved between the
mass of sight-seers until the eye grew weary of the
monotony. A company of Soudanese bowmen, who
were lately enlisted for the border wars always
going on, brought up the rear of the army. Then
very different figures appeared.

These were the craftsmen marching under their
several flags with emblems of their trades, and the
counsellors and judges of Memphis. Once more a
space intervened; and then, with censer-bearers
and choristers on either hand, came a superb ivory
inlaid car in which sat the Pagarch.

This was the title by which George was distinguished. His functions were of the first importance,
for he was Collector of Taxes, Sheriff, and Head of
the Finance. He controlled the public administration, the taxes and police, the municipality and
public works of the great city, which even in those
days of decadence displayed, to use the phrase of
our own Gibbon, "the magnificence of ancient
kings." On this day of festival he sat by the
side of the imperial envoy, a holy bishop carrying

in a bag of imperial purple the inestimable and
miraculous relic—the wonder-working fragment of
the true cross. Hitherto the emblazoned robes and
jewels, the armour and the weapons, had attracted
attention, but at last the eyes of all were fixed on
a man. Yet that man was not the Byzantine
ecclesiastic, who was a grey withered ascetic, his
shaven head half-hidden by the stiff embroidery of
a cope; it was George the Pagarch, who filled the
scene directly he entered on it. He wore a robe
of white, and carried in his hand a rod or sceptre
of office surmounted by a ring-dove, which was the
emblem of the Byzantine sovereignty in Egypt, as
a hawk had been the crest or symbol of the
Pharaohs. The same device appeared on the canopy
of his chariot and on the harness of his horses, and
was curiously connected with his title of office. He
was the most familiar figure in the whole procession,
and every eye had been looking for the delegate who
bore the relic; but beside the Pagarch most men
would have seemed insignificant. Thin, nervous,
and delicate of feature, rather below the middle
height, he attracted by the brightness of his eye,
his vivid gestures, and the mixture of grace and
command that every movement presented. His

bodyguard and ensigns closed the procession, which
now halted in the middle of the great square. Then
at a signal from Celadion the trumpet sounded and
the soldiers formed in two lines on either side of St
Gabriel's Church. The guilds of craftsmen divided
and branched off to the right and left. Then the
military music ceased and the chants of monks and
priests arose. Singing the glorious psalm which was
first sung when David brought the ark from the
house of Obed-edom, the long array of acolytes,
choristers, priests, and bishops descended the steps,
and, halting midway, met the venerable delegate,
who, supported by the Pagarch, carried the holy
relic with trembling hands into the great church.
There, after solemn service and a celebration of the
Adorable Mysteries, it was confided to the perpetual
keeping of the Bishop of Memphis and the clergy,
priests, and deacons of the Church of St Gabriel the
Harbinger.

It was high noon when the solemn service was
over, and the square baked in the white scorching
sunshine. The people, who had been awed into
silence while the ceremony was going on, had grown
impatient, and were surging to and fro, eager for the

departure of the great ones. For with them would march off the legionaries who had been penning them in behind a wall of steel for some four or five burning hours. At last the time of release came, and like water through an open sluice the mob flowed out into the thoroughfares, shouting, laughing, and gesticulating in the delight of recovered liberty.

CHAPTER II.

HOW THE PRIEST MENAS WAS ROBBED OF THE SACRED CHALICE.

"Take care — keep back — you have crushed my foot."

"Dog of a Jew! do you push before an ordained deacon? Things have come to a pretty pass."

"Saints and angels! shall we ever get home without broken bones?"

"Keep your blue hands off my new silk chlamys, you dyeing-vat!"

"A drink of water. Hand it down to me, and I will see if I have a copper-piece for you."

"I can't reach it. The press is carrying me well off my feet."

"Take care of the old man. It is the holy priest Menas."

"A blessing on me, father. Benédiction from a priest is better for the rheumatism than all the drugs in your shop, apothecary."

"Not if he is a Jacobite."

"Oh no. Of course that makes a difference. Blessed be the saints! we shall get cured of all our ailments now we have got a fragment of the true cross in our city."

These and a hundred cries like these rose from the hustling and tossing crowd as they pushed and trampled and jostled to get out into the open square which the removal of the cordon of soldiers had opened to them, only to find their way instantaneously blocked by a cross-stream of people coming from a side-street. Heat and pressure were no respecters of persons. The sedan of the chief magistrate's wife was crushed against the fruit-seller's ass, and the richest Hebrew in Memphis found himself struggling with a huge parsley-crowned prize-fighter. A pedagogue was a target for a hail of peach-stones delivered by some of his urchins who had climbed to the frieze of a convenient portico. Huge black slaves were trying with rhinoceros-hide whips to make a way for a grand Justiciary; but the spirit of the people was roused, and the negroes were disarmed, knocked down, and yelling under the lashes of their own courbashes in the twinkling of an eye.

"Down with you, heathen pigs! Shame, shame on the Christian who keeps black swine to strike the free citizens of Memphis!—guardians of the relic of the true cross."

In vain did the unfortunate judge endeavour to pacify the multitude by abject apologies, and at the same time to outvoice the loudest of them in abuse of his negroes. The whole scene was agitated. The tempers and humours of the crowd had been held in check too long, and now found furious vent in violent banter and rude horse-play. The donkey-boys with heavy sticks were fighting and pushing for fares, and the citizens who tried to bargain with them were shouted at and mocked as niggards and hucksters.

"Who would haggle for a miserable obol on a day like this?" cried one.

"The miser Harpax, who rolls in gold-pieces, to be sure," answered another.

"Shame, shame, shame!" shouted the chorus.

"Take my Eutychus," said a third boy; "the red velvet saddle will match your ladyship's robe to

a nicety. Nay, then, save an obol and foul your
dainty buskins in the mire."

The tide of men, women, and children, horses,
mules, and asses, surged through the streets; but at
last, by little and little, they dwindled away down
side-alleys, or took shelter in their homes or the
houses of their friends, and the lictors had time to
pause and wipe their hot faces, and to look ruefully
to the cuts and bruises they had received in the
cause of order.

In one narrow street at some distance from the
church lay a victim of the festival whose case was
piteous indeed. This was the priest Menas, who, as
we have seen, had been recognised and compassion-
ated by the crowd. He was an old man, who served
one of the most ancient churches in Babylon,[1] and
who had not ventured out to take part in the spec-
tacle, but to adminster the Holy Eucharist to a sick
man in a distant suburb. He was usually reckoned
too old and infirm to perform any outdoor duties,
but in order to let younger priests share in the
pageant he had undertaken this mission, and faith-
fully performed it. He had hoped to get back
through side-streets which he knew, while the multi-

---

[1] See Note B, The Roman Fortress of Babylon.

B

tude were occupied in the great square; but the office with the dying and the subsequent consolation of the friends had taken a longer time than he had expected, and he found himself entangled in the dense mass of human beings at the moment when they were released from their imprisonment between the lines of soldiers.

The result was that he was hustled and thrown from his mule. Some friendly hand dragged him out of the middle of the road under the shelter of a block of stone, the headless and legless body of some ancient Nile god, and thus he escaped being trampled on. He had fallen into a swoon, and lay on his side. His long white beard was covered with mire; his high forehead was gashed with a sharp stone; and his robe was torn and draggled; but he held fast the golden chalice used in his ministry, and kept a fold of his sleeve wrapped tightly over it.

After he had lain some time the street cleared, and only a stray passenger or two was threading his way through the narrow alley, which, as it did not lead to a frequented part of the town, was then wellnigh deserted.

The world has not much chauged since the days

when the Master told the story of the "Good Sam-
aritan," and the worshippers who had crowded the
great church that day were as disinclined as men
had been six centuries before to translate the lessons
of the Gospel into act.

Noon had gone by. For an hour only two groups
passed. One was a courtier attended by two beautiful boys—one carrying his state mantle, the other
holding a parasol over his head. He moved carefully, picking his way through the mire, and chiding
his page for choosing such a disgusting way home.
He came suddenly on Menas and uttered a pettish
cry, for his golden-fringed buskin was stained with
the little runnel of blood which flowed from the cut
in the priest's forehead.

"Whom have we here? Some holy man who has
taken more wine than he can carry. Well, we will
let him sleep off his fit and wish him joy of his wak-
ing. Hold the parasol slantwise, Hylas. At present
it shelters your own head and leaves mine to be
baked by the sunbeams. Make haste or we shall
be late at the Pagarch's." And the great man went
his way.

The next passenger was a richly jewelled and
floridly painted lady borne aloft by four slaves in a

high sedan or litter. The foremost of them stumbled in his swinging stride over the unhappy priest's foot, and got soundly rated by his mistress.

" That is the second time you have nearly dropped me into the street. First it was into a dust-heap, now it is on the top of some diseased beggar. You will pay for this when you get home. What are you stopping for ? "

" There is a poor man grievously wounded," said a female slave, who was nearly fainting in her attempts to keep pace with the bearers, and who had signalled them to stop.

" Very likely. There are sure to have been brawls and fighting-bouts on a day like this, and you are glad enough to loiter in the streets to avoid the whipping I promised you. It will be sundown before we get home at this rate. Forward ! I shall have no time to bathe and dress for the Pagarch's." And the rich banker's wife swept on with her panting retinue.

An hour passed, and a humbler figure than these checked his hurried step before the fragment of granite and looked at the prostrate figure it sheltered. The new-comer was an austere man in a black robe, who discharged the office of a precentor in a chapel near the White Church. He said nothing, but stopped at once and knelt by the side of his unfortunate brother. For an instant it seemed as if he would obey his first kind impulse, but he checked himself and rose hurriedly.

" It is not my place to keep breath in the body of a heretic. There are enough of them and to spare, and every one that aids or succours them is guilty of their sin and will share their condemnation." So saying, he arose with an effort that showed his heart was softer than his creed, and departed to sing evensong in the choir of St Theophistus.

The priest's footsteps had scarcely died away when a very different figure approached. This time the passenger was not a person of rank or religion. He was a tall young man with a tunic and robe of black and a peaked cap and yellow girdle, which marked him for a Jew even when the light was too uncertain to see his features. He came stealthily along with a deprecating bend of the head and a noiseless step. Like the others, he stopped before the prostrate Menas and at once recognised him. He felt his pulse. He cautiously rolled back his large covering sleeve and drew away the sacred chalice. He felt it, weighed it in his hands, and examined closely and

carefully the chasing, the monogram, the figure of
the Christ in high relief, the five onyx stones. Then
he lifted the robe and felt if there was any other
precious vessel beneath its folds. The attempt to
rifle the treasure he was so jealously guarding awoke
Menas. He opened his eyes and clutched the hand
of the robber with a tight clasp. The Jew struggled,
but he did not want to loose his hold of the chalice,
which he held in his right hand, and so he was hampered and could not use his full strength to get free.
Though the contest was unequal, for one man was
old and weak with loss of blood and the other in full
vigour, the fact that the youth had to hold the cup
as high as he could out of the other's reach, and that
the old man had both hands free and was able to
battle passionately with the thief, placed the former
at a disadvantage. Of course it would have been
easy to throw the sacred cup out of reach and to
stun the priest with a single blow, but this the Jew
hesitated to do, and indeed, when he found such
unexpected resistance he seemed for a moment in-
clined to give back the stolen property, and to
pretend the attempt had not been a serious one.

"Be quiet, father; I thought you were a peaceable
old carle who would understand a frolic, instead of

which you are fighting like a demoniac or a wild cat
for a few ounces of gold, which you shall have back
in a minute if you will take your grip off my wrist."

"Liar! You would ravish the sacred vessels and
put them to abominable uses. Restore the chalice
or beware my ban. Hands that have wrought less
abominable sacrifice than yours have been blasted
in the act. The God who could wither the arm
of Jeroboam can speak a word of power at which
your arm, stalwart as it is, shall shrivel and shrink.
Help! help! To the rescue, ye faithful!"

The cries, which were uttered in a voice wonderfully strong and vigorous, were at last heard, and
an answering shout and hurrying steps told of assistance at hand. Flinging himself free by a savage
effort from the nervous hold of the priest, the robber
dashed off down a side-alley which led in the direction of the Jews' Quarter.

Meantime the new-comer, whose voice had reas-
sured Menas by his answering hail, dashed upon
the scene down the steep street, stopped himself
by clutching the granite block, and swung round
to face—his father.

"Marcus! my son!"

The eyes that had been kindling with fire and

passion gushed out with tears, and with a great
sob the old man fell back. In an instant, however, he recalled his loss.

"God and the saints be praised for guiding you
here, but haste or it will be too late. Follow the
villain, who ran down that street to the left—no,
not the first turning, the second—and take from
him our golden chalice set with onyxes that he
has reft from me. Run; I am well and need no
care. Get the holy cup back, my son. He has
start of you, and is as fleet of foot as Ahimaaz."

Without pausing Marcus hurried off. He was a
runner famous in the stadium, sound and strong
in wind and limb, and though it was growing dark,
and he was a stranger to the winding and uneven
street, he soon came in sight of the robber. Perhaps the Jew repented the impulse which had
prompted him to take the cup, and was anxious
to avoid discovery. He could not be under any
mistake as to the rapidly diminishing distance between him and his pursuer, and so he turned suddenly round, and flinging one cloaked arm across
his face to prevent recognition, dashed the chalice
in the face of Marcus, and making a clever feint
as if he were going to take shelter under a neigh-

bouring portico, turned suddenly down a narrow passage leading to the river and disappeared. Though disappointed at not being able to secure and punish the robber, Marcus was glad that his main object, the recovery of the chalice, was secured, and resolved to waste no time in a fruitless pursuit. He hurried back to his father, and the sight of the cherished cup acted like a medicine on the spirits of the old priest.

"Thanks to the Virgin and St Sergius, sacrilegious hands have not been allowed to retain thee, O thrice precious treasure of the Lord!" he said, folding it carefully in the silken veil, a corner of which he pressed reverently to his lips.

By the help of his son he then rose and mounted his mule, which had strayed into a street close by, and was contentedly browsing on a heap of berseem dropped by a chariot-driver. The old man was too much shaken in body to bear being carried at a brisker pace than a walk, and so father and son proceeded slowly homewards. They dwelt at some distance from Memphis, in a house near the ancient Church of St Sergius, in the midst of the Roman fortress-city of Babylon.

CHAPTER III.

ARMENOSA.[1]

FOR several days Marcus was in close attendance on his father, but after a week of careful nursing the old man declared himself well enough to go out, as he was anxious to see the Pagarch on business of pressing importance. He had, however, overestimated his strength, as he found when he attempted to rise and dress himself, so a compromise was effected, and Marcus was commissioned to go and ask the great man to name a day when he would be disengaged and able to accord to Menas the favour of an interview. The relations between the two fathers were intimate. They had been schoolfellows, and had both been intended originally for the ecclesiastical office.

[1] See Note C, Armenosa.

They had read the same books and shared the same enthusiasms. The theological questions which seem to us perplexing enigmas, and often insoluble riddles, were the dominating studies of the age, and the two students sought to unravel their perplexities with equal ardour. Menas was more reverent and perhaps less alert of brain than his companion. His character was pure, high-minded, and simple. Less versed than his brethren in the intricate doctrinal disputes that formed in that age the daily bread of religious life, he was often able to mitigate rancour by reference to the Master's words. His charity and self - sacrifice were boundless, and he was known as "the good priest Menas" not only in his own community, but in the congregations of the hostile Melchites.

In periods of burning religious controversy such spirits are always found, and their influence is wide and beneficial. Their conduct is liable to misconstruction, and they are sometimes stigmatised as lukewarm and even treacherous by the zealot priests who head religious movements; but the respect of the sober-minded laity compensates for the distrust of their brethren, and when they are called away they leave a gap which those who have depreciated them during their lives are often the first to acknowledge.

Menas with consistent humility had refused preferment, and lived on as the priest of the venerable Church of the Pure Lady Mary in the Roman fortress, with his son and a few poor families around him; but his personal character and the protection of the Pagarch gave him more real weight than was possessed by many archpriests and bishops who strove to vie with their Greek rivals in outward splendour.

We have already caught a glimpse of the Pagarch, and the many folds of his complex character will be unrolled as we trace the events that developed them. For the present it may be said that he was holding his unique position with difficulty, and that his utmost skill was required to balance conflicting interests and to maintain the equipoise between strong and bitter factions. Though a Byzantine official, and conforming outwardly to the religion of the State, he was of Egyptian blood, and his sympathies were with the Jacobites. During the Persian invasion he had remained in high command, and had amassed great wealth. He had been foremost, however, to welcome the Emperor's reconquering troops, and had even accepted the religious document known as the Act of Union, by which Heraclius sought to reconcile his Jacobite and Melchite subjects. But all this had not been enough. He was further required to remit the arrears of tribute due to the Emperor, and with this demand he was both unable and unwilling to comply. Part of the money had gone to bribe the Persians that he might remain in his office, much had been spent to supply the demands of a greedy and corrupt secret service department which was always discovering plots and counterplots, and a very large proportion had gone—as he hoped—for good into his own coffers. Now he saw his position with Heraclius threatened, yet to comply in full with the Emperor's demand meant absolute ruin. He had enemies at Court who poured insinuations into the Imperial ear, and he had received despatches from headquarters threatening inquiry and throwing out vague hints of impeachment and supersession. He knew well the methods of the Court, and had contrived to send them lately large sums; but to do so he had stripped himself of much of his household gold, as he dared not increase the taxes of the peasantry

lest they should join with the Greeks against him.
The gift of the holy relic to the chief church in
Memphis was a sign of imperial favour, and he
hoped it was an acknowledgment of the immense
private sacrifice which he had made. At all events
there seemed at the moment a renewal of Court
favour, and he knew the populace of Memphis too
well to be ignorant of the fact that he owed to
this impression the glowing welcome which had
greeted him at the festival. For some time before,
he had observed on occasions of public display
signs that his popularity was waning, and he
guessed accurately enough that the languid huzzas
of the Memphis mob were hints of suspected dis-
favour at the capital. Knowing how unwise it
would be to allow this impression to harden into
a conviction, he had doubled his largesses, and
pressed on Heraclius through the clergy the request
for a gift of some relic from the Holy City. He
had succeeded, and was satisfied on the evening of
the festival that nothing had been left undone to
secure two objects, — the re-establishment of his
peace with the Emperor, and the gratification of
his Egyptian subjects. There was one burden on
his mind and conscience. He had, in obedience

to the dictates of an impulse apparently wholly inconsistent with his character for statecraft and policy, taken a step which, if known, meant absolute ruin.

The dread of this action being discovered, and published or conveyed privately to the emperor, haunted him day and night. It made him nervous, moody, and uncertain, and many hinted that nothing but some wizard spell, or the glance of the evil eye, could account for the strange fits of gloom that at times clouded the brightness of the most energetic intellect in Egypt.

There was one person, however, who had the skill to lift and lighten the Pagarch's mind, and that was his daughter Armenosa. She could remove, finger by finger, the strong hand which hid her father's face, and drag him out to make her a flowerball, or to watch the leafy boat or Moses' ark her playmate Marcus launched on the waters of the great river. Indeed the only persons who could approach George in his dark hours were Menas and the boy and girl who had grown up together, and who were only now feeling that they were children no longer.

Marcus therefore set out on his visit to the

palace with a much lighter heart than most of the
good citizens of Memphis would have carried in
their breasts had they been bound for the same
place.   For in spite of his courtier-like grace of
manner when he condescended to grant an interview, the Pagarch had purposely hedged himself
round with extraordinary pomp and ceremony.   The
minute etiquette of Constantinople was copied in
Egypt, and after waiting in anterooms, and being
handed on from vice-chamberlain to chamberlain,
and from secretary to secretary, the suppliant was
often only allowed to prostrate himself before the
great man, and leave his petition in the hand of a
deputy - remembrancer, who required to have his
recollection kept alive by purses of gold, or he
would inevitably forget all about it.   No such cold
reception awaited Marcus.   He entered the garden
unchallenged, and was at once taken by a smiling
black page into a summer-house, where he imagined
his master was reclining.

On pushing aside the silk curtain, however, Marcus uttered a cry of pleasure that, in spite of his
affectionate feelings towards him, the sight of his
father's stately patron would hardly have accounted
for.   The picture presented when the embroidered

veil was removed was exquisite from its combina-
tion of flowing lines and delicate colour.

The summer-house was eight-sided, and curtains
of the hue of the autumnal vine-leaf hid five of its
windows, and softened the warm colour and splendour of the after-glow which was enriching every
light and deepening every shadow in the outside
landscape. Without, the river was turquoise, the
distant hills cornelian, the sloping bank an emerald.
But when once the threshold was crossed, the senses
were suffused with a tender and restful twilight, for
the glare had been tempered to suit the dreamy
languor of the beautiful girl who sat on a high
divan gazing out at the shadowy shapes of the
pyramids, but who, at the voice of Marcus, sprang
from her seat and hurried to meet him, with a
quiver of joy in her voice there was no mistaking for any note save that of love. She was an
Eastern maiden; but her mouth and chin were different from those of Egyptian women, and were
fashioned on Greek lines. Her lips were full and
imaginative, her forehead small. The eyebrows and
lashes were deepened, in the fashion of the day, with
a slight trace of the dyer's pencil; but there were
no disfiguring henna-marks on the nails of her nar-

C

row hands, and she was unweighted by the clinquant chains, bangles, bracelets, and brooches which at that time encumbered the movements of ladies of rank at home and abroad. Her garment, of the soft tint of the blush rose, was shaped like a classic tunic, and a peplum of pearl-grey hung from her shoulders and fell in folds to her sandalled feet.

"Marcus," she said, taking his hand with an air of frank welcome, "I did not expect you to-day. Indeed," she added, with a pretty, pouting smile, "I had given up expecting you altogether. You have stayed away from us so long. But I really thought it was my father. He should have returned from the council-room an hour ago."

"I thought to find him here," said Marcus; "and since you are expecting him I may wait with you a while, may I not? I have a message to him from my father."

"The good Father Menas is well, I trust?" asked the Pagarch's daughter, as she seated herself and signed to Marcus to do the same.

Informally the two were betrothed; but though the Egyptian women were still allowed a freedom and given an education to which their unhappy descendants are strangers, it was not in accordance with etiquette that the motherless Armenosa should receive him alone. The presence of her companion lady, silent and apparently unobservant as she seemed, at the other end of the summer-house, gave, therefore, a certain constraint to the intercourse of the two young people who so short a time ago had played freely in the gardens together.

"My father is better, but by no means well," said Marcus, "or he would have come himself with me. He met with an accident on the festival day, and has not been able to leave the house since."

"Indeed. Oh, Marcus, how grieved I am!" exclaimed Armenosa. "How was it — what happened?"

Marcus told the story of the priest's misadventure, of the attempt at sacrilegious robbery, and of his fortunate arrival at the critical moment. He added that Menas desired to see the Pagarch without delay, and that he had come to ask if an interview could be arranged.

"Time was when you were not so formal," said the Pagarch's daughter, smiling. "Are not my father's doors ever open to his oldest friend?"

"No," said Marcus, with a bluntness which startled the beautiful girl into a perception that something

was wrong. "Three times in the last month he has
crossed the river only to be told that the Pagarch
was busy and could not see him. And my father is
not strong enough to come now unless he knows
that he will not have his journey for nothing."

"Is it so indeed, Marcus?" asked Armenosa, with
tears springing to her eyes. "Truly, I had feared
something was amiss with my father of late, and
something must be very much amiss if he has been
avoiding speech of the good father. Oh, Marcus, I
had forgotten my anxieties at sight of you, and yet
I had been longing so for you to share them!"

"Tell me, my sweet," murmured Marcus, in tones
that a discreet lady-in-waiting could avoid hearing,
"you cannot suppose that I had any thought of
reproach for you in my mind? What have you
been fearing when I have been unable to come to
you?"

"My father is so changed, Marcus, you would
hardly know him for the man who bade us be happy
that sunny day in Rhoda only six weeks ago. Of
course there have always been times of trouble, even
since the Persians were driven back and the rule
of our most august Emperor was restored. We
thought everything would be bright in future, did

we not? Yet I cannot discover that anything has
gone wrong. Was not our glorious festival the other
day a triumph for the Pagarch above all? Did you
mark him as he rode in state, a king indeed among
our people? The Greeks had no such figure to show
in the whole pageant, though they had gold armour
and cream-white horses and the lines of legionaries
to make a show withal. No one looked such a hero
as my father as he sat in his chariot dressed in that
simple' white robe with the ring-dove staff in his
hand. How they shouted and applauded him! Do
you know, I even felt jealous—as if the mob were
claiming a share in him to which they had no title,
and were taking him away from me to whom he
belongs,—my darling noble father, whom none of
them can know and value as Armenosa does. I
could scarcely sleep for happiness that night. But
on the very next day the cloud came down again.
I had seen it on his brow often of late, but I knew he
had many affairs of state to trouble him, and hoped
this festival and the honour shown him by the Emperor would bring all right. I could have wept before
him when I saw him gloomy and depressed, wander-
ing alone in the intervals of his labours instead of
coming to forget his troubles with me. But I would

not add to his distress, so I have striven to smile;
but it was hard—and you came not, Marcus."

Marcus ventured to take her hand and bend
towards her with eyes of love. "Did not my
pigeon bring you my greeting and explanation?"
he asked. "Ah, I feared some evil had befallen
him when he did not return. But you knew—you
must have guessed, my dearest one."

"Yes, yes," said Armenosa, blushing through her
tears; "I did not suppose—I knew some good cause
must have kept you. But I wanted you to help
me with my father. I thought if the good Menas ·
came—— And you tell me he was refused admittance! And yet my father spoke of him only
yesterday with such love in his tone. It must be
a mistake. Beg him to come soon. I will ask my
father to fix a day, that there shall be no more mis-
understanding between the two whom we most love
and reverence."

"We have both reason for pride in our fathers,"
answered Marcus; "but it needs all my trust in their
wisdom to submit to the delay they have imposed
between us and our great happiness. Six months
more! How will they ever pass?"

"No, I must not hear any murmurs," said Armenosa, with a lovely blush. "It is against the compact we made in the garden at Rhoda when our troth-plight was sanctioned. We agreed that we should not rebel or rail against the rule, but admit that our elders had right and reason on their side. Besides, I want you to be the brave one to-night, for it is I who have the hardest lot. This day week you know I go to my aunt Barbara at Heliopolis."

"That was only a threat in case we were not obedient and tried to see each other oftener than on the permitted days."

"No, no, my Marcus. It was the decision of the fathers in any case that the six months before the wedding were to be spent in the Nunnery of the Holy Tree at Heliopolis, of which aunt Barbara is Mother Superior. You won't love your wife the less because she comes to you fresh from the midst of a holy sisterhood, strong in the strength that comes from fast and vigil kept beneath shadow of the very tree that sheltered the Pure Lady Mary and the Child Jesus."

"I do not want you any holier or better than you are," said Marcus, petulantly. "No fast or vigil or nunnery can make you more lovable than you are, and they will keep you from my arms six weary months. I keep my word and bear it like a man,

but you must not expect me to smile at it or call it
anything but needless cruelty——"

"Silence! silence! not a word against the parents
we were praising a minute ago. I must charm away
the spirit of rebellion with a song if my spoken words
cannot exorcise it."

"You know I like that better than anything in
the world; but, before you touch the cithern"—he
held it at arm's-length out of her reach—"promise
me one thing."

"What is it?"

"I will tell you. In the holy house of Mary you
will be safe—*there* no harm can reach you—but be
careful not to stray beyond the precincts. Heliopolis
was the city of the old idol-worship. There men
bowed down to devils, and offered incense to beasts
and birds and creeping things. My father has told
me that the Israelites learned there the worship of
the calf Mnevis, for which they deserted the service
of the true God. Our forefathers called the gods
Ra Harmachis and Isis Hathor, but these were the
same as the plague-sender Apollo and the wanton
Aphrodite. But besides all this there was from days
of old, centuries before Father Abraham came to
Egypt, a tree at Heliopolis to which men offered

human sacrifices and for which women wove hangings, as they did in the time of Manasseh, King of Judah. So keep, my dearest, keep within doors, or at least in the convent garden. There no powers of evil can assail you. You promise me this?"

"Yes, if it will make you happy I will promise it. But have you forgotten that when the holy Jesus passed through Heliopolis with His mother, flying from the rage of Herod, all the idols bowed down before Him and did Him homage? It is faithless to believe in the powers of evil when we have the Lord of lords for our shield and buckler."

"I know not, dearest, nor do any of us know, what liberty is still permitted to evil spirits."

"They have no power to withstand the cross of Christ."

With these words she reached her hand to the cithern and sang—

Sweet Love said, "Canst thou bide with me,
    And Time's dull burden carry,
Nor falter though full wearily
    The hour of wedlock tarry?"

Then Patience in her suit of grey,
    With eyes of meek reliance,
Came softly down to point the way,
    And teach my heart affiance.

But as the days grew long and dark,
 And light seemed breaking never,
While Love a-cold in stranded bark
 Wept baffled of endeavour—

Fair Faith with starry aureole crowned,
 And heavenward-pointing finger,
Cried, " Oh ! Love's triumph shall abound :
 Faint not, nor fall, nor linger."

As the last line of the song died away, the silent lady-in-waiting rose from her seat and went out upon the terrace. This was the signal for the lovers to part.

" It is uncertain when my father will return. You must not wait. I will give him your father's message. If he were well I would bid you wait in the *deipneterion* and share his evening meal, but it is impossible to say when he will come home. Business often detains him until midnight, and when he reaches home he is too tired to talk, and goes to his chamber at once. Good night."

Sadly and wistfully they looked in each other's eyes ere the final kiss was exchanged.

" Farewell, my queen. All angels watch over you. When we meet next there will be no more long partings."

He held her very close to his heart, then hurried away down the avenue of orange-trees.

The Pagarch's garden was not laid out in beds and parterres intersected by walks, but was in the fashion of the East, carelessly ordered, yet full of delicious roses, and hedged round with thick plantations of orange, myrtle, and lemon. Here and there were painted summer-houses covered with convolvulus, now closed and veiling its azure glory; and amid groves of white and pink oleanders rose clusters of Corinthian and Ionic columns surmounted by pediment and architrave with tangles of fragrant jasmine twisting round their fluted shafts. In the distance, against the flushing sky, could be seen the delicately pencilled outlines of the palm-orchard, which was the glory of the Pagarch's estate. The gardens were full of unexpected glimpses of lawny expanses and of irregular avenues converging to various centres and leading up sometimes to an obelisk, sometimes to a plashing fountain.

Marcus, who thought he knew every winding alley, rustic grotto, and pillared alcove in the domain, took the road he usually took to the gate of exit, but the gardeners had been busy lately in diverting the path so as to lead from the palace

direct to a small marble edifice, apparently a chapel
or oratory newly built. This was masked by large
trees, and thus Marcus met with a double surprise:
first, he found that the road did not lead to the
gate; secondly, that he was confronted by a building of exquisite workmanship which he had never
seen before. A light was burning, and the priest's
son from religious habit turned in to say a prayer.

As he bent the knee for a moment on the door-
step he thought he heard a slight movement within,
and entered cautiously. His first impression was
that the place was an utterly different one from that
which he had expected to find. He had supposed
that he was entering an oratory or chapel, and
looked for the usual furniture, the holy picture of
the blessed Virgin, St George or St Mark, the cross
and prayer-desk with rosary and missal. But the
walls of the little chamber were perfectly bare,—
its only furniture a silver candelabrum shaped like
a serpent, and a heap of papyrus scrolls. In the
midst of the room stood Armenosa's father, no longer
clad as at the pageant with official vestments, but in
a long black robe. He was studying intently a huge
parchment chart which lay on the floor, on which Marcus could see marked the figures of stars and planets.

Startled at the sight, and feeling that he intruded, he stood irresolute. But the Pagarch had not heard him enter. He was busy tracing the astral signs with an ebony staff, so intent on his task that he neither saw nor heard. Awe of the chief of his nation had been inculcated on Marcus from childhood, and he would never have dreamed of spying on his privacy. Besides, the studies in which he was engaged were clearly not those of which he desired a witness. Marcus therefore retired as silently as he had entered. Fortunately the turning he took on leaving the building was the right one, and he soon gained the garden gate, and reached home an hour before midnight.

CHAPTER IV.

HOW GEORGE THE PAGARCH VISITED MENAS AT BABYLON.

THE Pagarch debated whether it would be better to see Menas in his own palace or in the priest's house. He decided, after much thought, that it would be the safer course to visit him in Babylon. The rooms of the palace in Memphis were large and opened into each other, and there were plenty of places where eavesdroppers might post themselves. Then, again, chance words might reach the ears of gossiping slaves, or visitors of rank might interrupt the conference by sudden calls. So, after thinking it over, he sent a message that he would come down after evensong in the cool of the summer evening and visit his time-honoured friend. The priest was somewhat disappointed:

his life was monotonous, and he would have en-
joyed the change of scene. It was one of the
few pleasures of his life to visit the stately house
in Memphis, and see the statues and rich furniture inlaid with mother-of-pearl, and handle the
manuscripts blazing with azure and gold illumination, and to rest by the fountain in the garden
and listen to the singing of Armenosa. He realised, however, the motives of the Pagarch, and
knew better than any one else the extraordinary
difficulties of his position.

The communications that must pass between
the two related to matters of vital importance,
and he pleased himself with the hope that he
might be invited to stay in the palace later in
the year, when the tide of public affairs was
ebbing, and the great man was secure of comparative privacy.

Within a week of the visit of Marcus to Armenosa the Pagarch, in a simple robe and attended
by one strong slave, got off his mule at the low
door of the priest. The house was close to the
church, with which it was connected by a trellised
gallery, and was dominated by the lofty bastions
of the fortress, within the cincture of which it

stood. Its walls, like all those in Babylon, were
very thick, and the iron-guarded door resembled
the entrance to some rich treasury rather than
the abode of a humble priest. In fact, though
the priest was personally a poor man, the church
possessed large stores of plate and jewels, the
offerings of the religious; and as the Melchites
were fierce and greedy and ready to spoil their
rivals at the least provocation, precautions were
necessary. A watchword was exchanged between
the Pagarch and a deacon who was in attendance;
then Marcus, who was waiting, came from the
porter's lodge, and kissing the hand of his father's
friend, bade him welcome to his poor dwelling.

The upper room in which Menas sat was nearly
dark, but the windows, which had been closed
all day, admitted the little air that was stirring
through holes in the shutters. The chamber was
lighted by a silver lamp hanging before a picture
of the Saviour rising from the tomb. A high
seat covered with matting occupied three sides
of the room, and in a corner of this Menas was
reclining. The two friends exchanged a few in-
quiries; Marcus handed them some sherbet and
then withdrew, shutting the door carefully.

"I have asked to see you, my friend, for my mind
is torn with fears and forebodings, and in the course
of events I cannot expect to be long in this world.
' The keepers of the house tremble, the strong men
bow -themselves, and those that look out of the
windows are darkened ' — all the signs of the end
that the Preacher reckons up are coming or already
come upon me, and I must speak, even though the
words I utter should be grievous and painful in
your ears."

"Open reproof is better than secret love.   It is
the part of a friend not to spare his friend's faults
to his face, as it is his duty to be silent concerning
them behind his back.   But do not think I am un-
accustomed to censure though I have lip - service
and flattery enough in my palace yonder.   I am
no stranger to rebuke and blame.   The reptile liars
and slanderers of the city, and the august calumniators who sit behind the Emperor's purple chair
and by every post, menace me with ruin if I do
not bribe their silence.   These, O Menas, prevent
my hours from gliding by in the Elysian bliss
that fools believe to be the lot of every one who
holds a sceptre.   My days are weary, my nights
sleepless.   I would gladly exchange my palace for

D

a monastery. If it were not for Armenosa, a cave-tomb in the Thebaid or a cell beside the Natron lakes should bury all the years that are left to the Pagarch of Egypt."

"I know it, and I can tell you exactly how long you have had this distaste of life. It dates from the day when you began to distrust your holy faith and to look out of and beyond it for support and help. For months there has been a distance between us, growing wider and wider, until from a narrow rift it has stretched into a chasm, and from a chasm it has broadened into a gulf. You have been silent and unhappy. The holy services you loved have been neglected on the plea of the claims and duties of business, public and private. This, my brother, has not been the real cause. Must I tell you what it is? Will you not confide in me? Must I show you to yourself? Will you not pour out your grief? I ask you not as confessor to penitent, but as friend to friend."

At the first words of this appeal the Pagarch set his features in firm lines as of one determined to resist all entreaty, but when the priest ended he laid his hand on the hand of Menas and spoke in a tone pathetic from its naturalness.

"Should I have spoken to any living being save you as I spoke but now? You know how, when I was a young man, my heart went out to others, and what an effort it has cost me to stop the natural flow of frank speech and franker feeling, and to insulate myself as the island castle is insulated by the lake that girdles it. I had to learn first reserve with some, then suspicion of all. I had to hold men apart, and to watch every word, gesture, smile, and frown — to teach my face to mask my dearest feelings, and while I revealed nothing, to scrutinise every eye that drooped its servile lids before me. If I am cold and hard, the traffic with my fellows has made me what I am."

"No one expects the ruler of men to be free of tongue. Silence and haughty carriage are proper to the part you play in the world. That necessity we have admitted ever since you were raised to the rank you now hold. I did not ask this interview to learn that dignity befits the Emperor's representative, and that a politician must keep his own counsel. Do not let us fence and fight over the outworks of the citadel. There is a secret weighing on your breast. I have learned by means

not to be revealed what it is. Only I ask you, for
the sake of your duty to your God and your nation,
to pause before you take one step — though it be
but an inch long — on the downward road. You
took precautions that seemed to defy detection.
You used as tools wretched mutes, and you took
care that no single scroll of legible writing should
remain to witness against you. But the mysterious providence of God has revealed the secret to
me. The bird of the air that carried the matter
reached my hands, and I know you have sought
to bring the armies of the False Prophet into
Egypt. You have exchanged messages and gifts
with Mohammed, the enemy of your God, the
denier of your Saviour."

Menas had dreaded the moment when duty should
oblige him to speak this word. He had at first
resolutely denied the accusation against his friend
and had only yielded to evidence that it was utterly
impossible to resist. He had prayed and striven to
see if there was any conceivable alternative between
charging him with his treachery and incurring the
guilt of criminal compliance, but he had found no
middle course. It had been forced upon him that
the trusted representative of the Emperor, his own

close friend and schoolfellow, had taken the first
steps towards the betrayal of Christian Egypt to
men who denied Christ. It was then clearly his
duty as an ordained priest to disregard all the ties
of past intimacy, to banish all tender recollections of
older years, and to tell the truth whatsoever consequences might follow. Menas had tried to picture,
as he lay awake pondering over the burden laid
upon him, the expression of George's face when the
terrible charge was first launched against him. He
had feared lest the convicted traitor should rush out
from his presence and, like Iscariot, put an end to
his own life. He had prayed that, if it were possible, the dreadful accusation should be put in any
other mouth than his. And now that he had taxed
him with his infamy, he hardly dared to raise his
eyes to see the effect of his words. To the priest's
utter astonishment, however, the arraigned traitor
replied in the tone of one relieved from a painful
duty, and made no perceptible attempt to repel the
charge.

" You have only anticipated me a few hours, perhaps minutes," said the Pagarch, " in mentioning
this transaction. When you sought this interview I
purposed to tell you of what I had done, and to lay

bare the state of my mind to the only human being
I can trust. You were absent in the desert-convent
when I opened communications with the Prophet, or
I should perhaps have told you what I purposed to
do. The resolution was not taken hastily, or without many and fervent prayers. It was the outcome
of the doubts and fears of years. I have bent my
neck too long to the tyrant at Constantinople. I
have seen for too many years this people of Egypt
crushed, enslaved, insulted, and tortured by the Melchite devils, while I have been obliged outwardly to
conform to their heretical rites. I have seen the
poor taxed and ruined, the priests insulted, their
most cherished doctrines mocked and ridiculed, and
vile names hurled at them. The nunneries where
their holiest and purest women sought refuge have
been broken open on charges that only leprous hearts
could invent and lying lips speak. These things
have I seen, and I have kept silence. The ancestors
of the men who built this castle, the idolatrous Babylonians, did not evil entreat God's people the Israelites more foully than Melchite prelates and Melchite
soldiers have treated us whom they call Jacobites.
So I say the time of endurance is over. The day
of submission and sufferance is past and gone.

Henceforth, as we are too weak and too divided to
resist without foreign aid, we must summon it and
cry, 'Islam to the rescue!' Remember the soldiers
of the Man of Mecca have not been stained with
blood as are the Greeks. They hold a pure but an
imperfect creed. Who shall say that it may not be
mine to teach them what is lacking? They believe
in a God of righteousness and truth, they are tem-
perate and just. May not this Mohammed be the
destined deliverer after all?"

He paused and looked eagerly to see if his appeal
had in any way touched the heart of Menas.

"No, no—a thousand times no," replied the priest.
"Whatever is right, I am certain that this your act
must be wrong. It cannot be God's will that one
body of Christians should call in a heathen to fight
for them against another body of Christians. And
who is this camel - driver that he should be summoned to take part in the armed debate of emperors
and the controversies of holy churchmen?"

"Who is he?" said the Pagarch. "A like question was asked often in this land when Moses defied
the power of Pharaoh, and in later years when the
disciples of Jesus defied the tyranny of Rome. I
tell you God has raised this man up as He raised up

Moses. The scimitar in his hand is God's instrument as much as was the rod that turned into a serpent and divided the Red Sea when Moses grasped it. I am not deceived. Voices superhuman as well as human assure me that I am right. This man has been marked out as the Deliverer by signs, and by wonders, and by war. On the night of his birth the palace of Chosroes was shaken, and fourteen of its turrets fell. The fires of the Persians were extinguished, which had never been extinguished before for a thousand years, and the Lake Sawah sank. He was helped by the angel Gabriel at Bedr. He conquered in thirty battles. To resist his followers is as idle as to oppose a raging torrent with a wall of platted straw. Do not ask me more, but I tell you, O my father, that in addition to the signs of his victory which all the world can see, I have heard voices and seen sights which there is no mistaking. Tongues that speak no lies have spoken to me; tokens that cannot deceive have been shown to me, and not to me only, but to one in whom even you place reliance. Yes! I say men in comparison with whose knowledge mine is blank ignorance look to the Man of Mecca, to the son of Abdallah, as the restorer of religion, as the saviour of Egypt."

"You speak in riddles," said the priest, bitterly. "All these dark sayings hide projects that you dare not avow, and prelude acts you dare not call by their right names. Treason and apostasy are the demons with whom you are trafficking, though they come to you with visors on their faces and call themselves patriotism and reformation. I have listened long enough. Would I had died ere I heard from the lips of my oldest and most cherished friend the words I have heard to - night. There cannot be many years in store for me, and I have not used the past well, God knows. I have been a negligent shepherd, and have loved my rest and my child before my Master's service. Chastening was needed, and Thou, O Lord, hast sent it in the shape that Thou knowest to be best, but would God I had died without knowing what I do know. Would God I had been trodden under the feet of the Melchite crowd, when I lay prostrate in the streets of Memphis, rather than hear what shall come upon this people at thy hands. The sounds of their greetings, the voices of their flatteries, are in your ears. How will you feel when those sounds are exchanged for the wailings of your brethren over desecrated altars, and the curses of women given over to men to whom the wolf and the hyæna could teach mercy?"

"I did not expect you would see as I see," said the Pagarch, "but I did expect you would trust me. There is no choice, therefore, but to disclose what I would willingly have kept secret even from you. Listen to one word which even in this thy private chamber I must whisper in thine ear. All this is *not* my vain dream. It is the firm faith of ——" He bent his head and whispered in the priest's ear.

As he received the mysterious communication a strange change passed over the old man's face. Though he had denounced George's new and extraordinary policy, and started aside like a broken bow at the bare idea of a fusion of parties so diametrically opposed to each other as the Jacobites and the sons of Islam, the vivid conviction and burning zeal of his old schoolfellow had not been without effect. For years Menas had been accustomed to look up to the ruler of Egypt with pride and admiration. He had, as we have seen, gained an accession of personal consequence from his intimacy, and the family tie that was soon to connect

them more closely than ever endeared him to the
old man, whose heart was singularly affectionate.
While he had poured forth the vials of his righteous
indignation against the sophistries of the Pagarch,
the thought of his son Marcus and his love for
Armenosa had caused his voice to falter and break
in spite of himself. And now George claimed the
sanction of a name which to a true son of the
national Church of Egypt was above all other names
on earth. For the moment Menas was stunned into
silence. He sat with his face buried in his hands.
The Pagarch, who, in spite of the bold face he had
assumed, had found the interview full as trying as
he could have feared, seized the occasion to end it,
and leave the poison of his last suggestion to work
in the priest's mind. Before Menas could recover
speech he rose to go.

"We have said all that can be said. Whatever
happens we shall be friends. Good night. Marcus
will see me across the court, and I have servants waiting at the postern," and he quitted the
room.

"He never left me before without asking my
blessing," said the priest. "Could I have given it

to him if he had sought it? Could I have with-
held it? O send out Thy light and Thy truth,
that they may lead me."

And he knelt before the picture of the Christ and
wrestled in prayer until the morning broke.

CHAPTER V.

FATHER AND SON.

ELIEZER the Jew, the father of Reuben, lived in a quarter of Memphis which was remote from the great square, the fashionable churches, and the lake frequented by pleasure-takers. He knew that if one of his nation showed signs of wealth he was sure to be accused of violating some civic or religious law, and mulcted with a heavy fine to the public treasury. If he escaped these legal penalties, he was compelled to bribe informers or tax-gatherers to avoid being denounced to the magistrates, imprisoned, and perhaps tortured. The Jew then chose an obscure suburb near a huge broken statue of a hippopotamus god, which was regarded as haunted and dangerous. Here he had built himself a strong house, with chambers in which he could store his

gold and silver, his pledged jewels and his parchment securities, and here, tired and ill at ease, he
arrived late in the afternoon of the day on which
the Pagarch visited Menas. He had no wife living,
but dwelt with his son Reuben and an old cripple
who acted as servant. Many of the Jews made up
for playing the part of paupers abroad by luxury at
home. Eliezer's house was bare and poverty-stricken,
containing nothing save necessary furniture of the
rudest kind. Against these sordid surroundings his
son, who was pleasure-loving and expensive, chafed
and fretted. To-day he had come home from watching the splendid show made by the sons of rich
Greeks in the stadium, and his sense of exclusion
from all this gaiety was gall and wormwood to him.
A dinner of one dish, sorrily served, and the thrifty
contents of a small flask of sour wine, aggravated
his ill-temper, and when Eliezer arrived he found
his son cynical, sullen, and defiant.

He remained silent while his father ate a like
meal to that which had disgusted him, and it was
only when the old man rose and muttered from
habit the usual form of thanksgiving after meat
that his sulkiness relieved itself in a sneer.

"If you matched your grace to your feast it would

have been two words long at the most. No grace say *I* until you broach one of those jars of Falernian that have been gathering dust and cobwebs in the cellar these seven years. After a flask of that I may feel disposed to say a thanksgiving."

"To sing a lewd song to Bacchus or Venus rather. Reuben, every day you fall lower. For lighter acts and words than yours men have been cast out of the synagogue. You think you blind me, but I know what you have done and what you plan to do. Be warned; you are watched with keen eyes. I know of your attempt at theft; I know of your mad passion for a Gentile."

Reuben had not expected this, but he determined to brazen it out.

"Well, and if I did pick up a piece of plate that chance put temptingly before me. Are not the Christians fair game, and am I not doing a pious act when I convert their goods to the use of the chosen people? Is all the gain to be on one side?"

It was not easy for Eliezer to reply, as his son was putting into coarse words the creed he himself had taught him: besides, he had that lurking admiration for boldness common to crafty subterranean natures. Craft always secretly worships force.

"Well, well, at least be warned," he added, and there was no threat in the tone this time, only a note of earnest entreaty. "Be warned. I am not deceiving you. There is danger from those who will have no mercy. I dare not quarrel with the Gentiles yet, but in less time than you guess we may drop the mask."

"Not until you secure the church with the tomb of Jeremiah in it for a synagogue?"[1]

There was a sneer underlying Reuben's question that stung his father to a fury.

"Mock anything but that," he said. "I have sinned, plotted, tampered with things holy, but that has been the one pure aim of my life. My father Ezra told me on his deathbed that far away in this land of old devil-worship was the tomb of the holiest of our prophets, and that it was in the hands of the Gentiles. I have resolved to get it back. Directly my father was dead I left the Holy City where we dwelt. I journeyed, I starved, I toiled for that one object, and now I have gold enough to buy it from the Nazarene. Let me hear the holy language read over the sepulchre of the prophet; let me know that

[1] See Note D, The Jewish Synagogue at Old Cairo.

the end is wrought through my means. That will be an atonement acceptable to God. If only I see that day, I die in peace."

" But why traffic with the Christian ? His hold is loosening every day over Egypt. Wait and you will get good terms from the Moslem."

" I must work while the Cross sways Egypt. The Christians, Jacobites, Melchites—all will sell themselves for gold. The sons of Islam are uncorrupted by greed. Men who live on a handful of dates and a mouthful of water are not to be bribed. It is your silken pagarchs and your epicure priests who are my commodity."

" I wish, O most austere father, you would for once class me with these reprobates, and open your purse and cellar to relieve the wants of your off-spring."

He seconded his appeal with a comic gesture of supplication.

"Never ! What have I done to father a mime and a wine-bibber ? "

" Not the last, for you take precious good care I get no wine to bib. But one word. I have not been absolutely idle. Callinicus at least gives

E

me a good character for working hard at his
mystery. I have sweated and grown thin over
his furnaces at Heliopolis for the last week, and
he bids me tell you that he has an order for one
hundred casks full of the *you-know-what* from
Celadion. It is to be conveyed to Rhoda and
stored carefully. He bids me ask you, shall the
casks be marked H or B?"

"B is safer," said Eliezer after a pause. "I dare
not trust this new fire demon within the city lest
it destroy what I would preserve with my life.
So you are learning how to make this war-fire.
The knowledge may stand you in good stead some
day. There is a time to break down and a time to
build up; you are born for the time to break down."

"I cannot say that I am learning the secret
from Callinicus. The cunning Egyptian sets me
to grind his chemicals and watch his furnace, but
the ingredient on which all depends I know not.
When you advanced him the money to purchase
the shop at Heliopolis, did you not stipulate he
should teach me all he knew?"

"I will speak to him myself on that matter.
Now I must to my study. I shall see the Pagarch,
to-night. If I hear by word or sign from him

that you have dared to approach his daughter, I have means to punish that you will not be able to escape."

Eliezer then retired to a chamber on the roof of the house, and was soon absorbed in drawing out a horoscope he had promised to give George, who had for some years employed him as his confidential agent. He sketched the diagram with the rapidity of a master of science; then laid down his reed pen and took up the threads of a reverie which, woven together, formed a plan of as complex a pattern as was ever wrought in a plotter's brain.

"Does the end draw nearer?" he asked himself. "Yes; and will it be accepted as an atonement if I can reach it? The great rabbis have told me so, and, at least from mine own people, honour, worship, fame, are promised me. The worship of the one God in whose name Moses triumphed over Pharaoh will be set up again in Egypt, and it is Eliezer who will bring it back. And the sin of Iscariot shall George sin, and the names of both shall flame together blazoned in fire unquenchable in the book wherein the doom of the accursed is written!"

A noise from below broke in upon his reverie. He rose and looked over the parapet of the roof, and saw Reuben in the act of leaving the house. According to his custom, Doeg, the deformed serving-man, had wrapped himself in his rug, and settled to sleep before the door. Reuben in going out had waked him, and then the servant had tried to hold his young master back. Angry words were passing as Reuben struggled to free himself from the old man's clutch. Eliezer heard the quaver of remonstrance, and the impatient curse with which it was answered.

"Why do you lie like a watch-dog for every one to fall over? Let go my cloak."

"I am no dog, though you and your master give me the language and the food of one. Where are you going? To the Gentile woman and the Gentile wizard. Stop, I will call your father."

"What care I? Let go;" and Eliezer heard a short scuffle, a fall, and a cry of pain.

His son had struck the old man's arresting hand and flung him to the ground. For an instant Eliezer hesitated. Should he go down and try to detain Reuben? At least he would see if the old man were injured. He heard him rise,

however, and go grumbling back to his lair—the
mat on the threshold. And Reuben was out of
reach, flying fast across the moonlit sand until his
shadow was swallowed up in that of the great
hippopotamus-god that rose up like a rocky mountain between him and the gleaming streets of
Memphis.

CHAPTER VI.

CALLINICUS.

THE scene changes to Heliopolis.

Through a thick cloud of furnace-smoke and an atmosphere heavy with the smell of chemicals a man was dimly visible. He was the master of the Jew Reuben, the philosopher and architect Callinicus. The room in which he sat was not far from the spot where the rose granite obelisk which marks the site of Heliopolis now stands. Against the wall of a ruined temple[1] Callinicus had built a brick house of moderate size, and fitted up the largest of four rooms with the apparatus of his trade. Compared with the carefully made and well-adjusted instruments of a modern chemist the machinery of the Egyptian was rough and

[1] See Note E, Callinicus.

unserviceable; but with such means as he had
Callinicus did good work as a pioneer in science,
and unquestionably stood on the border - land of
great discoveries. The invention of the Greek fire
seems incontestably to have been his. Enthusiastic
to a degree, he constantly ran risks of ghastly
accidents, so zealous and regardless of consequences
was he in pursuit of his studies. His face, which
had never been handsome, was seamed by scars.
He had lost an eye, and all his hair, even his
eyebrows and eyelashes, was singed off. Still the
face, though ugly, was not repulsive. A queer
cynical smile curved the big lips, and the one
seeing eye took in the humours of the world as
well as its tragedy. Callinicus, when we peep in
at him, had just finished a dish of red mullet from
the lake of Tinnis, and, after quenching his thirst
from a pitcher, settled himself in an attitude favourable to digestion and repose. He leaned against
the wall, doubled his thin legs under him, crossed
his smoke-engrained hands over his stomach, and
inclining his head over his left shoulder, passed
into a state of dreamy reverie, like a Buddha entering Nirvana. He slept in great peace for the
space of an hour; then he awoke gradually, and,

in the transition - time between sleep and wakefulness, put his reflections into the shape of a
fragmentary murmurous soliloquy which seemed
like the continuation of a dream.

" I have given my precious apprentice one day's
holiday, and he is not likely to show up for a
week unless he has to give leg-bail to a husband
or a creditor. It is the plague of philosophers
that their experiments want coin, and so they find
themselves under the yoke of the money - lender,
who saddles the advance with some infernal condition that counterbalances the benefit. Eliezer
said he would accept no share of my profits, but
insisted on my taking his prodigal Reuben as a
make-weight. He hopes the young fry will worm
out the mystery for himself, but I will lay odds
on an Egyptian baffling a Jew any day. He has
never seen the yellow powder, and knows not
where it is stored, though he treads on the stone
that covers its receptacle every day; and without
that the great invention is nought — and, by He-
phaistos, what an invention it is ! Fools will call
it cruel, savage, satanic, but that is because they
are fools and judge according to their folly."

He was interrupted by three knocks at the door

—the two first following immediately on each other, the last given after a space during which one could count ten. He rose with a yawn, prolonged apparently with two purposes: first, by a lingering and delicious farewell to defer as long as possible his re-entrance into the troublous world of wakefulness; and secondly, to exasperate the patience of the visitor who was waiting for admission into the house. At last he unbarred the door, and Reuben entered with a curse on his master's dilatoriness; for though he inwardly respected Callinicus as much as he was capable of respecting anybody, to bully and swagger were parts of his brutal nature, and he asserted himself by airs of superiority over his employer and by coarse banter of his odd appearance. This afternoon the master's grotesque face, with its red eye blearing through the darkness, struck the pupil as so like a comic mask which he had seen lately in a pantomime that he burst into a laugh. The acrid smoke-reek turned it into a loud sneeze. When he had recovered from this Reuben spoke.

"Hail! most learned master. I am returned before you expected me, and as it is too late to work, let us come out of this den, which smells

like Acheron and all the rivers of Tartarus, and
get a breath of fresh air."

As he spoke he brought out two stools, one for
himself and one for the philosopher. Callinicus,
however, took his seat on the head of a stone ram
which he had placed on one side of his door,
handed Reuben his pitcher, and watched him
empty it with a mingled expression of jealousy
and wonder.

"I always tell my friends, who devoutly believe
you have sold yourself to the devil, that if you
had you would have stipulated for a handsome
face in exchange."

"Beauty is of two kinds. There is the loveliness of the outward shape, and the loveliness of
the intellect. My eyes——"

"Eye you mean."

"My eyes, I repeat, may lack the lustre and
fire which are proper for an actor or an orator,
but they have been darkened and dimmed by researches into the mysteries of nature; and my
fingers——"

"Those you have left of them."

"My fingers, I repeat, have become hard and
callous by working in the elements amidst which

the god Ptah, whom the ancients worshipped at
Memphis, laboured for purposes far less benevolent than those which occupy Callinicus."

"I fail to see the benevolence of inventions
which will multiply the number of the slain in
every battle a thousandfold, and cause men to
depend more upon chemistry and arts diabolic
than on the strength of their muscles and the
prowess of their hearts."

"You are a tyro, and fail to see many things
which to those experienced in science are obvious
as the sun at noonday. But listen, and reply to
the questions which I shall address to you, and
if there be any virtue in the method of Socrates
I shall convince you out of your own mouth."

"I am all ears."

"Are the majority of men brave or cowardly?"

"Cowardly."

"Assuredly. Yet do they not desire to appear
brave? And thus when called on to fight they
accept the challenge?"

"Yes."

"And put on armour, and listen to heroic
speeches, and blow trumpets, and pretend to be
eager to fight?"

" Yes."

" And if by the use of certain things they can
slay whole armies of the enemy and lose few of
their own number, will they not rejoice ? "

" Yes."

" And be eager to fight again ? "

" Certainly, as long as they are sure of a successful result."

" Rightly said ; but when the enemy shall ob-
tain the things, or THE THING, by the employment
of which against them they met with such dis-
asters, will they not rush to arms and retaliate
on those who before were victors ? "

" Yes."

" And what will be the result of the second
battle ? "

" Great loss on both sides, and the slaying of
many more men than the nation can afford to
lose."

" And then will men be eager to go to war ? "
Reuben was silent.

" I say they will be for a time ; for those who
are beaten will be angry, and those who are
conquerors and have made great gains will desire
more. But after a time, when many men are

killed, not only soldiers, but artisans and merchants, and those who till the ground — for all will have to answer to the war-levies,—then will nations grow weary of fighting, because, owing to THE THING which makes the carnage so great, war will be the most terrible scourge that there is, and men will cease from it."

"Something like that is written in our books, wherein it is said that a time should come when swords should be turned into ploughshares and spears into pruning-hooks," said Reuben, dreamily.

"So the lore of the Jew may point to that which the science of the Greek shall achieve. But enough of dialectics. Let me hear immediately why you have come when your services are not needed, since I know very well that some purpose of your own has to be served, or you would not leave your boon companions to seek me while you have a single coin of your month's wage in your purse."

"I should not certainly, but coins take unto themselves wings and fly away when usurers clamour and the dice have forgotten the way to turn up sixes. However, all will come right soon if you will only help me. You know I love the

richest and loveliest girl in Memphis. Her father's
consent cannot be got, so I must do without it.
You can help."

"I?—never. The part of Thersites I might play,
for nature has fitted me for it, but I have no
qualification for the character of Pandarus."

"Pandarus! Heaven forbid! I only ask you
the loan of that cunning helot Hydrax for a
couple of hours to take a message to the Convent
of the Holy Tree."

"Is that the prison of the Memphian cynosure?"

"For the present, yes."

"If that is all, you may have Hydrax. He is
now gone on an errand to the city, but he will
be back before sunset. Now as I must go to
work again at 'midnight, let me take the other
half of the nap you so inhumanly interrupted;"
and he curled himself up on the ground and
went to sleep instantaneously.

Reuben waited patiently until he was assured
by the philosopher's snores that he was unconscious, then stole into the house and began to
look eagerly amongst the jars and bottles on the
shelves. As we have seen, he was perfectly well
aware that he only partially shared the great

secret, and he lost no opportunity of searching for a clue that would unravel it. In his eagerness he spilled a jar of ill-smelling powder, and before he could replace it he was aware of approaching footsteps and of the darkening of the doorway by the body of a man. Motioning to Hydrax (for it was he) not to waken Callinicus, he stepped across the prostrate sage and took the slave to a spot a few paces from the house. Here with much gesture of head and hands the two had colloquy with each other for about half an hour. Then they parted—Hydrax in the direction of the balsam-groves amidst which rose the towers of the Christian monastery, Reuben towards a small fountain by the roadside, near which he had tethered the horse on which he had ridden out from Memphis.

CHAPTER VII.

IN THE CONVENT OF THE HOLY TREE.

QUIETLY and happily the days glided by, with
Armenosa safely bestowed, as her father hoped, in
the Convent of the Holy Tree. Long before the
flight of the Christ Child and Mary His mother, the
spot where the convent stood had been regarded as
sacred. It was connected with an ancient cult,
and miracle and legend blended with its authentic
history. To the Christian of the seventh century all
before the era of the Saviour was dark and terrible.
The old world was the devil's world, which Christ
had come to change and mend. Marcus said
what everybody thought when he spoke of the old
demon-worship lingering in those palmy groves and
giving voice to those carven idols. All this was to
be buried in silence, or never spoken of save in a
whisper; the event to be remembered was that the

Blessed Virgin, or, as the Egyptian Church called her, the Pure Lady Mary, and her Divine Son had rested under the ancient sycamore which grew in the convent precinct, and that when Herod's slaughter-men came in pursuit of them a spider, Arachne-like, had spread a wondrous web over the hollow in the trunk where they were sheltered, and hid them from the fury of their foes until the tyranny was overpast.

The Mother Superior of the holy house was Barbara, Armenosa's aunt, a woman destined to exercise after her death a far-reaching influence. For was not her dead hand, enclosed in its silken case, with its many wrappings and swathings, to be placed under the altar of a church bearing her name, and to work cures of epilepsy and palsy, of which the fame was spread throughout the whole preaching of St Mark? In the days of her flesh she was a grave kindly woman — devout in her prayers, punctual in her long fasts, and not sparing her nuns the scourge of godly discipline. Life under her rule was regular and hard, but she was not, as were many of her class, cruel or given to favouritism. She spared not others, because before she rose to her present rank she had not spared

F

herself, and she was just and charitable according
to her lights to all save the Melchite pretenders to
orthodoxy, whose condemnation, she believed, though
it lingered, was not slumbering. Armenosa was her
one link with the outside world. She saw her
seldom, but she loved her more than she acknow-
ledged, and much more than she considered it right
to reveal to the sisterhood. Indeed on Armenosa's
arrival at the convent on her periodical visits it was
the Mother's wont to exhibit to her nuns her niece's
embroidered peplum, and gilded sandals and jewelled
bracelets, as the gauds and bedeckments wherewith
Satan lured the daughters of this world, and to bid
them add special thanksgivings to their evening
devotions that they were free from the temptations
to such excess of apparel. It is true that in private
the aunt questioned her niece minutely as to the
price and quality of each robe, gem, and armlet; but
after having been examined, fingered, and held to
the light for a whole evening, the trinkets were consigned to their cedar-wood chests, and Armenosa was
enjoined to wear sober raiment during her stay, save
on feasts of the saints, when it was permissible to
adorn oneself.

On the present occasion, as it was the last visit

that Armenosa would pay the convent before her
marriage, her aunt had a curious struggle between
her desire to make her sojourn a time of chastening
and penance and her curiosity to see the fashion of
the garments she was preparing for the bridal
ceremony. Then, though extra vigils, fasts, and
prayers were enjoined and enforced, the hours of
silence were lessened, and the Mother Superior spent
many days in the cell assigned to her niece.

Thus after the morning instruction of the novices,
a task which invariably tried her temper, Barbara
would seat herself with a sigh of fatigue on the one
chair in Armenosa's cubicle and address her somewhat in this fashion :—

"It needs patience, indeed, to listen to the mistakes of those girls, specially Appia and Lycia, who
grow worse every day. I am wearied out bending
over their copies and correcting them. No, thank
you," as Armenosa placed a cushion behind her back.
"No, no ; such luxuries are not permitted save in
case of infirmity, though my back aches so that I
might indeed plead for some indulgence this morning. Kneel, child, and say your psalms, remem-
bering to bow the head thrice as I bade you at
the *glorias*."

Armenosa knelt and repeated the seven peni-
tentials without mistake or correction, while the
Superior closed her eyes in pious meditation. The
exercise over, she sighed again yet more audibly
than before, rubbed her eyes, and continued—

"Repeat them this evening, and the devotions
for the commemoration of the Holy Justina along
with them. By the way, there was a monogram
of a curious pattern embroidered on the green
silk robe you showed me yesterday. I would
have it copied by Sister Thekla, to whom the
saints have given a skill in needlework, though,
alas! a temper none of the sweetest. It would
suit well for a device in one of the four corners
of the banner she is working for the arch-priest
of St Mercurius."

Armenosa fetched the silk and held it dutifully
in various lights, while her aunt became so
absorbed in examining its shape and quality, and
in contrasting them with the fashions of her own
girlhood, that she forgot for twenty minutes at
least to look at the sacred initials which she had
at first been so anxious to study.

This is a sample of many mornings spent in
the convent. Then came the long services in the

chapel, the simple meals in the refectory eaten in silence, while a sister read the Acts of saints and martyrs. Then the hour of recreation in the high - walled garden for those who had wrought their tasks and performed their penances, and then the work amongst the many sick and old and poverty - stricken who dwelt in the mud-hovels round the convent. It was here that the sisterhood showed at their very best. Barbara never gave a sidelong glance at the gauds of the outside when binding up some gangrened or ulcering limb. Thekla's snappish voice was modulated as she lulled to sleep some fever-wasted baby whose cries were torturing its dying mother. Appia and Lycia atoned for many pain-ful pictures of saints with eyes asquint, and martyrs with wry necks and splay feet, by bathing ophthalmic lids and poulticing sores and wounds, with the cheerful tireless patience that only the one great Master teaches. Then when the work was done, and the evening light deepened the red of the granite obelisks of Heliopolis, and burnished the twisted trunks of the sycamores, and flashed on the crosses and aureoles of the saints whose images surmounted

the convent chapel, the little group of women
walked home, chatting cheerfully of their work,
and their patients, and their heavenly patrons
and patronesses, suffused with a beautiful light
in heart and spirit, even as their bodies were
embathed in the tremulous splendours of the
after-glow.

Then came the service answering to compline.
Then each nun retired to her mat in a little
cell, which had a crucifix and a holy picture for
its only ornaments, and slept with a rosary between her tired fingers until the bell summoned
her to begin a day the counterpart of that just
ended.

Thus passed several weeks. This resting-time
was a blessing to Armenosa. She did not know
until she entered upon it how much she needed
a pause for quiet and meditation. It was true
that her life in Memphis was secluded compared
with the lives of Western women in the modern
world, but it was one of alternate outward
ceremony and inward anxiety. Her place was one
of distinction. Her father, for reasons of policy,
and perhaps from preference, kept up much state.
She had to exchange with the wives and daughters

of high officers the long visits which occupy
time and weary the flesh by the perpetual re-
pression they require. And in her heart she had
as constant indwelling fears as to the change she
had observed in her father, and vague doubts as
to his intentions about her marriage. Before
everything else she knew he was ambitious.
Though she understood one side of his character,
she was aware there were many leaves of the
difficult book she could not read, and for some
time she had been haunted by a fear that some
of the complex motives connected with his intricate policy might suddenly induce him to bar
her union with Marcus. Her love was deep, the
growth of years of companionship. Her father
treated her betrothed like a son, and had never
opposed the engagement; but there was a feeling
of distrust, deepening and widening, lest some
sudden change of policy should break in and
dispel the peaceful love - dreaming, as so many
love - dreams had been dispelled in that cruel age.
The contrast between the life of sweet love she
longed for and her Memphis existence was held
up to her every day as in a mirror by the talk
of the great ladies she visited. Intrigue, false-

hood, shameless selfishness — these she saw all
around her save in the few moments she was
allowed to spend with Marcus. These were
usually her only times of unmixed happiness,
and now, though she could not see him, there
was nothing to jar upon the inner life of hope
which was bound up in him. She could forget
and banish the hateful serpent shapes of scandal,
envy, and impurity, and feel that she was preparing herself for *him*,—the bride adorning herself
for the bridegroom. The traces of weakness in
the sisterhood — the lingering looks worldwards
that she detected in the Mother Superior,—what
were they to the garish lies of that society she
had left behind her when she crossed the Nile?

She was soon to require all the supplies of
strength that the round of holy service and the
guileless companionship had given her.

It was a spring evening; the nuns were returning from visiting their poor, and were in sight of
the convent gate. They were walking through
the brown dust with weary feet. The last few
minutes of rough road always seemed long, but
it was a point of honour not to complain of it.
There had been a khâmsin wind blowing all day,

scorching like a furnace-blast, and covering with impalpable sand every corner of the convent. Within, novices with their busy feather-brushes had been removing the defiling enemy from altar furniture and oratory. Without, the rose-trees in the garden were blighted and burnt up. In the mud-huts the patients down with fever had tossed all day in parching misery. The visit of the brave Sisters had lightened their pain, and the presence of the Lady Armenosa, who had come with them all of her own accord, had been a very wellspring of comfort, as was Elim to the old wanderers.

With a sigh of relief they approached the wooden gate.

"I think the wind is freshening," said sanguine Sister Euphemia.

"It always lasts three days," said gloomy Sister Sophia.

"What do you want?" said the Mother Superior to a strange figure who crawled out from behind some tamarisks and barred their progress.

He was a beggar of loathsome shape. One arm was wrapped in rags and splints as if it had been recently broken. He crawled rather than walked,

dragging a paralysed leg after him, and oaring
himself with two brown hands covered with noisome
spots like leprous marks.

"Help! ladies, help!" whined the wretch, "in
the name of the holy Lazarus who lay full of
sores at the rich man's gate! Help, in the name
of St Lydia, and St Dorcas, and St Dorothea! My
child is sick — very grievously tormented. He is
despaired of by the leeches, but I know if the
Lady Armenosa would come she could do what
all of them, including St Æsculapius himself,
could not do. The touch of a betrothed maiden
is a sovereign cure, says——"

"Says who?" asked the Mother Superior, severely.
"You have been going to the witch again. Woe unto
this people who go after enchanters and wizards and
mutterers, and not to the blessed saints and martyrs
whose virtues have an efficacy beyond all gold and
rubies. Say where you live? We will send to assist
you, if your story be a true one, early to-morrow."

Her parched skin and tired limbs were drawing the poor Superior for a moment from the
path of duty. It had been a hard day, and
visions of food and rest had been rising pleasantly
before her when the beggar broke in upon them.

"Oh, send her! Lady, do not put me off!" said the wretched object, laying his noisome hand on the hem of the Mother Superior's garment. "Come, and deny not the prayer of the poor destitute. It is my only child, my chaplet of lilies. Even as Isaac was a laughter and a joy to Sarai, the wife of Abraham, so is my boy Namin to me. Send her, I beseech you."

"God forbid that the Sisters of the Holy Tree should be deaf to the cry of sorrow, or sluggards when called to an errand of mercy. I will go even now, without waiting for a morsel of meat or a draught of water. I will go," she added, with a look of rueful resignation,—"yea! though I faint by the way."

"Nay, Mother," said Armenosa, "this is not fitting. You require rest, and are needed to preside at the service of Benediction. Let *me* go. I am the youngest and strongest, and perhaps, if the poor boy has set his heart on seeing *me*, he may take medicines from my hand more readily than from any other of us."

Sister Sophia murmured something about her readiness to go, so indistinctly that no one noticed her.

Judging from the look of relief on the Superior's features that there was a chance of gaining her end, the beggar redoubled his importunities.

"I see the blessed saints are helping me. Come ere it grows dark, O lady of charity. My child lies close by, behind the first balsam-grove, beside the red pillar." The red pillar was a huge block of rose granite which had once formed part of one of the pylons of Heliopolis. It was about half a mile from the convent gate.

"It may be well for the girl, whose life has been one of softness and ease, and who will dwell henceforth in the luxury and pride of life, to taste the cup of bitterness and to carry the cross of self-denial for a space," said the Mother Superior, half to herself and half aloud; then she added hurriedly, as anxious to get the matter settled anyhow—

"The blessed Virgin be with thee. There are medicaments in this basket, and Michael the sub-janitor will follow thee. Come, Sisters."

And sighing deeper than ever, Barbara gathered her flock about her and entered the convent. Armenosa followed the beggar, who twisted him-self along at such a pace that the girl, who was more exhausted than she had imagined, could scarcely keep up with him.

Michael, the sub-janitor, was fast asleep when summoned by Sister Euphemia. He heard her directions very imperfectly, for he was deaf as the Psalmist's adder, and grunted his acquiescence; but he resolved to finish his supper of bread and cucumbers before starting: so when at last he set out on his way, Armenosa and her guide were out of sight. As it was impossible to know which road they had taken, he returned after walking a few yards, and was soon snoring on his mat.

Armenosa walked rapidly on until she reached the plantation of balsam shrubs, successors of those which were famous in the days of Solomon, King of Israel. It was now nearly dark, and her guide moved on so fast and kept so far ahead of her that she could not make him hear. The shrubs grew thick to the right and left, and the road narrowed into a footpath between them. She saw no hut or sign of man's habitation anywhere. Suddenly, however, the beggar struck to the right, where a group of tamarisks, possibly the remains of a grove, surrounded the huge red

block that he had named as a landmark. Armenosa called to the man, and refused to go any farther,
as there was no house in sight. She stopped, fairly
frightened. The warning of Marcus came to her
mind, and she felt the tears welling up in her
eyes. She trembled, and tried to call to the guide,
but no words came. The Mother Superior had
charged the man with complicity with a witch.
Was she to be dragged to some devilish scene
of magic ritual? Was the beggar a fiend? She
made the sign of the cross, and pressed a medal
blessed by Menas, which she always wore, to her
lips.

Suddenly she was conscious of some one beside
her. In her panic it seemed one of the old brute
gods, but it was only a mounted man who had
come silently from the direction of Heliopolis.
Before she could ask herself why he was there,
the rider — a youth of lithe limbs and bold
bearing—dismounted, caught her in his arms, and
mounted with her in front of him. She screamed,
but a silk handkerchief was instantly twisted
over her mouth.

"Pardon me," said Reuben, for he it was.
"It breaks my heart to stop the tongue whose

music I love best in the world. But we must put a league between us and the poultry - yard yonder, or some of the cacklers will be guessing our whereabouts." A light touch of the stirrup sent the horse forward, and Armenosa was borne away into the darkness. She had no note of time, but it seemed hours since she was drawing near the convent gate in the quiet evening and the beginning of this wild race. The hideous guide, the dialogue with the Sisters, the red pillar, the seizure — all seemed pictures for a fever - fit. There was no coherence in it. Still it was real. She felt the tight bandage round her face, the hands clutching her waist. She heard the quick breath of the horse and the clatter of the hoofs as they struck some fragment of causeway.

On, on. There seemed no end to that ride, no light in that darkness. The movement at last loosened her eye - bandage, and she saw the horse's head and ears. Then it slipped a little lower, and she saw objects in front of her—lights, high buildings, walls, obelisks. Then the direction of the ride changed, and the horse stopped, panting and steaming.

Reuben called twice—thrice.

Then everything real vanished.

The facts that she was trying to fix in her mind in order to keep her senses disappeared. She had counted. She had tried to say to herself that she was seized probably by some robber who would detain her for ransom, and that she must be on the alert to save herself by courage or craft. Above all that, the one thing to dread was losing her senses. This, though nearly dead with fatigue, she had tried to keep before her. Any fall into unconsciousness might mean ruin. Her perils were strange, but they were from the hands of men. With the protection of the Virgin, while her lips could say a prayer or her fingers clasp the cross, she was safe from the powers of evil.

No!

At once the ground shook. Fires of every hideous colour — blood red, livid green — flamed up against the sky. Then came a crash, redoubled by the echoes. "The voice of Thy thunder was heard round about — the earth was moved and shook withal." The words she had sung in the chapel that morning rang in her ears. Then all was silence and darkness.   The horse plunged. The arms no longer clasped her.   She saw no more, she heard no more.   In her last passionate moment of knowledge so much was crowded in that it seemed there could never be anything more to know.

CHAPTER VIII.

AN OFFER OF MARRIAGE.

THE Pagarch had risen early, and sat in his favourite pavilion reading and re-reading a closely written scroll. It was not one of the Jews' horoscopes, but one of those formidable letters from Constantinople which Armenosa dreaded almost more than the mystic parchments. George, as we have seen, had successfully baffled the intriguers behind the imperial throne, and had obtained a signal mark of favour from Heraclius. This had been done at enormous expense, for the courtiers, chamberlains, and secretaries who guarded the avenues of approach to the Emperor were insatiable. Thus the sum that should have been devoted to the imperial treasury had been spent in illicit ways, and to make up the deficiency, money had been borrowed at ruinous

interest from Eliezer and his brethren. Now new
and startling tidings had arrived. Affairs had taken
a turn wholly unexpected. Heraclius proposed to
assume the command of the troops, and to lead
the veterans who had conquered Chosroes against
the armies of Omar. He called upon Egypt, the
wealthiest of his provinces, to supply money and
men, and hinted that a mark of unparalleled favour
would reward the loyalty and zeal of the Pagarch.
But as he read the high-sounding phrases and mag-
nificent promises George's face grew darker. He
rose and walked impatiently about the room.

"Is my fate never to be that of other men? We
are taught that misfortunes are blessings in disguise.
To me blessings are but veiled curses. Gifts of
honour, fortune, and preferment, that the rank and
file of men plot, struggle, and damn themselves to
gain, are to me messages of ruin. I have strained my
credit to the last *aureus* to glut the harpies of the
Chalkoprateia,[1] and now they cry More, more. Fresh
imposts are impossible. Egypt is burdened far beyond her powers already—poll-tax and land-tax,
and a dozen taxes direct and indirect, as well as
the coronary gold that was wrung as a 'free gift'

---

[1] The quarter of Constantinople occupied by Jew money-lenders.

from the poor wretches when Heraclius triumphed.
It is impossible. But if I fail to send the gold, the
old stories will be revived. They are known to
more persons than I once imagined. Everything *is*
known here, and then my refusal to help against the
Arab will be alleged as a corroborative proof of the
truth of the old story. He will not assist his
Emperor against Omar because he has trafficked
with the false Prophet. All will be discovered. Oh
the shame, the shame!" And George fell upon his
knees, his face buried in his hands.

Overwhelmed with passionate emotion, he did
not hear two low knocks at the pavilion door, nor
the noise of the lifted latch when the Jew Eliezer
entered. His face, as he peered through the door,
wore its old subservient smile, which, on seeing the
Pagarch's attitude, changed to a look of contempt
and triumph. The Emperor's letter was still lying
open on the table, and Eliezer glanced quickly at its
contents. Then he paused for a moment, looking at
the prostrate figure on the ground with the sneer of
a being who stood aloof from pity. With his first
spoken words, however, he replaced the mask of sub-
servience and became the Eliezer known to the
Gentiles.

"Rise, Illustrious! This is not the posture for the man whom kings delight to honour, and on whom emperors shower their richest gifts. I thought to find you in the midst of your slaves issuing orders for the grandest pageant Memphis has ever seen."

George rose and looked at him with a dazed expression. He had heard his words, but did not comprehend them.

"Rise, I say, Illustrious! This is the proudest day of your life, and a day which makes all those who glory in your renown rejoice with exceeding joy. Surely you have heard the news that all the city will ring with ere we are an hour older."

"Do you mean the news contained in this despatch, that the sacred Emperor will take the field in person against the Arabs?"

"No; I mean the tidings contained in a later despatch—not from Constantinople, but from Cæsarea."

As he spoke the door opened, and a slave entered and prostrated himself—

"A messenger from the sacred Emperor."

"Admit him."

A courier tanned with the sun, and covered from buskins to bonnet with dust, entered the room almost before the order to give him entrance had

left the Pagarch's lips, and handed him a tasselled
and embroidered case carefully sealed. His commission executed, he retired with the servant.
George took the case in his hand, pressed it to his
lips, heart, and forehead. Then he cut very carefully the purple silk thread with which it was tied
and drew out two scrolls. As he read his face quivered and flushed, and he almost dropped the paper
from his trembling hand.

"Is it not as I said?" asked Eliezer.

"The sacred Emperor commands that I give my
daughter to his son Constantine in marriage, and
urges that she be sent at once with a suitable escort
to Cæsarea. His Imperial Wisdom seems to believe
that this alliance will knit together more firmly than
hitherto the interests of Africa and Asia, and also
cure that melancholy wherewithal the heir to the
throne has been oppressed ever since he beheld
Lady Armenosa at a festival at Jerusalem two years
ago. And further, Constantine Augustus himself
writes to ask the hand of my daughter, and to urge
me to lose no time in sending her to him under a
sufficient guard, so that the marriage may be concluded before the fast, and on an auspicious day."

"Did I not tell you so? We of the nation have

early news of all things that concern the welfare
of our friends. Accept the congratulations of the
most devoted of your servants."

"Congratulations!" said George, bitterly. "That
word from you of all men living. Do you not see
that this means ruin, and nothing more? It is a
death-draught, though handed to me in a jewelled
cup."

"Death-draught! It is the elixir of life you are
bidden to taste. It is a cup full to the brim of all
men love—power, wealth, rank, victory, fame. You
are bidden step into the imperial circle. Your foot
is planted on the first step of the staircase that leads
to a throne. It is well known that the Augustus is
weak of body and mind. Even if he lives, he will
be your tool and instrument; and if he dies, who
knows that you may not grasp the sceptre that falls
from his hand."

The words were spoken with extraordinary fervour, and George was carried away by the passion
of them. After all, if the Jews would only help
him, the financial crisis might be tided over. The
father-in-law of the future emperor could not be
called to account as easily as a provincial governor.
But could he depend on Eliezer? Why was he so

hearty in his desire that he should gain this prize,
which meant enormous outlay ?

He asked himself the question as the other was
speaking, and the answer he received was so far
satisfactory. The higher his place, the larger his
fortunes, the surer would be his credit, and the
greater his capacity for paying high interest on his
loans. He said this to himself, and thought he had
read the Jew's motives; but the strongest of them
had escaped his ken. Eliezer loved his profligate
son, and dreaded above everything else his passion
for Armenosa. It was no figure of speech — he
would rather have seen Reuben dead at his feet
than married to the woman whom an emperor was
seeking as his daughter-in-law. Armenosa's betrothal once known, and the danger of his son's
marrying a Gentile would be over. He remembered, too, the love of Marcus for Armenosa; and,
strong in his hatreds, it pleased him to think that
the man who had detected Reuben in a villany
should suffer defeat. Briefly, the scheme in its main
object and in its incidents wove itself into his subtle
policy, and harmonised with the pattern of the piece.

"Jew, the spirit of Moses and Joshua fires you
to-day. Look at the reflection of our faces in that

steel mirror." He pointed to one that hung over
the ebony cabinet. "Would not you say *I* was the
man of action and energy, and you the timid grey-
beard, infirm of purpose and impotent of will. But
what is the truth? A crisis comes: I tremble and
hesitate, and see only danger in front of me; your
spirit mounts like an eagle, and looks beyond the
peril to the prize."

The blended speech of depreciation and flattery
which Eliezer began to stammer in reply was never
finished, for suddenly a man's voice was heard impatiently demanding admittance, and overbearing
the remonstrances of servants.

"What is this? who is this?" cried George, angrily.
Marcus burst in.

"I should say it is a gentleman who will leave
the room somewhat less haughtily than he is entering it," sneered Eliezer.

"Pardon me, pardon me," cried the young man.
"I know I am unmannerly, I know I am intruding
on hours sacred to state affairs; but I must be the
first to tell you she is saved, she is saved!"

"What does this mean? Who is it of whom you
speak? Fool! what ill wind blew you hither at a
time like this?"

"I have come because I feared you might hear that the Lady Armenosa had been abducted from the Convent of the Holy Tree."

"The Lady Armenosa abducted! Who dares lay hands on the Pagarch's daughter and violate a convent of holy nuns at one stroke? Do law and piety count for nothing in Egypt?"

"If Reuben's hand be here," muttered Eliezer aside, "may he be accursed with Hophni, Phinehas, and Absalom."

"She was abducted by a shameful trick, but the villain was struck down by fire from heaven, and I saved her and took her back to the holy sisterhood."

"She is safe then? All the saints be praised!"

Eliezer whispered in George's ear. He saw that in his joy at the news of Armenosa's safety the Pagarch was in danger of forgetting everything else.

"Well said. I had forgotten. There is an important question to be asked. What took you to Heliopolis? Was it not against the promise made solemnly, and understood by your father as well as by me, that you should not approach within a league of the convent? Did I not confine my daughter to the sacred precincts solely and entirely to protect her from your importunities? Did I not fear that, as my friendship for Menas threw you together, some dreams of ambition might cross your mind and lead you to think of Armenosa as of one who would listen to a love-suit? Explain, then, what took you to the forbidden ground; and if your tale halts in a single particular, were you my brother's son you should rue it."

A smile of pleasure lit up Eliezer's eye as he saw how every word stabbed Marcus like a knife.

"Might you not ask the young man to tell us some more about the fire from heaven?" he asked, sneeringly.

"Yes. What was all this? Let me have a plain tale plainly told."

Marcus was stunned. He had entered the room expecting the thanks of his father's friend, the blessing of his future father-in-law. He found the ground he stood on cut from under him; the love which was the essence of his existence spoken of as a delusion; the Jew whom he instinctively loathed installed high in George's favour, and urging him to commit the grossest injustice. It was the sudden conviction that Eliezer was gloating

over his confusion, and that every moment of hesitation was noted against him by the estranged eyes
of the Pagarch, that nerved him to speak.

"My plain tale I will tell. I was yesterday
riding towards Heliopolis. I came just after sundown to the balsam - grove. There I found the
Lady Armenosa on the ground insensible. I
brought her water, and after a time she recovered
consciousness. She implored me to take her to
the convent, and on arriving there I heard from
the Sisters how she had been entreated by a
crippled beggar to go out to visit a sick child;
and then I learned slowly and with difficulty, for
her mind was perplexed and her speech faltering,
that there was no sick person needing help, and
that, when at a distance from the convent, she
had been seized by a strange horseman and carried
some way on the road to Heliopolis. Then in
answer to her prayer, and by the special help of
St Barbara, the abductor had been struck down,
as she supposed, by lightning, and she saw him
no more. When she opened her eyes there was
no one near save me, but the tamarisks and prickly
pear bushes were blackened and burnt."

" I have heard of abductors and rescuers being in league when beauty was to be won by bold adventurers," said Eliezer.

" Jew, I will not bear this—give the Jew the lie. O Pagarch, as you are my father's friend, tell me I misheard your words when you said you knew not of my troth to Armenosa! Bid this man leave us, and be your noble self again. Say you spoke to test my loyalty. Say there has been a spell cast over me."

"Listen," thundered George, his voice resonant and his whole frame straining and quivering with passion. " Not to you or such as you shall my daughter be given. You have taken advantage of the fact that I was overburdened with affairs of state and could see my child seldom, to gain her heart and fill her brain with fantasy. But your practice is detected. It will pain me to break with Menas, the friend of my youth, but my daughter and my allegiance before everything. Yes! my allegiance to my sacred Emperor before my daughter."

He motioned the unfortunate Marcus to depart, and, taking the Jew's arm to support him, left the pavilion by a door leading to a private apartment. Marcus flung himself on his knees and clasped the Pagarch's mantle. It caught and tore as Eliezer slammed the door after him, and Marcus stood with the piece of rent silk in his hand.

CHAPTER IX.

THE CONVENT AGAIN.

PROSTRATE with fever, Armenosa lay in her cell in the Convent of the Holy Tree. The first shock had passed. Gradually what had seemed a nightmare was shaping itself into a series of separate impressions, and she was beginning to realise the order in which the events occurred. At first she hardly knew whether she had been carried off on a horse, or on some hideous monster with a steed's body but with the distorted face and shambling gait of the beggar who had acted as decoy. Then over and over again she heard the noise of the explosion and saw the flash of the fire, and then a figure, at one time like her patron saint, and at another time like her lover Marcus, bent over her with soothing words and healing touch. The remedies promptly applied

by the Sisters helped the cure. The febrifuge soon
allayed the more violent symptoms of brain excitement, and an opiate brought a refreshing sleep.
When the sunset rays quivered through the latticed
window and dappled the walls of the cell with a
golden pattern, the girl's mouth had lost its tense
and pained expression, and she smiled gratefully
at the Sister who sat by the bedside fanning her.

"Thank you, Sophia. I am stronger now and
the fever is lessened, but still I scarcely know what
befell me yesternight. Whose was the hand that
brought me hither? I heard the thunder peal, and
in the lightning St Barbara descended, but no saint
or woman bent over me when I awoke, but even
Marcus, the son of Menas."

"It was he and no other who brought you to the
convent insensible, and with no power to move hand
or foot. And, judging from the imperfect sight I
had of him through my veil, he was like the youth-
ful David, of a fair countenance. But I would know
more of the appearance of the blessed St Barbara.
Was she tall or short? dark or fair? and did she
carry her tower in her hand?"

"Verily all was confusion, and the sound seems
now not to have been like thunder, nor the fire like

ordinary lightning, but more like the flames which I
have seen in a picture of the destruction of Cora
and his company. But do not talk more of it just
now please, Sister."

And Armenosa turned her head wearily on her
pillow. The Sister continued to fan her for a while,
and then fell into a doze. She was awakened after
a time, with a guilty sense of having been asleep at
her post, by a knock and whispering voices.

Sophia rose, finger on lip, and opened the door
softly. She was on the eve of saying "Armenosa
is asleep," and forbidding the visitors to enter, but
sank into a profound obeisance directly she saw
that they were the Mother Superior and the
Pagarch.

"The lady Armenosa has slept well, I hear," said
George, "and I am come to take her to a place
where she shall be more safely guarded from fraud
and outrage than it seems she can be here."

"Though Armenosa has slept, she is still very
weak. I implore you to let her remain somewhat
longer in the convent. Twelve hours more will
restore her completely."

"I do not think any one in these days can
venture to say what will happen in twelve hours,"

H

said George. "Besides, it is a matter of high consequence that my daughter should be at once
conveyed home. There is no delay, and as this
road is perilous after dark, we will not waste time.
Prepare her for the journey — a litter waits
below."

A few days before, George would have shrunk
from a measure so violent. The least hint of
danger to his daughter's health was a word of
power with him. He had been always kindness
and courtesy itself to the holy Sisters and the
Mother Superior, but now all was altered. He was
mad with ambition. The dream of raising his
daughter to a throne intoxicated him. The strange
influence of Eliezer, gained partly by the power of
money and partly by his astrological predictions,
had dominated every softer passion, every gentler
impulse. He must carry out the Jew's advice at
once.

The Mother remonstrated passionately, forgetting
her awe of the Pagarch.

"Take her hence to-night! It is madness. No
physician would answer for her life if she is moved
thus early. The fever is not abated. Touch her,"

and she put her hand on the girl's hot cheek. "The fire is still burning in her blood, and it would be fatal to remove her."

"Father, what is this?" said Armenosa, wearily. "Send these strangers away; I would sleep a little."

"I have provided for all this. Socrates"—he beckoned to a grave bearded man who was standing on the threshold—"examine my daughter and see if she is fit to be moved. This," he added, turning to the Mother Superior, "is one of the imperial physicians. Whatever he orders we may do with the assurance that it is absolutely safe."

He stood aside while the man whom he had addressed as Socrates came to the bedside, felt the pulse of the girl, and with much show of care tested the temperature of her body. He then said slowly—

"The lady Armenosa will travel with safety indeed. The journey in the cool evening, if she be fortified with the remedy which I shall give her, will hasten and not retard her cure."

He then took a small phial from his girdle, poured its contents into water, and bade her swallow the

mixture. She fell asleep in a few moments. Then
the insensible girl was carried into the courtyard of
the convent, placed in a well-cushioned and cur-
tained litter, and, surrounded by a troop of the
Pagarch's guards, hurried to Memphis.

CHAPTER X.

HOW THE PEOPLE OF MEMPHIS CONGRATULATED THE PAGARCH.

MEANTIME by every means in his power Eliezer had diffused the news of the betrothal of the Pagarch's daughter. It is to this day a wonder how rapidly tidings are spread abroad in the East. In many cases now the money-lenders and usurers are busy agents in the work of circulating reports political and financial, and in the seventh century they had no rivals in the newspapers. At a hint from Eliezer or some powerful member of his tribe, every money-changer communicated the news to his customers as he weighed him out his silver. The customer retailed it to a knot of gossips as they paused to have their drink of sherbet in the cool colonnades. The barbers passed it on as they trimmed the beards of the rich youths whom Reuben envied. They chatted it over at the public baths, and then it ran fast until it reached the boxes at the circus and the symposia of the high officials. If, as in this case, it was a topic likely to interest the womankind, a few of the cosmetic-sellers and fortune-tellers, who were nearly all Jewesses, received the order of the day, and the languid ladies rose from their silken divans and bustled off in their sedans to make a round of visits, assured that for once even their rivals would welcome them.

Knowing well the weak places of George's character, it was Eliezer's policy to force him to despatch his daughter at once. He went direct from the palace to the houses of several of his rich brethren, and, by arguments suited to each, induced what we should now call a powerful syndicate to guarantee the needful money. This difficulty got over, he had nothing to fear but the tears of Armenosa.

"The fool dotes upon that girl of his," he muttered. "At the last moment he may start aside like a broken bow, and spoil the finest plot my mind ever minted."

He rightly judged the point whence resistance would come, and all through the night, while George paced his chamber with nervous steps, trying to stifle his conscience by every sophist argument, Eliezer was setting the machinery in motion which should stun the Pagarch, as he went out into the world next day, with a chorus of congratulations.

Fortunately for his plan, it was the levée-day, when George was accustomed to appear in robes of state and receive from early morn until high noon the crowd of officials in possession and officials expectant whose rank or birth entitled them to be presented to him. Never had he dreaded this ordeal more than on the morning when he was deemed the happiest man in Memphis. Pale, hollow-eyed, and weary, he allowed himself to be robed and prepared for the ceremony; but no rouge nor cosmetic could make the face look other than haggard, or the smile he tried to call up other than a mockery. As he took his station under the silken canopy a herald proclaimed his titles, and announced that he was ready to receive all loyal subjects of the sacred Emperor, to reward the good and punish evil-doers.

Contrary to custom, a unanimous murmur of greeting, swelling into a shout, echoed through the hall. "Hail to the Illustrious George! Hail to the father-in-law of our Augustus! Hail to the Glory of Egypt! Blessing, prosperity, and peace upon the house of the Pagarch! Blessing, prosperity, and peace upon the elect Lady Armenosa!"

It seemed as if the voices would never cease. At last, however, the general burst of congratulation died out, and the Melchite Bishop of Memphis, with his attendant priests, moved—a mass of flashing jewels and gold embroidery—up the hall. As they halted before the Pagarch's chair, the crowd became with one accord silent, and the Bishop spoke.

"We desire to be the first, O Pagarch, to offer our congratulations on the betrothal of your daughter, the virtuous Armenosa, to the illustrious Constantine Augustus, the well-beloved son and heir of our Emperor, the sacred Heraclius. The union will join the loyal province of Egypt with new and firm bonds to the imperial throne, and strengthen——"

The end of the speech, like many perorations, was inaudible. The Bishop was not sufficiently sure of George's or Armenosa's orthodoxy to say anything about "the faith of Chalcedon and the two natures," which were the phrases made and provided for such occasions. He therefore trusted to his chaplains, who, seeing his difficulty, shouted the formula, "God save the Emperor!" in sonorous tones, to veil the impotency of his conclusion. George was dazed. The image of his heart-broken girl and the consciousness of the lie he was acting rose before him. The praises sounded like hisses. Instead of servile courtiers bending the knee, he seemed to see mocking fiends jeering him as he walked to perdition. For one moment he was on the eve of rushing from the hall, imploring his daughter's forgiveness, and begging the pardon of Marcus and Menas; but the penalty would, he knew, be more than he could bear. He was pushed too far forward to recede, and by an exercise of his iron will he nerved himself to reply. A fluent orator, the words came readily to his lips, and the emotion visible before he spoke seemed only a becoming expression of humility at the extraordinary honour his sovereign had bestowed upon him. His enemies, who accused him of arrogancy and presumption, were disarmed by an exhibition of right feeling which was clearly genuine.

"Friends and fellow-servants of our sacred Emperor, I did not expect your greeting. Holy and reverend Fathers, I did not anticipate your congratulations. I had intended to announce this

command of his Sacred and Imperial Majesty to
my Council, and to ask the reverend the clergy
to put up solemn prayers that my child might
bear the responsibility and burden of the honour
bestowed upon her becomingly; but your zeal has
got the start of me, and, all unprepared, I am
asked to say first before man in the hall what I
would have desired first to utter before God in the
church,—I mean my sense of utter unworthiness
to receive the least of all these honours from the
imperial hand; and I would have asked you to
allow me to retire for a space, that in solitude,
fasting, and prayer I and my child might prepare
ourselves for this high decision and destiny: but
time presses, 'the king's commandment is urgent,'
and I must consult with the right valiant Celadion
and the Treasurer the Intendant of the public works,
so that not an hour be lost. Come with me then
to the council chamber, right trusty and sage advisers. To you, friends, I must say farewell, until
we meet at the wedding festival."

George then rose. His chamberlains and heralds
took their places, and leaning on Celadion's shoulder,
and closely followed by the members of his little

Senate, he passed within the curtains that draped the door behind the throne.

The courtiers hurried to their homes, but the crowd that always gathered outside the palace on levée-days was much too excited by the news to go home speedily or silently.

"Did you hear the holy Bishop was unable to finish his speech?" said burly Lampo, who as one of the palace tradespeople had squeezed himself in at the end of the hall. "He knows that the Pagarch has not got the orthodox symbol written up in that fine new oratory of his, depend upon it."

"Why, they say it is no oratory at all, but a place where he and Eliezer the Jew meet to cast spells and consult Diabolos," said the druggist, in a whisper.

"Better raise Diabolos than the anger of a Jew, you wine-vat," said a man in a leather apron. "Hold your tattling tongues, and listen for once to a man who knows which side of the cake has honey on it. What George believes is his own business; but if he did not humour the Jew, where would he get money? and if he does not get money, how can he marry his daughter to Augustus? and if he

does marry his daughter to Augustus, who will be
the gainers? Why, the dyers that furnish the
purple, the druggists that sell the perfumes, the
smiths that make the new cuirasses for the horse-
guards. So let us go across the square to the old
wine-shop and drink the health of the Pagarch
and his daughter."

CHAPTER XI.

A VIRGIN SACRIFICE.

OWING to the good offices of the Jew, who had supplied the Pagarch liberally with money, the Council despatched its business easily. The gifts and loyal addresses to the Emperor were voted, and the more important question of the number of men to be sent as Armenosa's escort discussed and fixed.

The Egyptian youth exercised in martial games and well disciplined were a numerous body, and to find an outlet for their energy was one of the constant objects of the Government. They were the very men to send on an expedition which might be called an armed pageant, as they were rich and splendid in equipment, and would make a gallant show in the wedding processions at Cæsarea. Besides, as there was always jealousy between the militia and the regulars, which now and then broke out into broils, Celadion pressed on George the importance of keeping up the Pagarch's dignity by sending a large escort with his daughter, really desiring to have a free hand in Memphis, which would be left practically under the control of his legions. Still, though the councillors had been unanimous, many hours were consumed, and it was not until the afternoon that the various seals and signatures were affixed to the documents and the ceremonious farewells taken. At last George was at liberty to visit Armenosa.

He had never dreaded an interview with her before. Lately, as we have seen, since the complications of his affairs and his enslavement by the arts of Eliezer, he had not found her society the solace and comfort it had been in former days, but still he had always turned to it. Hers was the one pure presence that had blessed his life. Now he was going to enter it burdened with a lie and fresh from an act of treachery to the man she loved. In the excitement of the morning, however, he had forgotten many of his scruples. The plaudits and compliments of the crowd were ringing in his ears.

So, hastily swallowing a cup of wine, he walked across the garden to Armenosa's apartments. At the door a hand was laid on his shoulder, and turning with a strange start, he confronted Eliezer.

"I pray you pardon me for frightening you. It is only Eliezer, who desires to know if all has gone well at the Council, and if there is any poor service you require of him?"

"Yes; all has gone well. No; there is nothing else. I go to my daughter Armenosa."

"You will find your work difficult with her. The young are easily persuaded to folly, hardly to wisdom. But I think I can help you here. Should she resist, give her this." He took from his pocket a small bag and drew from it a white stone. "Bid her look into it, and she may see something that will alter her mind; but recollect you are pledged, and there must be no going back. At all hazards she must leave for Cæsarea within a week."

The Jew presumed on his influence with the Christian, and presented himself at the wrong time. At that instant George desired to forget him. He was going to ask his child to rise to a high destiny. The motives he was to put before her

were those of religion and patriotism—motives by
which for the moment he believed himself to
be actuated. In one sense all that was best in
him was leading him to one of the worst actions
of his life. He had in an ill-starred moment become the tool of the Jew's arts, but the thought
of tampering by such unhallowed means with his
Armenosa revolted him. The word "must" in Eliezer's speech cut him to the quick, and he was
on the eve of a fierce outburst of passion, but mas-
tered it.

"No, Eliezer," he said, putting the magic stone
back with an impatient hand. "I will not use
any arts with my child save those of persuasion
and love. Leave me now. To-morrow I will
summon you."

"Be it so, Lord Pagarch. I desired to save time,
and my arts are certainties. May your eloquence
be as effectual." He turned away.

Somewhat ruffled by the interruption, George
took a turn in the corridor, stopped for a while
before a crucifix which stood in the recess, and
then with a composed face knocked at the door of
the anteroom to his child's chamber. One of her
maidens answered the summons and showed him

into the room. Armenosa was lying on a bed, her fever abated and her face less flushed than when we saw her at the convent.

Her father kissed her and motioned the maid to withdraw, which she did after placing a small cup, containing a cooling drink, where Armenosa could conveniently reach it.

"My child," said George, "I would have given you another day of rest, but the matter of which I must speak cannot be put off. Since we parted many things have happened. May I ask you to listen patiently while I recount them?"

"Dear father, I have been expecting you since morning. No nurse or physician could keep you from my bedside."

"Not now, for you are better; so listen. You have seen lately that I have been sad and uneasy. My heart has known its own bitterness. But it has not been hidden from me that you were longing to share it. Armenosa, you can do more than share it. You can remove it. Your father's honour is in your hands. By a word you can put me in possession of a happiness which I never dreamed of. One word and the toils that have whitened my hair, scarred me

I

with wrinkles, ay, filled my nights with remorse, will all be forgotten. I shall be overpaid a hundredfold if you will help me."

Vague fears filled Armenosa's mind. What was she to be asked to do?

"Dearest father, your honour and happiness are not in the keeping of a girl like me. They are high above the reach of envious hands. They are the glory and the pride of Egypt."

"They are not now, but they shall be here-after, if you will help me. You remember our visit to Jerusalem after your mother's death? You remember the stranger who accompanied us to Bethlehem, whose name I forbade you to ask? It was Constantine Augustus, the heir to the imperial throne, and your husband if you will have it so."

"Husband! Am I not betrothed to Marcus? How can I break my faith? O father, unsay this; call it a trial of my loyalty, a dream of delirium, anything but the request of George to his daughter."

"Armenosa, your love for Marcus was the love of a girl for a boy. I sent you to the convent to forget it, and had it not been for that ab-

duction, the secret of which I more than suspect
is known to Marcus, you would have forgotten
him by this time. No! The Emperor has de-
manded you in marriage for his son.   You have
the future of your father, your Church, and your
nation in your hands.   Read for yourself the
sacred Emperor's handwriting." He placed the
scroll in his daughter's hand.

"Write to him and implore him to spare me.
He will not want a loveless bride.   But no! *You*
cannot do that, dear father.   Let me go.   I will
kiss his feet.   I will implore him to spare me."

"To spare you from the highest rank, save one,
woman can reach, and within a step of the
highest of all! But no. My dear one," he said, in
that voice of irresistible music and pathos which
was one of his greatest gifts, "yours is not the
ambition which can be tempted by rank and
titles, by the purple robe and the jewelled
diadem. You remember rather that in this great
choice you are surrendering what you most prize.
You are giving up your heart's desire and
wrenching yourself away from all you hold
dearest for the sake of duty to your Church.
Constantine would be easily moulded by your

hands, and untold good to Egypt would follow.
This is not the path of pleasure you are called
upon to tread. It is the narrow path of duty
and self - denial, though the thorns are hidden by
the imperial purple. Yes," he cried, as if in a
flash of inspiration, " it is the path your Marcus,
if he be the true son of my Menas, would bid
you tread. For years we have had to bear an
imperial yoke laid on our consciences by an unwilling Emperor. Heraclius himself is too old to
recant, so for his few remaining years there may
be no change, but Constantine will be free and
unfettered by the past. He will be what you will
make him. Be the Esther of your Church and nation, and let the first act of your husband's reign be
to summon a council which shall cancel and blot out
for ever the false faith promulgated at Chalcedon."

" O father, if I could only believe this, there
is no sacrifice I would not make to gain this
end. If I could help you by vowing never to
marry, if I could serve my Church by penances
and vigils, by fasts, by scourgings, the flesh should
not shrink from pain or whip or hunger; but
God cannot require falsehood. How can that save
His Church ? "

"We are bidden to pluck out an eye and to cut off a right hand if they offend us. This love for Marcus is the impediment that hampers you in the heavenward race : cut it away — cast it from thee. Thou hast not yet resisted unto blood striving against sin."

The father rose as he said these words, with the gesture of one who had made his last appeal.

"If I could be sure of this."

"It is written, 'An evil and adulterous generation seeketh after a sign, and there shall no sign be given them'; but yet to God's servants it has happened that tokens for good and notes of guidance have been vouchsafed in the time of stress and perplexity."

He spoke in the dreamy voice of one communing with himself, and his eyes wandered over the room as if they sought for something. They rested on a picture of the crucified Saviour. Suddenly—whether deceiver or self-deceived, who can say ? but seemingly in an ecstasy of conviction—he pointed to it.

"Look, look, Armenosa! Doubt no more. HE speaks who cannot lie. HE commands whom you dare not disobey."

And as his daughter's intense gaze fixed itself on
the picture, whether by a play of light and shadow,
by a trick of imagination, or by some outside artifice
of one who overheard the conversation, the head
seemed to bow, and the right hand to disengage
itself from the nails and to extend its pierced palm
in benediction.

At the same time a handmaid entered and gave
a small scroll tied with a silken thread to her
mistress.

"This was given me by one wrapped in a cloak,
who hurried away after saying, 'Give this with
speed to the Lady Armenosa.'"

She opened it.

"A message from Marcus sealed with his seal
and containing the words, 'Obey thy father and my
father—a short parting—a long reunion.' God and
man speak. I dare not contradict them. I submit
to the Emperor's pleasure."

.   .   .   .

Eliezer spared no effort to hasten the departure
of Armenosa. George was feverishly anxious to
hurry on the preparations, dreading that some hindrance might arise at the last moment. Armenosa
herself lay on her couch obeying the prescription of

her physicians, uninterested by anything that happened around her. The tire-women and sempstresses and embroiderers lavished their skill on the prepara- tion of dainty veils delicate as gossamer, and mantles of state heavy with gold; tissues from Sicily, and brocades and damasks from Tinnis and Dabik. The jewellers spread their brooches and bracelets, necklaces and girdles of precious stones, to tempt her; but she lay with her eyes fixed on the sacred picture and her hands clasping her rosary, less like a royal bride than a corpse on a funeral bier. Menas made two or three attempts to see George, but the attendants always barred his entrance to the palace. Barbara, whose exultation in the high fortunes of her niece was unbounded, was admitted to see her; but the Mother Superior's congratulations found no response save an eager entreaty for her prayers.

Seven days passed. The excitement in Memphis was at fever-heat. The families of the young men who were to form the bodyguard of the bride-elect vied with each other in equipping their sons gallantly. The gifts offered by the guilds of artificers to the daughter of the Pagarch were unparalleled in splendour. The chariot of the bride was only to be compared to that in which Eudocia rode at the triumph of her imperial husband. The Egyptians love show and pageantry, and here was an occasion that dwarfed the procession of the sacred relic.

Both banks of the river were astir. The populations of Babylon and Memphis were provided with processions. For while the immediate *cortége* of the bride-elect assembled at the Pagarch's palace, the mounted escort was drawn up in front of the fortress of Babylon. It was arranged that the cavalcade was to travel at night, and rest during the heat of the day. The moon was rising, and showering over land and river a rain of silver light, when the horsemen formed in the great square. The multitude, as before, crowded every terrace and portico, and wherever foothold could be found there men and boys clustered. Flaming torches were suspended between the pillars of the churches, and huge lanterns hung from masts placed at intervals in the chief thoroughfares. The dyer, the druggist, and the butcher, with hundreds of their fellows, were exchanging banter and gibe as the great ones passed within the enclosure reserved for dignities. In a Memphis crowd there were always two parties— Melchite and Jacobite, orthodox and heterodox. To-day there was a cross-division, and those who lived by providing for the imperial troops, and those who belonged to the families whence the militia were drawn, tossed quip and mock across the square like ball-players in a tennis-court.

Such was the scene without; and within the palace, except in one chamber, all was merriment and minstrelsy. Musicians and banqueters filled the halls; for the Pagarch feasted the officers of his household.

But in Armenosa's chamber, beneath the mysterious picture of the Christ—which now showed blood-red in the light of a ruby lamp, while all else was shadow and darkness—the father and the daughter were parting. There was no screen between them now. He saw nothing save his great debt to her. She saw nothing save her resolve to do anything for him.

"My child, my darling," he said, as he held her face from him by a sufficient space to gaze into her eyes, "no emperor is worthy of you, and I am not giving you to an emperor, but to the cause of Christ. Be strong and of good courage. I shall know no rest until I hear of your safety."

"Promise me one thing," she said. "Be kind to Menas. He has been turned from the door during my sickness, and perhaps it was for the best, but do

not let estrangement separate us longer than necessary. Meet him as of old. Tell him I have followed no leading of ambition or vanity, but the
voice of the Lord and the beckoning of the Saviour's
hand. Show him this paper "—she gave him the
scroll stamped with the seal of Marcus—" and beg
him to pray for me at morning and evening."

" I will. May a curse and not a blessing light on
me if I fail to fulfil all you have told me ! "

The trumpet - call announcing that the hour of
departure had come drowned his last farewell. The
curtains were swung aside, and, leading his daughter
by the hand, George moved slowly along the corridor and descended the marble steps. They passed
through lines of courtiers and slaves to the portal
under which the white and silver litter was waiting.
Her maidens placed Armenosa on the pillows. The
Pagarch pressed on her forehead a last kiss.

A shower of roses, poured from above, hid her for
a moment from view, and the blushing and perfumed
leaves continued to rain down long after the heroine
of the festival had disappeared in the moonlight.

George made one stately obeisance as a sign to his
guests that the feast was over, and retired. The
departure of Armenosa was a sign to the crowd to

disperse. Many had skiffs ready to row across the river, in order that they might get the start of the cavalcade and see the reception of the bride by her escort at the Castle of Babylon. But the father ascended to the roof of the palace and strained his eyes in the direction of the bridge of boats across which Armenosa was to pass. The moving lights of the torches showed first like beacon-fires, then like stars, and at last diminished to sparks, getting smaller and smaller until not a single gleam was visible.

CHAPTER XII.

THE RUBICON.

ON the same day that the bridal cavalcade departed from Memphis a host of a very different character halted at Rhinacolura, the modern El Arish, within sight of Raphia. It was the victorious Five Thousand, with which Amr had resolved to conquer Egypt. The Arabs contrasted strangely with the cavaliers of Memphis and the legionaries of Constantinople. Around Armenosa flashed cuirasses of gold, and silver helmets with plumes of white ostrich-feathers. The housings of the horses were aglow with jewels. The very swords were sheathed in diamonded scabbards. Amongst the Moslem no gold gleamed and no precious stone sparkled. Dark sinewy warriors, clad in loose robes and snow-white turbans, their arms the scimitar, the lance, and the bow, they sat erect on their superb horses in long lines, silent, grave, and expectant. For though the evening prayer was over, the word had been given to remount, and none knew what command would next be issued by the General.

It was impossible to look at these wild warriors without awe. In little more than twenty years they had been transformed from irregular bands of horsemen, living at perpetual blood - feud with each other, into a strong united force that had defeated imperial armies and laid siege to the strongest cities of the East. These men, who seemed so ill - accoutred and poorly armed, had broken legions led by Roman veterans and mar-shalled under Roman discipline. Many had charged with Derar before Damascus. Others had defeated the Emperor's splendid levies at Aiznadid. The grey-bearded chieftain of one wing had knelt with the Prophet himself on the hill of Bedr. His lieu-tenant, a fiery young tribesman of the Koreish, had been the first to mount the breach at the siege of Cæsarea. One troop armed with heavy maces bore as their standard a smith's leather apron, to mark the fact that their captain had learned his trade at the anvil. In the van was the green ensign of Islam.

In the rear floated the Hamra, the blood - red flag
which sheltered those who surrendered and claimed
quarter on the battle-field. And between these two
banners there were representatives of all the tribes
of Arabia,—some lithe and wiry cavaliers capable of
enduring the extremities of heat, thirst, and fatigue,
others gigantic champions to whom the Samson-like
feats of Ali seemed possible. Here and there were
negroes conspicuous for wearing gaudier caftans than
the Arabs, but these were exceptions. The Arab
type predominated. There was a general likeness
in the warriors one to another, and all wore a look
of grave and fierce resolution, held in check by the
habit of obedience, but waiting only a word to burst
out into flame.

Thus they waited; for Amr, Zobair, and some
half-dozen trusted chiefs held a council, under a
group of palms a bow - shot from the army, and
there seemed not at first to be agreement between
them.

After a while, however, it appeared that the
objectors were silenced and the will of Amr pre-
vailed. Then the hands that had been clenched in
angry gesture opened in sign of acquiescence, and
salutations were made, and the General on his iron-

grey horse rode forward, with a sealed letter in his hand. Like so many of the heroes of fact as distinct from the heroes of fiction, Amr was not distinguished by extraordinary stature or preternatural strength. He was short, broad-chested, and broad-shouldered; but his head was of unusual size, and his mouth large and resolute. Still, by the magic of distinction Amr was marked out as a leader of men and ruler of his fellows. In spite of the stain on his birth, his father was of the Koreish, and he had been the companion and friend of the heroic Kaled. Not only a soldier, but an orator and poet, his tongue and pen had, before his conversion, been the terror of the Prophet. But, once converted, Islam had no more devoted servant. Strong in faith, burning with zeal unquenchable, and with a dominating will, he often aroused the jealousy of his captains. But as Amr thought the army thought, and in the cabals of chieftain against chieftain that arose in the short intervals of peace a speech from Amr crushed a rival in the council as his scimitar swept and scattered his enemies on the battle-field.

As he faced his men at that critical moment they all knew that he had triumphed in debate, had overborne timid advisers, and was about to lead them to spoils and victories richer and more glorious than they had known before.

"In the name of God, the compassionate, the merciful! The time has come to read the missive which Our Lord the Caliph Omar has addressed to us. Approach, O messenger, and give us the scroll of which the string is ˙uncut and the seal unbroken."

A tall man, who had stood a little aloof from the group of captains, placed a letter in Amr's hands. He kissed it and raised it to his forehead, then opened it and read in a clear ringing voice:—

"In the name of God, the compassionate, the merciful! Omar, Caliph of Islam, to Amr-Ibn-el-Asi, General of the Armies. We charge and command you, if you have not yet entered the land of Egypt, to halt and await our orders, by which it shall be seen whether you shall retire or advance. But if this our message is not read until you have crossed the frontier, then shall you lead our armies against the fenced cities of Memphis, Babylon, and Alexandria, and shall do unto them as thou hast done˙ unto Bosra, Damascus, and Antioch."

He paused to let the full meaning of the message

sink into the minds of those who heard it, and then, turning to the messenger, asked in a natural way the question, the answer to which he knew full well before he heard it—

" On what soil do I stand, friend ? Is it Egypt or Syria ? "

" When you crossed yonder torrent you left Syria behind you and entered the land of Egypt."

A murmur of distinct approval was heard throughout the host. Amr took advantage of the moment.

" O my brethren, we might have known what our master would command. It was not to be expected that the Caliph Omar, whom the Prophet (on whom be peace !) compared to Noah, the son of Lamech, in that he prayed for the utter destruction of the infidels, should now speak even as Abu Bekr, whom the Prophet (on whom be peace !) compared to Abraham, the son of Terah, who sought to save Sodom and Gomorrah. Now, as it is written in the Book of the Koran, 'The hour of judgment approacheth, and the moon hath been split in sunder.' Behold the sign is set in the heavens."

He pointed with his scimitar to the horizon,

K

above which, half-hidden by a blood-red cloud, the moon was slowly rising. The Arabs had too lately bowed before the heavenly bodies to be uninfluenced by this omen.

"God is great." "Mohammed is the Prophet of God." "Amr is the soldier of the Prophet." "Amr wields the sword of Kaled," resounded on all sides. Zobair,[1] whose jealousy of Amr was well known, curbed his rising anger hardly. He knew that Omar for many reasons objected to the immediate advance on Egypt, and that the letter Amr had so artfully produced was intended to delay his march and not to expedite it. But, as on many eventful days in the stormy history of the new creed, the readiness of the orator had decided the policy by an apt simile or a telling fable, and certainly hitherto success had justified many attempts as bold as that of Amr's invasion. The tide was too strong to be stemmed by any opposition the rival chieftain could offer. So he followed the example of the rest and rode sulkily off to his division. Meantime the signal to encamp was given, and the host began to picket their horses,

---

[1] His full name was Az Zubair ibn Al Awwam.

and to bring out of their wallets their simple
desert fare. In an hour the meal was done, and
the men, exhausted by a long march, had thrown
themselves on the ground, and the Five Thousand
were as silent as an army under the spell of an
enchanter.

CHAPTER XIII.

THE DREAM AND THE AWAKENING.

ARMENOSA and her little army moved slowly. The heat was so intense that they could only march at night, and the time taken in encamping and breaking up camp was long and wearisome. At last they reached the rising ground now known as Kantara-el-Khazneh, the "Bridge of the Treasure," and pitched amidst the ruins of an ancient town. The sun had risen some two hours, the morning meal was over, the men were asleep in their tents, and the horses picketed beside them. Armenosa's pavilion was pitched under the shadow of a huge sandstone block, once a sacrificial altar dedicated by the Pharaoh of the Oppression. The place was distasteful to her, as, in common with all those who were brought up with any strictness of belief,

she held the memorials of the ancient Egyptian
kings as relics of devil-worship. ˙Her adventures
at Heliopolis had confirmed this opinion, and she
ordered her maidens to draw the tent curtain over
the hieroglyphs on the slab, lest by unconsciously
looking at them she should pass under a spell.

The enthusiasm which had borne her up on the
day when she dedicated herself to the cause of
her Church and nation had not died out, for she
was steadfast and strong.   But the weary days
and nights, the formality of her surroundings, and
the absence of any one to whom she could speak
freely, were taxing her powers to the uttermost.
Would the old days ever come back ? She thought
of her father, and Marcus, and the good priest
Menas, and the garden of Memphis, and it seemed
as if years instead of days divided her from her
girlhood.   Then from reverie she sank into sleep
and dreamed a dream.

She was once more in a garden, and in one far
fairer than that which bloomed around the home
of her childhood. She seemed to have lived there
a long time.   It was beautiful with glowing roses
and plashing fountains, and musical with the song
of birds.   Her bower, which was wreathed with

jasmine and lilies larger and fairer than she had ever seen, fronted a broad river. On the farther bank of the river was another garden and another bower, and there, looking as he had looked when she had last seen him, was Marcus. He beckoned her to come to him, and as she was motioning to show that it was impossible, a barge of pearl and silver appeared alongside the bank, and she walked down the flowery slope to step into it. Then the sun was darkened, the earth shook, the river that had been clear as crystal became dark and clotted and of the hue of blood, while all around her there seemed to be a conflict and struggle of armies. There were no hosts of flesh and blood charging and clashing. She saw no palpable champions, and yet there were battle-cries and groans, and the indistinct shock of armour against armour, and steed against steed, the voices of generals issuing high commands, the whistle and hurtle of arrows, and then cries of pain and agony as of tortured fiends. And all the time the demon battle raged there were thunderings and lightnings, and the storm and tumult of elemental war. The din of the fray seemed as if it would never cease, but was taken up by an end-

less succession of combatants, and while it roared
through it all, when the lightning showed her the
garden and the river, Marcus appeared standing
on the opposite bank. *He* seemed real, and she
was conscious of *her own* reality; but the storm
of warriors that swept between them were spirits
of the abyss fighting against each other with a
fury and a hate that mortal men know not. Then
suddenly all changed, and as it grew light, and a
great rainbow of ruby and emerald spanned the
scene, while the river became clear and shining,
all traces of war vanished, and instead there appeared through a silvery mist what seemed at first
a bright cluster of flowers; but, when the sparkling films rolled away, the flowers were revealed
to be radiant angels sweeping upwards from the
ground to the azure heavens, and singing praises
to One who dwelt in glory, and whose symbol was
a luminous cross.

A feeling of delicious rapture possessed Armenosa
as she listened to the heavenly harmony. Exceeding calm, joy, and peace steeped her senses. But
again there was a vision of woe. Blotting out the
angelic shapes, surged up again, more ghastly than
ever with roaring sound and lashing foam, the sea of

blood. And in the seá were struggling horses, and broken armour, and drowning men. And the face of one of the men was turned towards her, and when she saw it she uttered a piercing cry and woke. . . .

In a moment three thoughts crossed her mind. It was only a dream, but it was not as other dreams are, for it was sent by the devils whose names were engraven on the altar slab against which her tent was pitched. It was going to be fulfilled, and the voices she heard ringing in her ear were calling her to see its fulfilment.

"Awake, Lady Armenosa. All are calling for you. There is news from the sacred Emperor. There is news from the Augustus. The messenger will give the scroll to no other hands save yours. Let me bind on the sandals. Fling over all the silver robe. The captains are waiting without."

So cried the tire-women, joining in a shrill chorus, while they laved, perfumed, and robed their startled mistress, who tried in vain to discover the cause of their panic. The impression of the dream was too vivid for her to shake it off. She was bewildered, between terror of the superhuman powers, and surprise at the passion of the human beings around her. Women usually mute, doing their offices with the precision of machines and the reverence of creatures of clay before a divinity, were hurrying her to make a toilet four hours before it was necessary, and ordering the mistress before whom they were usually prostrate.

" What means all this ? Darta, you are wont to obey me when I speak."

" There is a messenger without. The soldiers are clamouring. The Prefect bade me implore your Ladyship's presence. It will restore order in the camp."

Shouts and trumpet-calls interrupted her speech and emphasised her appeal.

" I am ready."

The curtains were drawn aside, and Armenosa showed herself to the soldiers. They were grouped in parties, talking eagerly with each other, and apparently paying little heed to their officers.

Within a few yards of the pavilion lay a superb bay horse, afroth with sweat and blood, in the agonies of death. By his side knelt a man in corslet and greaves covered with sand, haggard and gaunt, with one hand supporting the horse's head, and with the other carefully guarding a thick roll of red silk.

As Armenosa stepped upon the scene, the horse shuddered all over, a quivering spasm passed over its limbs, and he was dead.

The man rose with horror and despair in his face.

"Farewell, my good Dorkon![1] You had better die. Would that your master could quit himself of his troubles as easily as you have done. Pardon, lady, I knew not I was in your presence."

"You are weary and in evil case. Give him a cup of wine," she said.

The wine was brought, and the man drank it eagerly.

"Thanks! I have not tasted such a draught for years. Yes, I am in evil case, but there are thousands worse off than I, Marianus the standard-bearer. I come with ill-tidings that little suit with brides and bridals. That scroll will attest my truth. Abu Obeidah is in possession of Antioch, thanks to the dastards who guarded the iron bridge and the traitor Youkenna. The Moslem is master of Syria. The august Emperor Heraclius set sail for Constantinople two months ago, and his son Constantine left Cæsarea secretly, and followed his father. Some of us fought like men. Had there been a few

---

[1] The war-horse of the Emperor Heraclius was so called.

hundreds with hearts like Nestorius, my general, we should have conquered. As it is, I have kept my trust." He unfolded from its staff the crimson roll, and disclosed a gorgeous embroidered banner emblazoned with the figure of Christ on the cross. "There is the standard. Three infidels clutched it. Two I cut down. The third, a negro, got off cheaper, but I have a relic of him which will prevent his forgetting me." And he flung upon the ground a sinewy black hand cut off at the wrist. As it fell on the sand with a cold thud, a cry of horror broke from Armenosa's women.

"You will have to get used to worse sights than that, my dainty maidens, if Amr-ibn-el-As enters Egypt, as he will before a month is out."

"What is this? Let me see the scroll."

"Read, and you will see that the cause of Christ and the Emperor is lost."

"The cause of Christ is never lost. Our sins may have offended a righteous God, and He may in punishment have suffered our light to be quenched, but the servants of the false Prophet cannot prevail against the warriors of the Cross."

But even as she spoke she beheld again the vision of the blood - red sea, and heard the shock

of the mysterious battle, and the words of hope
seemed to die on her lips. To hide her face she
held the parchment which Marianus handed her
close to her eyes. It was from Constantine. In
a few sentences, written as he was preparing for
flight, he bade her forget him and ally herself
with one whose fortunes were happier. The message of farewell was rolled within a larger scroll
addressed by the Emperor himself to the Pagarch.

But meantime the news had spread like wild-
fire through the camp. There was no doubt that
something terrible had happened. The haggard
blood-stained veteran was no herald of victory.
The flag was not the captured standard of an
Arab general, but the ensign of their own Emperor. The word "Lost" passed from lip to lip.
Some flung down their gilded arms in panic.
Others saddled and bridled their horses, and cal-
culated how quickly they could measure the distance back to Memphis. Some of the cowards
and traitors, of whom there is a sprinkling in
every army, drew together and began to form a
plan to seize the treasure-waggons. In less than
an hour the mass of men, who had seemed welded
together by one motive and loyal to one chieftain,

were divided and scattered in groups, evidently distrusting, if not plotting against, each other. Owing to the jealousy between the militia and the imperialist army at Memphis, it had been impossible to place a commanding officer of experience in charge of the expedition. The officers commanding the citizen soldiery were all equal, and ready to resent the claim of any one of the number to the leadership.

Armenosa, who had lived all her life in the midst of Memphian society, knew the position of affairs only too well. It was in arranging such difficulties and toning down such animosities that her father had spent the most anxious hours of every day for twenty weary years. During the journey, whenever she presented herself, though the bride-elect of the Augustus, she had never distinguished any of her glittering guards by a note of preference. Now, however, a crisis had come. Her quick eye saw the danger. Ere the sun set, that ordered army might be scattered hither and thither, or, worse, the swords Egypt needed so urgently might be pointed at their neighbours' throats. The murmur of stirring mutiny, so unmistakable when once heard, was beginning to buzz

in the ear. Handsome Damien, Prefect of the
Blue Cohort, was moving amongst his friends, and
rich Menander, Prefect of the Green Cohort, was
sending his parasites to whisper his name amongst
the poorer officers who wore his colours. The
factions of Constantinople were not unrepresented
in Egypt, and if the party-cries were once shouted,
the encampment would be divided into two parties
at once, and the rival colours would give the pretext for which the disaffected were eager. Of course
the exact state of the case was only known to those
who had heard the tidings brought by Marianus,
but all understood that the Emperor had met with
a reverse, and that the object of the journey was
defeated. To the blue factions Armenosa had been
safe as the bride-elect of Constantine; now she was
simply a woman to whom they owed no allegiance,
and her gold and jewels were the booty of the
strongest arm.

All these thoughts, that were passing through the
minds of the men around her, she grasped in a
flash of insight. She saw what wanted doing, and
she resolved to do it. But first she must secure
attention. Near her stood one of her heralds with
a long trumpet.

"Blow three blasts," she said, and springing on one of the smaller altar-stones of the old Pharaoh, she waited until the trumpet - call ceased, then raised her hand to enjoin silence, and spoke thus :—

"Fellow countrymen! when you left my father's house in our city of Memphis you were the guardians of a woman whom the divine Emperor had selected for special honour. You were going to a wedding festival. Now God has ruled that you shall have a harder but a more honourable duty. You are to guard not Armenosa, daughter of George the Pagarch, but our ancient and famous Egypt, against the armies of Islam. God has seen fit to give the false Prophet victory. Antioch and Cæsarea are taken, and the enemies of the Cross are perhaps even now upon our soil. They will enter by the route which has ever been the one taken by invaders; they will seize the key of Egypt — Pelusium. Thither, then, I implore you, hasten. I with the Green Cohort will proceed with the treasure destined for the Emperor to Belbeis, and thence to Memphis. Should you want counsel how to repel these enemies, seek it of this stout soldier Marianus, whose valour has saved the holy

standard of our faith from the clutch of the infidel!" and in a sudden inspiration she seized the
silken flag, and pointing to the figure of the Crucified, exclaimed, "*In this sign conquer!*"

The right moment was seized, the right word
spoken. The appeal to loyalty and duty struck
the better sort, who echoed the great Christian
battle-cry with ringing voices.

Then the mass of waverers, who were waiting
to see which was the winning side, followed as
a matter of course. The jealousies and rivalries
were stopped from bursting out by the nomina-
tion of the man who was the hero of the hour,
and the immediate danger of the crisis was passed.
Armenosa saw that she had the army almost with
her, and that only a stroke was needed to clench
the last rivet which should hold them together.

"Give me your sword," she said to Marianus.

The soldier handed her his short, straight Roman blade, dinted with blows and blotched with
blood-stains.

She had stepped down from the block of stone
and stood beside it. Now she laid her hand on
the hilt of the sword and called the group of
officers to approach.

"Friends," she said to Damien, Menander, and the rest, "on the hilt of this sword, symbol of the Cross, swear to be loyal, true, and faithful to your captain, Marianus, so long as he shall be true, loyal, and faithful to our master, the sacred Emperor Heraclius, and to have neither truce nor traffic with the followers of the False Prophet or with the chieftains of Islam."

The officers, as if under a spell, obeyed her voice, and laying their hands on the hilt of the sword which Marianus presented to them, repeated the oath.

"And I in my turn," said the commander, "swear to exercise this my function without fear or favour, and to hold it only until an officer shall be appointed to the command by the sacred Emperor or his representative."

Armenosa then retired to her pavilion, and the officers waited to hear what Marianus would say. In a few words he thanked them for their confidence, and urged the need of instant action.

"There is not a moment to lose. The lady speaks words of wisdom worthy of a veteran general. We must march to Pelusium. Thither the enemy are hastening. There can be no doubt that they will

L

not be satisfied with Syria. Egypt is their next
prey. Unless we can fling them back NOW, their
grip will be round our throats."

Events had followed so quickly on each other
that the young captains had scarcely realised all
that was needed. Still, the blood-stained flag and
the severed hand were visible signs of danger
that struck them more than the most eloquent
battle-speech. A chivalrous admiration for Armenosa burned in many breasts, and had given them
an inspiring motive; but her distinct and unhesi-
tating advice, which allowed no time to debate,
had more weight than anything else. Marianus
assigned each his station, detached the green cohort
which was to guard Armenosa and the treasure to
Belbeis,[1] made diligent inquiry as to the route,
and an hour after sunset the larger body began
its march along the road that the alternate armies
of the patriot and the invader had traversed over
and over again since history began. Later the
smaller cavalcade moved, by the light of many
stars, in the direction of the ancient Pharbæthus.

[1] See Note F, Belbeis.

CHAPTER XIV.

BELBEIS.

THE Moslems entered Egypt in the month Báûnah,[1] which answers to our June. Through the fiery weeks of July and August their main army besieged Pelusium, while a lesser force invested Belbeis. At last the heroic struggle approached an end, and when the hottest month of the year had burned itself out, the city of Belbeis was a city of the dead. Armenosa had hastened thither only to meet a second messenger of ill, with tidings even more alarming than those which had been brought by Marianus. As she had foreseen, the troops of Islam were actually on Egyptian soil; but as she had *not* foreseen, Amr was marching straight towards Belbeis.

[1] Strictly speaking, the month Báûnah begins on May 26, and ends on June 24.

According to the practice of all previous invaders of Egypt, Amr had determined to make Pelusium his first object of attack, and he had put his army in motion with that end. But the information reached him that a smaller Christian force was moving at a slower pace than the main army, in the direction of the present Kantarah, to Belbeis. Years before he had listened to the Prophet's call, Amr had visited Egypt, and therefore he knew its geography better than his master. He satisfied himself that it would be wise to send one column along the coast to Pelusium, but that if he was to get possession of the treasure-waggons, he must make a dash to come up with the second or convoy army, if possible, before they reached Belbeis. This he had failed to do, and on arriving there he found the gates shut, and the little garrison prepared to resist to the uttermost. As always in their early wars, the Arabs were ill equipped for sieges, and the resolute garrison held him at bay for fifty days. Now at last the Christians were on the point of yielding, not to force, but to famine. Entering the town unexpectedly, they had not had time to provision it. Armenosa refused to allow the old and sickly to be turned out as useless mouths to the tender mercies of the Arabs, and the investment of the place was so close that no relief could reach the defenders. Now fever had shown itself in the town, and the supply of water was failing. A score of men had died in one day, and there was a rumour that a traitor had poisoned the wells. The corpses lay unburied and blackening in the narrow streets. The women who watched them were too weak to drive away the crows and vultures that wheeled and flapped about their heads, coming lower at every swoop. They had held out twelve days longer than they had thought possible, waiting for succour; and no succour had come. Hitherto there had been no mutiny; but there were fewer and fewer men at their posts every day, and the eyes of all were looking to Armenosa with a pleading piteousness that broke her heart.

The decision time had come. That very morning the conditions of surrender had been received from Amr, and indeed they were more merciful than might have been expected. She held them in her hand in silence for a space, praying for deliverance and light, but no light came. She had hoped against hope that aid would come on the day just over, for it was the feast of the holy King Hezekiah,[1] and she had read how he had laid Sennacherib's letter before the Lord, and how the Assyrian had raised the siege of Salem. But the commemoration-day of Israel's deliverance was over and done, and she looked for the last time through a narrow slit in the direction of Memphis to see if there was any sign of rescue. But there was none. She rose and clapped her hands.

"Bid the prefects Damien and Menander attend me," she said to the slave who answered the summons.

And in a few moments the two men who had once been rivals, but whom the common peril had made comrades, mounted the platform.

"Friends," said Armenosa, "I hold in my hand the message of the infidel. It is idle to pretend we can hold out longer. There is no help coming to Belbeis — I believe because our messengers have never been allowed to pass the enemy's lines. Read the conditions."

The two men took the scroll, which was in Arabic with a Greek translation, each authenticated with the seal of Amr.

"The infidel demands surrender before to-morrow

---

[1] The feast, known as the Rest in the Lord, of the pious and good King Hezekiah, occurs in the Coptic month *Mesre*, August.

at noon. He promises that the lives of the garrison shall be spared, but the treasure and the commander are to be given to the Moslems."

There was a pause. Armenosa broke it.

"You have done nobly," she said. "The defence of Belbeis need not fear to be compared with that of any of the Syrian cities. We have detained Amr fifty days, and we may be sure they have been well employed by my father and the valiant Celadion in preparing Babylon to resist the invader. It is impossible to save the treasure, but had we been able to carry it to Cæsarea it would have been equally lost to us."

"Truly the treasure is the booty of the conqueror, but how can we give up our commander to the infidel when you are our commander?"

Again there was a pause.

Armenosa knew what was in the minds of the two men. In the days of their old Memphis life they had been dissipated and selfish, caring little for honour or manliness, but she had taught them a new lesson. Already in those Greek hearts was kindled the sparks of the flame that centuries later in the Western world was to bear the glorious name of chivalry!

"I know what you would say, Damien. I know

what is in your mind, Menander. You dread to
trust a Christian maiden to the infidel. You feel
you would not dare to face my father if you had
purchased your safety by the sacrifice of mine; or
perhaps," she said, smiling, "you will not allow that
I have been your commander."

"No, no," cried Damien; "the honour and the
glory are all yours. In the council-room and in the
battle-field rule us, lead us as you have done, only
to-morrow let it be ours to deliver the sword and
staff of command to the conqueror."

"It may not be. I will finish the work I have
undertaken. With my maidens in mourning weeds
I will hand the keys of Belbeis to Amr. I have no
fear. Infidel as he is, Amr, as this scroll proves, is
no bigot like his master Omar; but if I am mis-
taken, and I fall into peril from him or any of his
captains, I have but to press this gem "—she drew
a jewelled signet from her finger—"and swallow the
drug this opal conceals to be safe from danger—and
from sin. The sword of Islam gives not such a quick
path to Paradise as this ring."

.   .   .   .

Next day, an hour before sunrise, the iron-studded
gates of the city were slowly swung open, and a

procession, strange and sad even in that age of
sorrow and tragedy, issued from its portal. First
came two heralds carrying in place of their wands
of office boughs of funeral cypress. Then an aged
man, the Melchite governor, bearing the heavy keys
of the city gate. Then alone Armenosa, robed in
black, her long hair unbound, her arms bare, and
her feet unsandalled. Next followed four of her six
maidens, for two lay fever-stricken and could not
move. All the women were ghastly pale, and walked
with feeble and unequal steps across the ground that
separated them from the camp, picking their way
amidst heaped-up bodies, dead steeds, and broken
armour. Then came the carts of treasure, still enclosed in the gilded boxes in which it had been
despatched from Memphis, but drawn tardily by
the few famished horses that were left to the
besieged. And last of all in long line the remains
of the bold garrison which had fought so well. The
men who had started two short months ago to take
part in a marriage pageant came forth haggard and
hunger-bitten,—some grievously wounded, and supported by their comrades; others newly risen from
sick-beds, and propping their tottering steps with
the weapons they were about to surrender. The

procession closed with a miserable crowd of such of the women and children as had strength to crawl out into the open to escape the stench and reek of the corpses within the walls.

Though they had started in close order, many figures fell out or dropped down by the way; and when Armenosa met Amr at his tent door, the five black-robed shapes stood out in the pale grey mists of the morning like embodiments of the lingering hours of night unwilling to leave that world of horror to the revealing cruelty of the sun!

Amr, just risen from prayer, watched for the approach of the General who had so heroically defended the position. He expected a veteran like those who had led the imperial armies in Syria. But no tall figure with high crest and flowing chlamys appeared, only those dark spectral women moved through the mist. His first thought was that it was a vain appeal to his clemency; his second, that it was some cunning piece of treachery. The voice that addressed him dispelled the suspicion.

"O Amr, General of the Arabs, we come as you have desired, to surrender ourselves, our treasures, and the keys of this city, on the conditions of the scroll you sent to us yesterday."

" Who and what are you ? "

" I am Armenosa, daughter of George the son of Mennas the Pagarch, Commander of the garrison of Belbeis, which I have held for fifty days for the illustrious Emperor Heraclius."

And then the conqueror saw that he had been held at bay and defied by a woman, and a strong passion of anger and shame came over him; but when he beheld the dignity of her bearing, and her mourning garments, and saw the light of her brave spirit shining through her tears, he held his hand before his eyes, and said—

" The wives of Islam are brave: notably the wife of Aban Ibn Zeid helped her lord in the field with bow and spear; but never, since our lord the Prophet (on whom be peace) brought us from ignorance to light, has a maiden fought for us or against us as thou hast done. Therefore fear nothing. If the word of Amr has weight with his master, his head shall fall rather than a hair of thine shall suffer."

CHAPTER XV.

THE LOOSING OF THE WATERS.

AGAIN Memphis was keeping holiday, for the great festival of the Loosing of the Waters had come. As in the case of the spring feast of the Smelling of the Zephyr, the rites and observances that accompany the autumn ceremony go back for their origin to hoar antiquity. They have undergone many changes since the days of the Pharaohs, as new races and new religions have successively held sway over the people. The ideas of a mythology long since dead reappear at intervals through the vesture of customs that are distinctly symbolic of Christian doctrine, and traces of the faith of the Cross underlie the superstructure raised by Islam.

First the old myth of the Marriage of the Earth and Water common to so many Eastern nations

found an expressive emblem in the act that every
year broke the barrier and admitted the fertilising
waters of the Nile to gladden and fructify the expectant land. But with the amassing centuries the
myth had been forgotten, and about it the annual
ceremony had gathered a variety of customs obscene
and licentious to the last degree. Practices grosser
even than those which up to a recent date disgraced the fairs in many of the cities of Egypt were
frequent, and had of course a demoralising effect on
the population.

The Church wished to purify the feast, and sought
to give it a religious character. She was unwilling
to lose the idea of a bridal, but she wished to cleanse
it from coarse associations and to connect it with
sacred memories; therefore the embalmed body of
a virgin saint was lowered into the water. Later,
perhaps at the time of which we write, a holy relic,
usually the hand of some martyred maiden, was
dropped with many ceremonies into the ancient
stream. Later still a cross specially blessed by the
Patriarch was substituted for the hand. This was
the history of the Nile Feast, called sometimes the
Benediction, but oftener the Loosing of the Waters.
Like the Smelling of the Zephyr, it was a great

popular holiday, but it had a religious side and a peculiar ritual.

The Pagarch, the Bishop of Memphis, and the high officers of State assembled early at the Church of the Virgin in Babylon. Hither the relic had been conveyed on the previous night, and had been watched by the two nuns from the neighbouring convent who had been most strict in their devotions during the past year. At dawn the Bishop received the holy relic and touched certain sick folk with it, then prayers were said and litanies chanted, and all marched in solemn procession to Trajan's Canal, where embroidered tents were pitched, banners streamed, and censers smoked with incense.

Now the Pagarch gave a signal, and suddenly, as if by magic, a hundred swarthy arms went to work with axes and mattocks, and in a few moments the dam of brown mud was cut through and the waters rushed in. Then a shower of gold-pieces was thrown into the ditch, to be scrambled for by the workmen with much laughter and shouting. Next the Pagarch and the clergy mounted a gilded barge, shaped like a monster ring-dove, and from its prow dropped the relic into the water. Then with a mighty fanfaron of trumpets and clash of cymbals the stately vessel moved slowly across the Nile, so that the great ones might take part in the second and statelier pageant which was to honour the city of Memphis. The chief feature of this was a meeting of George and Celadion, who, after a celebration of the Holy Mysteries, met in a rich pavilion outside the old Temple of Ptah. There they ate and drank and exchanged compliments. The children of the chief men of the city sang a hymn in honour of the day, and then the two great ones departed to receive their civil and military guests in the gardens of their palaces.

It was arranged that the early services in the Melchite and Jacobite churches should end at about the same time, and the subsequent processions through the streets were so timed that George and Celadion should enter the large decorated tent simultaneously but at opposite doors, meet before a sort of altar decorated with flowers, and after exchanging formal greetings take their state in the high gilded chairs. All the preliminaries of the ceremony had been carefully arranged, and nothing marred the order. At the same moment the music which accompanied the two processions was heard in the distance — one band coming from the great White Church, the other

from the Church of St Gabriel the Harbinger.
The strains were loud and triumphant, but as
they both played the same hymn in honour of
the Emperor, there was no rivalry. At last, as
the trumpets pealed loudest, the two heroes of
the day entered the pavilion. White curtains
looped with silver cords were drawn to admit
George, and scarlet curtains with golden cords
were drawn to admit Celadion. Both paused and
expressed in formal phrase their votive wishes for
the health of the Emperor. Then they embraced
and took their seats, having before them the altar
wreathed with flowers, and over their heads the
gold ring-dove, sign of the imperial sovereignty in
Egypt. The tent was filled with officers of high
rank—the judges, the under-judges, the Superintendent of the Board of Punishments, the city
councillors, the Superintendent of the Taxes, the
Inspectors of the Revenues, Markets, and Granaries, the Master of the Games,—all bearing high-
sounding titles in imitation of the ranks and orders
of the Byzantine Court, and all having degrees of
precedence assigned to them, which it was a grave
offence to transgress. Their mantles, their insignia,
the length and colour of their tunics, the number

of straps on their sandals, the angle at which they held their various emblems of office, — all were marked by special provisions in the great Book of Etiquette, which regulated questions of costume and carriage in the remotest cities and provinces of the empire. Egypt was then, as it has ever been, ready as a waxen tablet to receive superficial impressions, but constant in preserving underneath its immemorial type of character. This is absolutely indelible, and was written in the faces of the groups that ranged themselves on the white side of the pavilion. They were unmistakably the descendants of the men whose mummies lay in the tombs of Thebes, and who had held the rod, the scourge, and the scales when their captive slaves built the Pyramids.

Nothing could be more marked than the contrast between the Egyptian side and the Greek side. Straight eyebrows, high cheek-bones, full lips, were the marks of the faces that bowed themselves thrice at every mention of the august Emperor's name on the left of the two thrones. In spite of curled hair, chlamys, and buskin, the civic officers were by blood and heredity Egyptians. Behind and around Celadion every figure was European. Straight profiles,

M

fair complexions, and rounded limbs showed the
breed of the officers and men who practically garrisoned Memphis, Babylon, and Alexandria. Their
crested helmets, shields, and short swords were the
time - honoured equipments of the well - greaved
Greeks.

After the exchange of salutations between the
chiefs of the two nations, they seated themselves
at the same moment on their chairs. George raised
his staff of office. The city herald, crowned with an
olive chaplet, proclaimed silence, and a choir of boys
and maidens in white vestments ranged themselves
on each side of the altar and sang a hymn.

There was a pause after the last strain died away.
Then the choregus who had trained the singers came
forward and received two purses of gold from George
and Celadion. Slaves entered with wine and fruits,
and the ceremonious silence was broken by the
exchange of congratulations, praises of the grace-
fulness of the choric hymn, and hopes that the
dreaded Nile would be a good one. So well tutored
were the Greeks that not a word about the impending
invasion was spoken on their side, though once or
twice the ominous name Islam was mentioned by the
Egyptians. At last the signal for breaking up the

assembly was passed from the chamberlains to the heralds, and from the heralds to the captain of the escort. There was that peculiar pause of expectation which precedes the dismissal of such gatherings, each one assenting to his neighbour's remark as a hint to him not to continue the conversation. Then the talk slipped from a continuous buzz into a dropping fire of single sentences. Suddenly a cry beyond the power of ushers and heralds to silence was borne from the crowd into the great square. There was a confusion of sounds in which cries of fear, shouts of wonder, and summons to arms were all blended in a wild medley.

"The enemy! the enemy! Treason! George— Islam—Amr—we are betrayed! Cut them to pieces! Let them pass."

George, in spite of a tremendous effort at self-control, grew livid and trembled. Celadion laid his hand on his sword, descended the steps of the dais, and moved with his officers to the door of the pavilion, which was rudely torn open from without.

Through a lane in the crowd of holiday-keepers, trampling over all in their way, dashed a troop of Arab horsemen guarding a swift camel with a negro and a woman on its back.

The multitude of white-robed men and women
resembled a sea of foam-crested waves parting before
one of the huge high-prowed vessels that took their
name from the ship of the desert. The horsemen
halted in front of the tent steps. The dromedary
knelt, and George saw that the woman she carried
was no other than his daughter Armenosa. All
those who were standing near recognised her, and a
strange sigh of suppressed wonder passed from one
to the other. The negro dismounted and handed a
scroll to George. For a moment he hesitated to take
it, and asked himself if he could deny his knowledge
of the character; but a translation was appended,
and seeing, or fancying he saw, suspicion in every
eye, he said—

"Whatever this may mean, it is for all to hear.
There are no secrets between me and the enemy of
Egypt and the faith. Noble Celadion, read this
scroll, and then, if it is fitting, we will publish its
contents aloud."

Celadion ran his eye over the Greek translation,
and said dryly enough—

"The unbeliever has captured your daughter and
restores her to you, whether in good faith or from
policy the saints only know. Our feast must end.

St Michael only knows if our Nile will not run blood instead of water before many days are over. We must at once to Babylon. Leo," to an officer, "take a maniple and guard the Pagarch and the Lady Armenosa to his palace."

He whispered a further command; but George could not have heard it had he spoken aloud, for all the passion of his love for his child had broken out, and she was sobbing in his arms.

Then the crowd who were afar off as well as those who were near knew it was Armenosa.

"Read the scroll,—tell us what has happened."

"Proclaim silence, herald," said the Greek commander; and stepping back on the dais, he spoke with a clear ringing voice audible to all.

"We learned yesterday that the soldiers of the False Prophet have had some successes over the garrisons of Pelusium and Belbeis. But we resolved to hold our festival, as the solemn services of the churches wherewithal the feast begins may bring the blessing of God and of His saints on our counsels and our arms. We have not, however, ceased to make preparations for defence. Sooner than we had expected the armies of Amr have advanced, and have sent an envoy with the letter that I now read. ' In the name of God the Merciful, the Compassionate! Amr-ibn-el-Asi, servaut of Omar Caliph at Medina, to the illustrious George, called the Pagarch, greeting. Be it known unto you that your daughter has fallen into our hands, and might be held as a lawful prey and captive of our sword. But we desire not that there be war between us until thou hast rejected the terms that shall be brought to thee in good time. Receive the maiden pure and unhurt, and let our clemency teach you to submit, for you are not——' "

Celadion broke off.

" There are words here that it is not fitting to read before the people. They are addressed to you, and should be read privately."

But there was no choice. The people were stirred to a frenzy of curiosity.

" No! no! There is nothing to be hidden. Read," cried the mob.

George motioned with his hand. He had not resumed his seat, but still clasped his daughter.

" Have I your permission to read the whole message? Beware, I warn you. There is danger in it."

" Read, read!" shouted the crowd.

"Read if the scroll charges me with treachery. I appeal from it to the Emperor," said George.

"Hush! for the saints' sake hush, father!" said Armenosa.

Celadion resumed: "'Let our clemency teach you to submit. I speak to you as to one unto whom Allah has given understanding, and who art not like those who make unto themselves a god of the man Heraclius.'"

The Greek commander dropped the parchment with a gesture of horror that was not all acting, though the trick of expressing extravagant loyalty to the Emperor by gestures of abject concurrence in his praises, and by starts of horror at anything that could offend him, was stamped from their earliest years into the soldiers and courtiers of Constantinople.

"I had bitten my tongue in two ere it should have uttered such a blasphemy. Comrades, forget that you have heard me speak," cried Celadion.

"It is a plot to sow dissension amongst us," cried George; "a babe can read such a transparent artifice as this. Amr has restored my child that he may appear to be in accord with me. I ask you to be patient."

"No patience with traitors. Treachery! treachery!
The Jacobites are trafficking with the Moslem. They
deny the two natures in Christ, and they are in
treaty with the Moslem."

The old fanatic spirit was aroused, and the mob,
not knowing with certainty what had happened,
harked back to the well-known cry and the phrase
that came easiest to their lips.

The Melchites and Jacobites were rapidly drawing
together, one on one side of the square and the other
on the other, leaving in the midst the Arab horsemen
and the dromedary that had brought Armenosa.

Celadion saw he had gone too far. Again he
ordered the herald to proclaim silence, and directly
the clamour lulled began to speak.

"Citizens! the infidel has blasphemed our sacred
and immortal Emperor. He is upon us, inflamed with
madness and lifted up with pride because he has
overcome the fishermen of Pelusium and the
vine-dressers of Belbeis. If any citizen of Memphis
has trafficked with him"—he looked at George—
"vengeance shall not halt; but for that there will
be a time hereafter. Meantime I must hasten
to Babylon; our citadel is no Pelusium to yield
in a week. Depart each to his ward. I will hold

a council, and by noon you shall each know what duty is assigned you. The noble George accompanies me to the fortress and brings his daughter with him. Be our watchword *Heraclius.*"

He drew his sword and raised it aloft. At the signal he was girt with a ring of flashing steel. The legionaries waved their spears and clashed their shields.

Fearing some violence, the gigantic negro drew his scimitar and advanced as if to seize Armenosa. The Arabs uttered their shrill cry, and drew together as if to resist the attack they deemed imminent.

" Assure the envoy that his person is sacred," said George.

" I had forgot," said Celadion, and in a few words he bade the Arabs go in peace, promising to answer their master's message in due season.

Then, in strange contrast with its beginning, the Feast of the Nile ended. Some hurried away in panic to their homes to try and hide their treasures of jewels and money. Others went to their several wards to await their orders. Others ran into the open churches to pray. All asked questions of neighbours who knew as little as they did of the meaning of the strange scene. But in a crisis like

this there are always spirits who want to do something original. So, as George and his party left the
square, a few set their teeth and began to hiss.

One of these was Lampo the dyer. In a moment
a hand smelling villainously of asafœtida was put
across his mouth.

"Peace. Hush thy snakes' music," said Batalan
the chemist. "It may cause a riot. There is danger,
no doubt, but until the swords are out there is a
hope some glue may be found to stick them to their
scabbards. Our holiday is marred, but we may have
a merry Nile-cutting yet."

"A merry throat-cutting you mean. Have you
heard how the Moslems got into Bosra?"

"By the gate probably."

"No. By the treachery of Romanus. Have you
heard how they got into Damascus?"

"Perhaps I have, and perhaps I have not."

"By the treachery of Josias. And do you know
how they will get into Memphis?"

"By fools like you sowing suspicion among the
defenders."

CHAPTER XVI.

TEMPTATION.

THE noble George accompanies me to the fortress."

The significance of this sentence was only too clear to the Pagarch. At last his enemies had grounds on which to base their suspicions of his loyalty. For years he had struggled against the efforts of the Melchites to prove his complicity with the Prophet of Islam. Stories of the wildest kind were circulated to show the intimacy of his correspondence with Mohammed, and many of the tales still find a place in the pages of grave historians. No wonder, then, that prejudiced contemporaries believed them implicitly. Amr's treatment of Armenosa had produced precisely the result which he most desired. Whether a politic design or a

generous impulse prompted his action can never
be known. · At all events, he had by a stroke cut
the crafty webs that George had been weaving ever
since his elevation to the government of Egypt.
The hostile faction had a handle against him, and his
own friends began to waver in their belief in him.
That scene in the great square of Memphis could
never be forgotten. An imputation on the loyalty
of the Jacobite chief had been made in the most
public place, and had been left practically answer-
less.

The sentence in Amr's letter—"I speak unto you
as unto one to whom Allah has given understanding,
and not as I would to one of those who make to
themselves a god of the man Heraclius "—had, it
seemed, to those who heard it, only one meaning.
It proved that messages had passed between the
chief of Islam and the foremost Christian layman
in Egypt which depreciated the authority and dignity of the orthodox Emperor, for at that moment
the current rumours of the heterodoxy of Heraclius
were forgotten. These were private matters between
the man's God and himself. He who sat on the
purple throne the ruler at Constantinople was the
conqueror of the Persian sun-worshippers; he had

overthrown "Chosroes Iscariot, who was burning for ever in hell."[1] Complicity with his enemies was treachery to the faith.

Then a thought rose in men's minds which aggravated George's guilt. He had been lately honoured with extraordinary marks of royal favour. In spite of his leanings to the Monophysite heresy—for his outward conformity had always been regarded as a hypocrisy—he had been preferred to men of unblemished loyalty, and offered an alliance with the Imperial family. While they were enjoying his liberal largesses and gazing at his splendid pageants, the flaws in their benefactor were forgotten; but now that everything had failed, they felt that they had a right to reproach him as not only a traitor but an ingrate. He, forsooth, whom Heraclius had delighted to honour as none of the orthodox had been honoured, had been plotting against his lord and betraying the people committed to his charge!

Then, as men talked over the day's events, supersubtle brains devised a new reading of them. Had not George known of the imperial defeat at Cæsarea

---

[1] In these words Heraclius announced his final victory. His manifesto began, "O be joyful in the Lord."

when the wedding procession was sent forth? Was
not the diversion of the treasure to Belbeis part of
a plan to plunder Egypt, to bribe Amr? And was
not the price of this Judas-like treachery the safety
of Armenosa?

At any other time the religious passions would
have caught fire, a cry would have been raised, and
George the hero of yesterday would have been the
martyr of the mob; but now the duty of resisting
the Arab extinguished every other thought. The
city was in a panic: the fierce Outlanders had been
seen in the midst of Memphis. Stories of their wild
shapes and uncouth arms flew from mouth to mouth.
A crowd can usually only think of what they see.
Moslem spearmen were visible and tangible; George's
treachery might be only one of the thousand floating
accusations that always surrounded a high official.
And though, had the Pagarch appeared in any public
place, the crowd would have wreaked their fury on
him, in Babylon he was secure.

Yet it is doubtful if personal freedom from violence
compensated for the sense of indignity that dominated every other feeling in George's mind, as he
found himself alone in a tower chamber of the
fortress, a prisoner in all but name.

"This was the end of all." These were the words he repeated over and over again to himself as he walked to and fro. For this he had turned aside from entering the holy calling of the priesthood; for this he had relinquished all the happiness of domestic life; for this he had forfeited the regard of the saintly Menas, and wronged the loyal love of Marcus, and sacrificed his daughter's happiness.

A noble and unselfish man would have been full of remorse for the deadly peril in which his ambition had placed Armenosa. A religious and genuine man would have been full of gratitude to God for giving him so noble a daughter, and for saving her almost by miracle from a hideous fate; but George had walked so long in crooked ways, and party hate, the curse of his Church and age, had so long lorded it in his bosom, that he only saw a victory of the Melchites and his own shameful defeat. The triumph that Celadion's courtesy thinly veiled was complete. He, the Pagarch, was a detected conspirator, trusted by none; indeed the iron doors which his enemy had closed on him were his only protection from the just revenge of his betrayed friends. He saw how he stood clearly, and he faced the facts. . . .

But a man who has been fighting all his life soon

recovers from a blow, recalls the victories he has
scored in field or council, and rallies himself for
another throw with Fortune. Egotism always makes
its own wrong right. After a few hours' reflection
George had persuaded himself that his only mistake
had been temporising with the Melchites, and that
for his Church and nation there was one hope, and
one only,—an alliance offensive and defensive with
the invader. The soldiers of the Prophet, as he had
always believed in his heart, were going to win. He
would seek the first opportunity to communicate
with Amr. If possible, he would acquaint him with
the weak points in the fortress, and with the various
positions of the defenders, so as to hasten the capture of the place ; but in any case he would assure
him of his good offices in the future, and pledge
himself to make his people acquiesce in the new
rule.

Bigotry, interest, revenge, and all the voices that,
like Ahab's prophets at Ramoth-gilead, unite to
hurry men to evil, pressed on George at this crisis-
time of his history, and urged him to cast in his lot
with the foes of Christ. On the other side he seemed
to hear the appeal of his daughter's voice, solitary
as that of Micaiah the son of Imlah, pleading with

him to resist the tempters. As the struggle went on he instinctively put his hands before his eyes to shut out the image of her face, looking as he knew it would look did she guess the purpose in his heart. Since her mother's death Armenosa had embodied everything that was fair, honourable, and pure to her father. She had been to him a conscience. Her bright smile assured him he was right. If there was trouble on her face he felt he must be wrong. But those that were against her outnumbered far those that were on her side. All the years of hypocrisy and resistance to his better angel were allies and auxiliaries of the evil; and now he put aside the pleading face and the recollection of the victories it had helped him to win, and rose impatiently as if to do something that should put hesitation henceforth out of his power. For a moment, in the thick of the fight between the good and the evil principles, he forgot where he was, and fancied himself free to act as well as to resolve. Then it was borne in upon him that he was to all intents and purposes a prisoner. He saw the bare stone walls of his chamber, so different from the marbles and draperies of the palace at Memphis, and flung open the window to get a breath of air.

N

But only a hot blast scorched his face, and walls
and battlements, rising one behind the other, showed
him how completely he was debarred from the outer
world.

He could hear the hum and bustle of the people
in the narrow streets. Some pleasure-seekers, who
had not heard of the approach of the enemy, returning laughing and singing from the festival;
others, panic-stricken citizens, hurrying to bring
provisions within the walls. But the only moving
objects he could see were the helmeted head and
spear-point of the sentry passing to and fro in the
court below, and catching and losing alternately the
gleam of the westering sun.

Then followed a yet wilder panic of rage and
hate. He was trapped and shackled, kept in bonds,
while the great world game of empire was left to be
played by sworders and courtiers. But do what
they might, he was still the representative of Heraclius. In the last resort Amr must treat with
him!

The light faded out, and there was no glint of
sunset flame on morion or spear-head, but his passion was not spent. He walked to and fro in the
growing darkness, lashing himself into a fury, piling

up the wrongs he had suffered to justify the wrong
he was to do.

At last there was the sound of a key turning in
the door. It opened, and a soldier entered with
a lamp.

"The Jew Eliezer asks admission; he brings a
permit from the commander. Shall he enter?"

Before the consent was given the Jew had glided
into the room. Never in the days of his greatest
pride had Eliezer bowed so obsequiously.

"Do not mock me with marks of reverence," he
said, angrily, for the word "permit" had emphasised
the sense of his powerlessness. "I am a prisoner
and a disgraced man. You and your tribe lent your
money on bad security. Go and make what terms
you can with the Melchites."

"Hush, most Illustrious. These stone walls have
ears, and a stray word reported to Celadion might
mean ruin. I have with difficulty obtained this
interview, and the moments are golden. Listen
and trust me."

"Speak; let me hear if your voice agrees with
that of the unseen spirits."

"If they are spirits of truth, it must agree with
them. Once for all, know that the imperial sway is

over in Egypt. The mercenary legions will hold out for a few weeks or months, but the end is certain."

"When you last saw me you helped me to beggar myself to aid Heraclius."

"I suffered more than you did; but I confess I was wrong to try and uphold the tyrant. Strong in self-conceit, I set myself against the counsel of our wisest rabbis, thinking by bribery to win back the tomb of Jeremiah. I have been punished. I should have known, when Heraclius issued his edict against our nation at Jerusalem, his doom was sealed, and his fate was to be like that of Sennacherib and Heliodorus. I know now that it was blind folly— nay, worse, it was falsehood to my people to help him, and I have been punished. There is no resisting what is written, and the gold I gave you to aid the Christian has strengthened the Moslem. Egypt is given to Islam. This fortress will only keep him back for a while, then—what follows depends on you. At once renew friendship with Amr. Tell him he has an ally in the heart of the citadel. Assure him at once before it is too late. A word *now* before he has conquered will be worth a thousand words when the breach is in the wall and his standard on the tower of the Beacon."

Eliezer stopped for some reply often, as he poured out his appeal in a voice nervous with passion, though studiously subdued, indeed at times almost a whisper; but George remained looking at the speaker like one dazed. He was struck silent with wonder at the suddenness with which another hand, as it were, had seized him, and was dragging him across the line he was on the eve of passing alone.

There was no daughter's voice to warn him. Conscience had let go the helm. The bark was caught in the rapids, and hung for a moment in suspense; then, oarless and pilotless, was carried away by the whirling waters.

"You say to me what they all say," he murmured, dreamily.

"Assuredly there is no hope elsewhere. But we have only a few moments. Write me one word to Amr assuring him of your good offices. Tell him that his foes are the Melchites only, and that the Jacobites (save a few fanatics) still look to you for guidance."

The Jew drew from his girdle a small writing-case, took out a slip of papyrus, and placed a reed pen in George's hand.

He wrote almost the very words Eliezer whispered in his ear.

The paper was scarcely signed and superscribed
when they heard the key turn in the lock.   Eliezer
thrust his prize into his breast and rose.   The
sentinel entered and announced that the hour granted
for the interview was over, and motioned the Jew to
go out before him.

Then George was left alone.

The darkness closed on the solitary man as he sat
with clenched hands and shut lip, stern in his resolution to baffle his rivals though the price of his
triumph was the wreck of his nation and the slavery
of his Church.

.   .   .   .

It is not easy to estimate the weight of consequence which that night's decision involved.   To
George the Pagarch, a mysterious figure whose true
name had until lately almost dropped out of history,
was committed far more than the future of Memphis.
It is not too much to say that had a united front
opposed Islam at that critical hour, the tide of Arab
conquest would have been rolled back.   Alexandria
with all its wealth of learning would not have fallen.
Constantinople would have been saved its six years'
siege.   The military spirit of the Greeks, which was
crushed by the second capture of Alexandria, would

not have died out, and the part played by Constantinople in the future would have been worthy of her
Roman origin. George first set the fatal example of
trafficking with the Moslem which in later years
wrecked the crusader kingdom in Palestine and sold
Spain to the Moors. He first taught the Arab that,
though foiled in battle, he need never despair of
victory as long as Christendom was divided against
itself.

CHAPTER XVII.

THE PRIEST'S SECRET.

AND now began the work of preparation for the siege. It seemed as if sufficient victuals and war material would never be brought into the fortress to enable the garrison to hold out as long as they hoped to do, and the constant messages of scouts and spies bringing word of the near approach of the enemy warned Celadion to hasten the laggards by naming an hour when the gates should be finally closed.

The priest Menas had been working hard all day amongst the poorer people, comforting the women and children, a large number of whom it was necessary to send out of Babylon, and seeing to the conveyance of the most precious vessels to places of secrecy and security. An hour after sunset he had finished his more pressing tasks, and sat with Marcus in the room where we first saw him.

"Had you not better go to rest?" said Marcus. "You have had a weary day."

"No, my son," he said. "I have sent my reader away, and asked you to come here because I have yet to do the most important work of all, and I must have your help in it. Lock the outer door, so that no one may intrude or overhear. Come nearer and listen. To day I have despatched by trustworthy hands to Memphis and the convents the most costly and holy chalices, patens, flagons, and consecrated vessels that we have inherited from ancient days; but the treasure of treasures remains, and that I will intrust neither to Church nor monastery. You and you only, my son, shall know where it is concealed. The priest of this church, the oldest in Babylon—perhaps in the world—is a guardian of a copy of the Holy Gospels which was partly written by the hand of the blessed evangelist St Mark. I received it from my predecessor Zacharias, who had it from the holy Molatius, who received it from Sergius the Martyr. This must never be touched by the infidel. If it is God's will that Egypt pass under the power of Omar, as Palestine and Syria

have done, we must bear it as a chastisement for
our sins; but this most sacred volume must be
deposited where no sacrilegious touch can defile
it. If God grants us peace, you will seek the spot
where it is hidden and give it to his Holiness the
Patriarch. If it is discovered in the meantime, the
finder will read in this scroll which I shall bind
round it, under what penalties he takes it from its
case or shows it to any other eyes save those of
Benjamin or his successor."

"Where will you find a place of security? The
world is given over to bloodthirsty and deceitful
men, and the spoiler's hand is everywhere."

"I have thought anxiously. There is one spot
and tomb in the desert not far from here, guarded
by images set up by the old devil - worshippers.
It is shunned of all, as though the lightning had
blasted it."

"Was there not a booth there long ago, dwelt in
by a holy hermit?"

"There was a booth or the relics of one until the
great storm wrecked it. But the dweller there was
no holy hermit; he was a parricide who fled thither to
hide himself, and at last died by his own hand. This
has added to the ill renown of the place, and makes

it safer for our purpose. Besides, who knows but the presence of the blessed Evangel may help to remove the curse."

Thus saying, he took a lamp from the table and beckoned Marcus to follow him to his sleeping-chamber. Then he unscrewed a bracket which supported a crucifix over the head of the mattress on which he slept, and disclosed a small door in the wall. This he opened, and putting in his hand drew out a silver case wrapped in folds of embroidered silk. This he reverently kissed himself, and then held it to the lips of his companion. The silver case was tightly closed, so that no portion of the sacred writing was exposed to the air.

"I have seen it once," he whispered; "but then it was shown to me after forty days of fasting and prayer by my predecessor Zacharias (equal to angels), on the Easter Day before he entered into his rest."

Then he motioned Marcus to be silent, and after closing the small door and replacing the crucifix, they quitted the house.

The streets were crowded with people, and piled with huge barrels and crates of provisions which were being brought in at the last moment. The officers, however, kept the mob in tolerable order with strokes of their vine-sticks; and as the priest was recognised, and supposed to be going to visit some sick or dying penitent, a passage was respectfully made for him, which would have been accorded to no one else. Turning sharply down an alley, he soon gained an unfrequented street and reached the city gate, which was open.

They were not unwatched, though the throng of citizens were occupied with their own business, and hurrying to get it finished before it should be too late. Two eyes, sharp as poniards, peering from behind a money-changer's counter, were fixed on the priest and Marcus, noting their every movement. Their owner, Eliezer, knew that many sacred vessels had been conveyed away already, and he guessed that Marcus was carrying silver or golden treasures of especial value to some hiding-place outside the walls. He did not hesitate a moment, but called to a slave who sat outside the shop to close the shutters, and not to expect him at his evening meal. Then he joined the crowd, and slipping and gliding through its intricacies in his snake-like fashion, regained sight of the men he had sought. When once the gate was passed he followed at a cautious distance, keeping to the left and moving parallel

with the two at a pace which was exactly adapted
to theirs.

Once in the desert, Menas paused and rested.
There is no twilight in the East, and it was quite
dark. Indeed it was not easy to find any landmarks
or guiding points. They left the ruins of the village
of Troja, devoutly believed to have been founded by
Menelaus, to the left, and walked as fast as they
could. As they got out of reach of the noise of the
busy fortress-city behind them there were no sounds
except the occasional cry of a jackal. The silence,
and darkness, and mystery of the place, seemed to
forbid speech, and they exchanged no word. Suddenly Menas stopped.

"There is something stirring behind us," he
said.

Marcus had heard nothing, and they moved on.

The sky was clouded, and the few stars that were
visible lacked the usual clear-cut, gem-like brightness of the Egyptian night. It was sultry, and there
was a trouble in the air that filled the two men with
a sense of the neighbourhood of unseen powers other
than the shapeless darkness and the buffeting wind.
Their tread made a muffled sound, save when the
hurrying feet struck against a stone.

"I wish we had a moon to light us," said Marcus. "It is hard to know if we are bearing towards the tomb. Surely it is farther toward the left."

"Fear not; I shall be guided aright. If the moon shone, we should be liable to be seen. I have a lantern which we can light when we come to the place. The ground is beginning to rise. We are not far from the end now."

But with Menas the spirit was stronger than the flesh, and he had to halt and take breath many times as he traversed the long sandy ascent. The hot wind in their faces made the task harder than it would have been otherwise, and the older man often needed the support of the younger. They tried to pierce the darkness, but heavy slumberous clouds covered the sky, and hid the few stars that had been visible. There was no distinct horizon-line, and the objects that seemed for a moment outlined in front of them altered their position and shape so often that the disappointed eyes refused to be cheated by cloud phantasies, and distrusted the reality of the actual hillocks and mounds until they were absolutely fronting them. The powers of the priest had nearly given way, and he could only clasp his hands in thankfulness when the tomb, the old treasure-guarding god, and the few palm-stems, relics of the outcast's hut, were at last reached.

"Rest, father, for a few moments. You are faint and exhausted. Lean against this slab and take breath."

The old man obeyed, and remained for some time motionless as the stone that supported him. The moments of perfect quiet reinvigorated him, and after lying apparently dead for a while, he rose with a long-drawn sigh of relief.

"I am strong," he said. "Now let us light the lantern, and be careful. The wind is gone down, and that wall will shelter us while I get a light."

After some delay and many vain attempts the flint-fire was struck and the lantern lighted. It showed a cavity in the side of the hill large enough to admit a man, and inside the entrance there were hieroglyphs and symbols partially obliterated.

"Stoop and enter; after a while you will find yourself in a chamber. In that there is a stone coffin, the lid of which you can slip aside. Put the precious case enclosed in its wrapping into the coffin, and note well the paintings that are above the sarcophagus, that you may know it again. Stay; unfold the silk and read the scroll I have tied round the case."

Marcus read—

"This case, containing the Gospel of the holy evangelist St Mark, placed here on the feast of the assumption of Isaac the son of Abraham, in the month Mesre, in the year three hundred and twenty-one of the righteous martyrs, when the armies of the infidel approached the city of Memphis and the fortress of Babylon, by the priest Menas. O thou who lightest upon this treasure more precious than fine gold, give it unto the holy hands of the Patriarch who shall then bear sway in the preaching of St Mark. In this be faithful, as thou lookest for mercy in the day of the Lord."

The reader paused as he asked himself, "Would his be the hands that should open this depository and take out the sacred scroll, and when and how should he visit the spot? Or would the secret be disclosed in distant years when he was dead and forgotten?" He thrust aside these thoughts and forced himself to obey Menas mechanically. He took the case, then entered the passage, groped his way into the larger chamber, and found the coffin. By a vehement exertion of strength he slid aside the narrow but heavy lid. There was no corpse inside,—nothing save a few withered lotus-flowers. He placed the silver case in the coffin, readjusted the lid, and returned.

He found Menas listening intently, with one finger on his lip and the other raised to command silence. Marcus held his breath and uttered no sound. He could hear nothing except a slight rustling amidst some brown wood.

"It is a lizard moving amongst the dry palm-leaves," he said.

"The noise I heard was too loud for that."

"It is a fox. They are common enough here. I have caught them often in a trap when I was a boy."

There was a still longer pause of suspense, but all was quiet.

"I must have been deceived," said the old man. "You have deposited the treasure in the place I told you of safely? But I know you have, my son, for you have never failed me yet in duty or obedience. We have done all we can, and must leave the issue to God."

He blew out the little lantern and prepared to return. The wind had fallen, and the whole desert prospect seemed lighter than before. The shape of the hillocks and the ruins that dotted the sand here

and there were now dimly seen. They walked
faster than when they were going from the city, as
the ground sloped downwards and was easier for
the old man's breath than the ascent, slight though
it was.

They had not gone far before a curious figure rose
from behind the pile of palm-trunks and stones that
formed the ruins of the hut. It was thin, sinuous,
and clothed in a long yellow robe. There was no
mistaking the Jew Eliezer.

"I am glad I came," he muttered. "These two
Nazarenes are hiding some treasure in that tomb.
I will not search for it now. In the days to come
the wealthy man who is wise will be as one of the
poor. It will be hard to keep jewels or gold from
the clutch of the Arabs. All the nation are sending
their plate and stones of price to Italy. All the
money left us after the advances to George I have
laid out in grain. But that neither Pagarch nor
commander shall know yet. In the siege they will
soon feel the bite of hunger, and then they will come
and crouch to me for a morsel of bread as they did
to Samuel the prophet." So saying he set his face
towards Babylon, and entered the city a few moments after Menas and Marcus.

CHAPTER XVIII.

THE COUNCIL OF WAR.

FROM the west tower of the Castle of the Beacon
the modern traveller who is venturesome enough
to climb it sees stretched before him the Saracenic
splendours of Cairo—the mosques and minarets, the
tombs and the palaces, of nine Mohammedan dyn-
asties. Above all he sees the marvellous Citadel
Mosque, like the palace of a magian enchanter or a
pageant dome of cloud-land. On the September day
in the year 639, Marcus, looking intently, beheld
nothing but fawn-coloured sand alternating with
waving palm-groves. The boundary was the Mokattam range of hills. Between lay vineyards and
patches of verdure in green strips, and then sand,
nothing but sand. Above him wheeled the Egyptian
kites with their flapping wings; from below rose

the stir of awakening life in the busy town that
clustered round the fortress. He strained his eyes
until they were weary. It seemed as if those he
expected would never come. At last from behind
the sandhills, in and out between the stems of the
date-palms, he saw a thin moving line. Here and
there a patch of colour, then a flash as of steel or
brass touched by sun-fire. These specks of light
became a sparkling unbroken line, sending out rays
like a procession of tiny suns. Next figures moving
steadily came out. White is the prevailing colour
of the riders. Then the undulating sandhills inter-
vene between them and Marcus, and the ground
swallows them up. He closes his tired eyes to rest
them for a moment, then fixes them on a nearer
point where he knows the line will next appear.
He waits some time, but when once it emerges all
is distinct and clear. Not a line of white robes and
starry radiating steel, but an army of which each
unit is a warrior joying in the neigh of the battle-
steed—longing for death beneath the shadow of
swords.

"They have come at last," said a deep but trembling voice. It was that of the Pagarch, who had
mounted the stairs and come out upon the platform

unheard, while Marcus was absorbed in watching the approach of the host.

"I must give the alarm. They will be upon us before we are prepared to meet them!"

"Wait. All the preparations that can be made are made. Cannot you trust our Melchite commander for that? The valiant Celadion has his outposts who will fall back in exemplary military fashion when they sight the enemy. There they are."

And as he spoke Marcus saw a squadron of cavalry in gilded helmets and corselets gallop across the sand and make for the shelter of the suburbs. No horsemen pursued them. The Arabs halted in a long line with their faces toward the town; then, at the shrill word of command, changed their formation and drew up in the shape of a widely extended crescent. They remained perfectly silent—not a chain jangled, not a steed stamped. Then a cry louder than the last rang out, and in a moment every trooper had dismounted and stood beside his horse. There was yet a third cry, and the white turbans were all prostrate on the sand. It was the hour of prayer, an auspicious and happy hour for approaching within sight of the goal of their enterprise, and every heart in the host beat high with the assurance that it was an omen of victory. They repeated their prayers, made the proper genuflections, then rose as one man. The sight bore in upon the mind of Marcus the great lesson which, as we read the history, stamps itself on our minds—

"These men think one thing, believe one thing, hope one thing. We are only agreed in hatred of those whom we should love."

"We need keen swords in our hands, and wise counsel in our heads, to repel the attack of such a host. But God and His holy angels are with us, and we will not despair."

The Pagarch said nothing in reply, but strained his eyes to observe the character and further proceedings of the enemy.

. . . .

There was no slackness in the preparations of the besieged. All day boats were crossing the river, bringing provisions and material from Memphis. Men and asses laden with grain crowded the bridge of boats. The defences of the island of Rhoda were strengthened by numerous stockades, and strongly hooped barrels, said to contain some new and mysterious projectile, were stored in the high-walled granaries on the side of the island farthest from the castle. Huge catapults were swung on the battlements by heavy chains. Sheaves of arrows were laid in readiness near every embrasure, slit, and eyelet-hole of the walls. Cart-loads of enormous stones from the quarries of Tourah were brought in and hoisted by cranes to the catapult platforms. Iron kettles and ladles to contain boiling oil were ranged close by the catapults. Every available inch of room, even ledges and window-sills, were filled with cross-bow bolts. One courtyard was devoted to the smiths with anvils and hammers ready to repair injuries done to the headpieces and coats of mail. But the greatest care was taken with the fosse or ditch which encircled the castle. This had been thick sown with sharp iron spikes, spear-heads, and jagged nails. To render it more difficult to pass, pits were dug in it, and these were filled with pointed steel rods, like modern bayonets. Over these pits were placed thin planks and mats covered with earth, so as to tempt the besiegers to trust them as safe footholds. Then it was hoped that the front-rank men, writhing and struggling in these infernal traps, would delay their following sufficiently to hold them as a mark for the arrow volleys and crossbow-bolts. In a word, as the

Arabs would try to carry the walls with a rush, the Greeks by preparation and tactic laboured to render this impossible.

The work was terribly hard. All day the naked sun was ablaze in the sky, scorching and blistering the brown flesh of the slaves who dragged the heavy machines along the sand or struggled with them through the zigzag alleys of the stifling fortress. Bruised by the vine-stick of the legionary, bleeding from the hide-whip of the taskmaster, tortured by the pressure of weights which always fell with cruel incidence on the weak place in each man's body, stung and bitten by mosquitoes, half-poisoned by filthy flies, the Egyptian worked as he had worked under Pharaoh, doggedly and hopelessly, in dust and blindness, reek and sweat, never for himself, but always to strengthen the conqueror of yesterday against the conqueror of to-morrow.

It was the last weary day of a week of weary days. Extra rations of bread and fish had been served to the labourers, and half the effective force of the garrison, consisting of soldiers who had been resting during the day, were turned out to guard the battlements. Many of the rank and file had not seen any service save that afforded by keeping in order the

Jacobite factions, but they were officered by tribunes and centurions who had conquered the Persians under Heraclius, and who still moved with the gait and bearing of men who fought under the eagles of all-conquering Rome. Four of these chief captains— Leo, Michael, Nicephorus, and Phocas—were summoned by Celadion to meet in a hall of the fortress, called from its containing a portrait of the Emperor the Room of the Picture, there to take final counsel and decision.

Though Celadion had exchanged his silver armour for a serviceable coat of mail, and his delicate buskins for plain leather sandals, there was enough of the courtier in his voice and gesture to show how different had been his training from that of his associates. The four officers were men of the time, compounded in varying proportions of fighter and theologian. Leo was nearly all soldier and Phocas all bigot, whereas Nicephorus had moods and moments when casuistry overlaid his militarism like the filigree pattern on his armour, and Michael's orthodoxy was tempered by quotations from profane writers.

When all were seated the commander spoke thus :—

" Comrades, it is likely to be our good fortune to

defend this post for our orthodox and adorable Emperor against the heathen worshippers of the False Prophet. Drunk with some successes over the Syrians, they have sent their swordsmen to attack this imperial province. But they forget that it cost the Persian Cambyses ten thousand men to do what they are attempting with five thousand. We cannot wish anything better than that they should dash themselves against this rock. We are brave, we have had time to prepare for their reception, and I will not anticipate anything but victory. I have called you together to ask your counsel. To-morrow the enemy will with their usual insolence summon us to surrender. Shall we parley with their envoy from the walls or admit him into the fortress?"

There was a pause: the veterans had sneered and shrugged their shoulders during the ornate flourishes of the preface, but the practical question with which their commander ended set them thinking, and being Orientals, they did not ask themselves first, as a Western man would have asked himself, Which of these two plans is the wiser, and which shall we do? but, What second motive has the commander in his mind prompting him to ask this question? and they concluded aright that he desired to see if any had trafficked with the Moslem; for a traitor would desire to admit the enemy's envoy, but a loyal man would parley with him from the walls. And the four high captains, who were really loyal, having no desire *for* or interest *in* treachery, said with one voice, " Open not the gates, O valiant commander. Hold no speech with the infidel save from the walls."

And all held up their right hands, and Celadion, making a pause as if to assure himself that they were unanimous, said—

" It is well."

He proceeded—

" To you, Nicephorus, who are our stratopedarch, I give command of the northern bastion; to you, Michael, the west; to you Phocas, the east; and to you, Leo, the south. Is this wise in your eyes ? "

Again he paused, again they held up their hands, and again he said—

" It is well."

" And now," he said, assuming a more confidential voice, "I have assigned you your places, I assume my own. Should you need help at any post, I will not fail you; but while you are fighting the enemy without, I shall watch the enemy within. I have taken the first step. The Pagarch, who has given me his parole, sleeps to-night in the house of the priest Menas, with whom he has placed his daughter. But he has not regained his freedom. To-morrow he will find quarters suited to his dignity prepared for him in the northern bastion—thy charge, Nicephorus—and he will not leave them. New locks were put on the door yesterday. The keys to fit them are in my girdle." He flung them on the table with a jangle of iron that woke the echoes of the arched roof. "Does this please you, comrades steadfast and orthodox?"

For a third time he paused, and a third time they held up their hands, and said—

"It is well."

"The last matter is this. You know Callinicus of Heliopolis. He has toiled for years to compound a certain war-fire which shall do in a moment what our arrows, crossbows, and mangonels take months to do. It will burn up an army like the lightning of heaven. Of this I have a secret store laid up on Rhoda. Does it please you that we bring it to the citadel?"

The proposal was received very differently from the former ones.

"Callinicus is a sorcerer," said the burly ignoramus Leo.

" He who mimics the lightning shall perish by the lightning," said the epigrammatic Michael.

" We might use it against the Moslem, though not, I think, in a war with Christians," said the scrupulous Nicephorus.

" A monophysite Christian is worse than a mono-theistic paynim," said the dogmatic Phocas.

To assent to this proposition or to deny it was equally dangerous, and none of the four was disposed to touch the gantlet thrown down by the last speaker.

" We will trust to our own weapons then. I did but desire to know the pleasures of your valiancies. We are of one mind in all that is important. Now to sleep, that we may be ready for to-morrow."

The commandant rose. The four captains saluted him by touching their winged helmets, then bent the knee to the portrait of the Emperor which hung on the wall, and departed to their several quarters. Celadion stood for a moment in a reverie after he was left alone.

" In spite of your wisdom the war fire shall be at hand. The priests tell us these Koran-readers are the spawn of Sathanas, and the hot flame will only give them an early taste of the climate they are destined for."

CHAPTER XIX.

THE FIRST ASSAULT.

"BLESSING and peace; blessing and peace, blessing and peace." Thrice the call to prayer resounded, in strange contrast with the work to which it was the prologue.

Then reverently and quietly Amr's little army performed their devotions. Not an inclination of the body, not a lifting of the hands, not a movement of the feet, was omitted. As they worship in the mosques to-day, they worshipped in the plain where those mosques were to cluster so proudly a few years later. Every man dismounted, stuck his spear in the ground, and standing beside his horse, copied each bow and genuflection, each word and tone of his commander. Then Amr spoke—

"Comrades, we have offered the Nazarenes who

dwell in the city such terms as are fitting. We have offered them life and peace if they become the followers of the Prophet (may God bless and save him), and if they are rebellious and obstinate, the sword is drawn and the arrow-feather at the bow-string. Fear not the number of the enemy. It is written in the Koran, even in the Sura called 'the spoils' revealed at Mecca, 'If there be one hundred of you who persevere with constancy, they shall overcome two hundred; and if they be a thousand of you, they shall overcome two thousand by the permission of God, for God is with those who persevere.'"

As he ended, the whole line moved forward until they were within bow-shot of the walls. Then suddenly and all at once the arrow-storm hailed on the defenders. If a Greek spearman showed himself on the battlements, if a single eyelet-hole in the wall showed the flesh of a face or the glint of a morion, it was a target for an archer who never missed his mark. Then steadily, under cover of the discharge, Zobair, and Abadah the gigantic negro, hurried forward, with lash and goad and prick of lance, a mixed gang of blacks, Copts, and fellaheen whose charge it was to drag the huge palm-trunks that were to bridge the moat and batter the gates. Twelve enormous masses of timber crashed and scraped and rolled along, impelled by hundreds of naked wretches for whom there was imminent death in front and certain death behind. The sun blazed overhead. Amr's officers had not had time to choose only able - bodied men, and weaklings fainted and dropped out. The ropes of palm-fibre often broke, and had to be pieced again, causing recurring delay and discouragement.

The attack was to be directed against the east gate. Here half a mile of burning sand had to be covered by this primitive siege-train, and for the last two hundred yards they were fully exposed to the discharge of darts and arrows from the walls. Owing, as we have seen, to the perpetual vigilance of the Arabs, the Greek bowmen were at a terrible disadvantage. Still some of the showers of shafts poured into the midst of the crowded gang of men who dragged the palm-trunks, and pierced the straining breasts of the slaves who acted as team-leaders. If a man dropped, his replacement caused further harassment; for when a halt was called, for however short a time, to drag out the body of a disabled man, the whole team stood at gaze, and were easily riddled by arrows and missiles innumerable. At last the foremost of the line of palm-trunks was brought within sight of the moat. The bottom of this was defended, as we have seen, by sharp spikes and spear-heads, but these had been concealed with layers of planks artfully covered with earth and shrubs. In all such manœuvres the Greeks were masters, and no effort had been spared to make the fosse-work look natural and safe. It seemed a pit of brown Nile mud, with shrubs of prickly pear tufting its sloping banks. All looked so secure that Zobair ordered the rear men to push the trunk down the slope, and the front rank to jump into the fosse, divide, and be ready to drag it up the opposite side. If groups of four or five had gone down into the treacherous ditch this might have been done. Indeed a few lithe Arabs actually crossed the planks without their giving way, and scrambled up the castle side of the fosse. But in their zeal to obey their leader a troop of fifty men rushed down together. The false stays cracked beneath the weight, and in a few minutes the fosse was a mass of bleeding, struggling, writhing bodies.

The first rank lay spiked on lance-heads, nails, and calthrops, while the second rank, pouring down

P

upon them in masses, pinned their comrades on the
bed of torture and death. Paralysed at the sight,
the Arab archers forgot to maintain their fire, and
the Greek slingers, seizing the opportunity, poured
volleys of heavy stones from the battlements on the
choice troops who were protecting the teams. At
the same time the bowmen from the slits and eye-
let-holes in the flanking towers showered arrows
with jagged points on the shrieking, cursing mass of
bodies that struggled in the fosse.

Celadion and Phocas watched the success of their
device from the battlements.

"Don't waste your arrows, men. That tall fellow
has as many shafts in him as Sebastian, while there
are two devils who have climbed up under the
cactus-bushes this side with whole skins. Ha! the
crossbow-bolt has knocked them over."

"I pray your Excellency not to liken the circumcised infidel to a holy saint and martyr of the
Church. Such random words can bring no blessing
on us, and the day is not won yet. These men show
more fight than the Sun-worshippers."

"Thanks for thy reminder, good Phocas. By St
George, that black fellow must be under the protection of Sathanas himself. He seems to enjoy our

archers' welcome as if it were a girls' rose-pelting on a holiday."

"It is he they call Abadah, doubtless from Abaddon, the home of the fiends infernal. But see, he retreats."

"It is only to rally his squadrons. Look, he has cleft to the chin that man in Syrian head-gear who was turning to fly. Now he brings up another team, and they are fixing the palm-tree as a bridge to span the fosse. It will cost some men to fix it if our bolts fly straight and——"

A sharp cry interrupted the speech, and Phocas fell heavily with a clatter of steel on the pavement beside his chief, the blood flowing profusely from an arrow-wound in the mouth. The temporary panic which had seized the Arab archers had passed, and arrows, aimed with the same fatal accuracy as before the interruption, came hailing in at every crevice. Celadion drew out the shaft and called to two soldiers to carry Phocas to the surgeon. He stayed to ascertain that the wound was not serious. This done, he returned to his post. On the spot where Phocas had fallen he found the Jacobite Marcus.

"How," he said angrily; "I ordered you to keep

in your father's quarters.   You risk arrest by trans-
gressing my commands."

"I should have risked the fate of Egypt had I
obeyed them.   We are attacked on the south side.
This assault made with such show is not led by Amr.
The Moslem general himself is at the gate of St
Sergius."

"The gate over which your chief and future father-
in-law is imprisoned, and where the Jacobites are
herding.   And *you* bring me news of this."

"I do; but on the way I alarmed Leo, who was
in a sound sleep.   The walls are lined by this time,
and Amr will fail, as Zobair and Abadah have
failed."

The cry "To arms!" and a shrill trumpet-call
broke further speech.   Celadion saw that the alarm
had not been given a moment too soon.   The picked
troops of the Arabs were forming for the attack,
marshalled by a figure on an iron-grey war-steed,
who was evidently Amr himself.   At the moment
Celadion and Marcus gained the battlements a rain
of arrows whizzed and hurtled round them.

Then a band of twenty men with shaven heads
and half-naked bodies, wild with the drunkenness
of battle, singing a strange chant of which the only

word audible was the name of Allah, plunged two
and two into the fosse, carrying on their shoulders
a long scaling-ladder fashioned of rope and cane.
Either by accident or knowledge, they chose a spot
on the earth-covered platform which bore their
weight, crossed with incredible quickness, and began
to fix the ladder against the wall. One man, seemingly of prodigious strength, knelt while another
climbed on his shoulders. A third clambered on
the back of the second, and was actually within
reach of a low window barred with iron, to which
he prepared to bind a rope. A feat which at any
other time would have seemed the trick of a troop
of acrobats, appeared then a military exploit whereof
the success meant ruin. Marcus rushed down the
tower stairs and dashed his poniard into the
frenzied face that stared at him through the
grating. The face changed to a mass of blood and
disappeared as the man fell backward, toppling
down his two supporters with yells of pain blending
with their battle chant.

But now a like fate to that which befell Zobair
overtook the troops of Amr. Whether chance or
secret advice had led the twenty to choose the point
for crossing the fosse which they selected, and where

the planks were well supported, can never be known;
but even if the timely arrival of Marcus had not
baffled the attack, it would have failed owing
to the fiery fervour of the Arabs. Instead of
adventuring across the fosse at one narrow point
and in a line of two and two, a mass of swordsmen
crowded down the slope, to fall as their brethren
had done on the points and jags of the hidden
chevaux-de-frise. There was a repetition of the
carnage; but as the desperation and fury of the
picked soldiers were greater than that of the others,
the wounds inflicted were more ghastly than those
received at the northern tower. Veterans who had
fought in all the battles of Islam, and who had seen
the scimitar of the Prophet flash in the front of
twenty battles, were not to be disheartened. They
poured over the bodies of the impaled men; they
fought through the chaos of writhing limbs and
gashed faces which formed a bridge of bleeding
trampled humanity; and then found themselves
baffled by the tall masses of Roman masonry that
fronted them, stark, sheer, and impregnable.

Amr saw that his first attack had failed, but
before he gave the signal for retreat he determined
on one desperate venture. He did not imagine that

it would succeed. It was written that Babylon was not to fall on that day, but he saw that something was required to sustain the courage of his men. It would give them something besides the slaughter of the morning to talk over in their tents. It would supply a strain for their singers and a story for their tale-tellers of which he should be the hero. The zeal of the little army needed to be kept at fever-heat, and hitherto the campaign, though successful, had been barren of high exploits. Amr resolved to cover the morning's repulse with a feat of daring which should set ablaze the fire of his minstrels and strike dumb the prophets of disaster. He took a rapid glance to see what he could attempt. Any effort to effect a lodgment was hopeless. He guessed by the steam rising above the battlements that the defenders were getting ready their caldrons of boiling pitch to pour down on the struggling mass in the fosse, and before this was ready he must summon out of reach of it as many of his brave men as could struggle back. He foresaw that the soldiers who would pass that pit of horror would be few. He could not give them victory that day, but he could give them an omen of victory on the morrow.

As we have said, a few of the forlorn-hope had

struggled across the fosse, and, gasping from the
passage, stood dazed before the solid walls which
faced them. Every window and arrow-slit rained
barbed and poisoned shafts. No frieze, or cornice,
or gargoyle stood out for hand to grasp or rope to
coil round. The ten (for the zealots had lost half
their number) stood round their scaling-ladders like
shipwrecked sailors on a reef. While round them
surged the blood-red wave tossing on the narrow
shelf, they stood on the wreckage and the war-drift
of the battle. As it was, there seemed no retreat
for them. One or two might by a miracle recross
the fosse over the bridge of bodies; but the rest
could not escape, and the first stream of boiling
pitch that poured over the battlements must scald
and shrivel to death the men under it. But the
eyes of the Greeks might be diverted from the
defence for a moment, and in the instant of slackness the Arabs might retreat. Every man of these
Dare-alls was a treasure to Amr as the signet on his
right hand, and as it was, their failure had dashed
the courage of his followers. He saw all this in
an instant, but he saw something else. Just below
the barred window so nearly entered there was
a small doorway long disused and built up with

masonry. Over this doorway was a narrow niche once occupied by a figure of St George, and in this a gilded crucifix wreathed with flowers had been placed in honour of the Nile festival. Amr pushed ahead of his men, thrust past those who were hesitating on the brink, and, leaping from his horse, dashed into the fosse, crossed on a fallen tree-trunk, and scrambled up the other side. Then with his poised spear he aimed at the crucifix, and struck it full in the midst of the superscription scroll. The whole feat was transacted in a moment. The cry of horror from the Greeks was lost in the victor shout of the Arabs as their hero *recrossed*, sprang into his saddle, and, waving his hand in air, called on all to follow him. In the panic of astonishment, as he had foreseen, the rain of missiles ceased, and nine of the forlorn-hope scrambled back across the fosse. In the sweep and swing of achievement he carried all before him. It seemed to the fierce religionists that they had gained their end. They forgot in that mad moment that Babylon was untouched, and that they had been foiled and flung from its walls like surf from the shore. They only saw the fragment of the cross sticking on Amr's lance-point. The symbol of the Nazarenes had been overthrown. Under the screen of this exploit the champion of Islam drew off his men. Zobair and Abadah had suffered too heavily to remain longer under arrow-fire, and, leaving a pile of dead and wounded to fester in the sun, they made for their encampment. At first they had thought the shout announced some real success, but Amr's flying figure seeking his tent told them that he had fared no better than they had, and had only raised the note of triumph to cover his discomfiture.

CHAPTER XX.

THE SIEGE.

ARMENOSA had viewed the battle from the tower of
the Beacon. She was thankful that the enemy
had been foiled, but the sights of horror she had
witnessed recalled Belbeis. Images of ghastly combats when the scimitar cleft the spear, visions of
faces transfixed with arrows, shapes of rearing
horses gushing with blood from stabs of lances,
all crowded in a welter of horror before eyes to
which hard sorrow had denied the respite and relief
of tears. At last, when there was nothing more to
see and the end had come, she crept down the stairs,
hurried through crooked passages and winding
streets, and entered the Church of the Virgin. It
was almost dark, but a gleam of sunshine lighted up
the pictured saints. Michael's brandished sword

and Stephen's golden censer were touched with
fire. She knelt before the picture of the Christ
and covered her face with her hands. Of the many
holy places consecrated by legend and miracle in
olden Babylon, that was the holiest spot of all.
Here, according to immemorial tradition, the blessed
Mary and Jesus had rested, and the spot was specially sacred to Armenosa, for in the font beside the
altar she had been baptised by Menas. Here she
had often prayed in girlhood. Here she had received
the holy mysteries with her mother shortly before
her death. Here she had prayed with Marcus before
her simpler maiden life was absorbed in the public
career at Memphis. And now in her day of tribulation she came back to the old shrine to see if there
was a ray of hope for her Church, her father, or
her lover.

It was long before a word of prayer would come,
and she knelt as motionless as the pictured saints
around her, until even the single sunset gleam had
died out and the darkness had settled down. At
last the fountain was unsealed and she was able
to pray. Her devotions ended, she rose to leave
the church, when a footfall she would have known
amongst a thousand struck her ear, and a man

carrying a lamp entered and stood beside her. There was no voice that thrilled her as this voice did, for it was the voice of her lover.

It was their first meeting since he had carried her, senseless and fainting, to the Convent of the Holy Tree. In the interval she had been snatched from him, by her father's ambition, to become the bride of Constantine; she had been the champion of her nation and a captive to the infidel. As in the never-to-be-forgotten dream, a river of blood seemed to have separated her from him. But now, though that river still surged round them, he held her in his arms, she looked up into his face.

"Dearest, it seemed as if we should never meet. I have longed to see you, but dared not after your father told me you bade me forget you, and that for our Church's sake you gave your hand to Constantine."

"Marcus, had I not your own words?"

She took a small scroll from a locket she wore round her neck and put it in his hands. "Yes, your own words, 'Obey thy father and my father—a short parting, a long reunion.'"

"I never wrote those words," he said.

Then a dread that had been slumbering in

Armenosa's mind awoke never to be lulled to sleep again—*her father had deceived her.*

But even this suspicion could not mar the joy of that sweet meeting. All the old days came back, and they instinctively sought the inner shrine together.

Then, after kneeling for a short time in prayer, they went into the outer court of the church and sat a while hand in hand as they had sat as children.

"When I heard of your danger I hated myself for not having gone with your escort. I could have disguised myself, and to have been near you would have been everything."

"I could not have expected *that* after the letter you thought you had received from me. But I prayed for you so during the days when we were shut up in Belbeis."

"Tell me of that. All Egypt rang with your name. I was proud to think my queen had done so bravely!"

"No, no. Let us talk while we can of the present. Every moment is precious. Tell me of our General. Is he hopeful of help from the Emperor? Is there danger of our having to yield to Amr? O Marcus, Marcus, anything but that!" and she hid her face on his shoulder.

He soothed her with gentle words, and cheered her with brave ones. Then the time came to part. They had only been together for an hour, but it seemed an age of joy, for our happiest hours are not always our shortest hours. They lingered for a while in the porch, and as they said "Farewell" the star of love, clear-cut as a gem, came out in the glowing sky.

This was the only uninterrupted meeting of the lovers for many weary weeks. Individual hopes and sorrows were swallowed up in the work that absorbed all the energies of old and young, men and women, in the beleaguered fortress.

.   .   .   .

The days and weeks that followed the first unsuccessful assault were terribly like each other, only that as time went on everything grew harder to the besieged. The daily routine of duty was more difficult, as the watches had to be kept with reduced numbers, giving to each sentinel a longer spell of duty than he could well bear. The losses in withstanding the constant assaults, as well as by disease, were heavy. The most unhealthy time of the year was approaching, and the soldiers suffered terribly from the heat. Amr never for a moment relaxed his efforts, and not a week passed without an attack. The times of these attempts the Arab chief endeavoured to conceal by a hundred oriental stratagems; but the Christians were well informed of all that went on in the camp, and were only once surprised. The attempt was repelled, however, and a chosen band of Amr's " Dare-alls " were once more repulsed. Later Marianus contrived, under cover of the night, to establish a position on a neighbouring hill, still keeping open communication with the Nile. From this point of vantage a most harassing arrow-fire was poured on the Arabs whenever they attempted an attack in force. On the walls the mangonels and ballistæ were worked with extraordinary skill and precision, and the losses of the besiegers were heavy. Several of the chiefs among the foremost in fame and fervour were killed or wounded, crushed by the huge missile stones hurled from the battlements.

Ever since the day when he had given him timely warning of the enemy's movements, Celadion had treated Marcus with confidence. The prejudice the general entertained against him was dispelled, and he won a high place in his regard. Two loyal natures usually understand each other, and before the siege had lasted a month Celadion trusted the young soldier as thoroughly as he did his veteran captains. There was another reason for his liking the society of Marcus. With the Byzantine officers Celadion felt himself bound to adopt the exaggerated phraseology which was proper for a courtier. It was expected at Constantinople that the conversation of a loyal servant of the Emperor should be seasoned with quotations from the poems of George of Pisidia and Theophylactus Simocatta, and Celadion found it difficult to recollect any lines from those poets that suited the present crisis. At any other time he would have delighted to compare the six Persian Campaigns of the sovereign to the six days of creation,[1] and to pour on Amr all the epithets of abuse, classical and ecclesiastical, that he had been accustomed to bestow on Chosroes; but just now the struggle was too real and the chance of victory too small for this rhodomontade, and the commander talked little to his fellow-countrymen. In fact Leo, Phocas, Michael, and the rest respected the chief for throwing off the courtier and appearing "plain soldier"; but he had been so used to the disguise

---

[1] This is the theme of the 'Hexemeron, or Poem on the Six Days of Creation,' by George of Pisidia.

that he was ashamed to appear without it save to the
unsophisticated Marcus.

Wherever fighting was going on Callinicus was
to be found suggesting and directing the operations
of the defenders,—now altering the angle of some
huge crane-like machine so that it might act with
truer aim; now supplying stones and bullets to the
soldiers who were slack in working their engine;
at other times superintending the boiling of the
oil or water that was to be poured scalding hot on
all who tried to scale the walls. But his triumph
was the invention of a contrivance by which the
iron ladles formerly wielded by hand were swung
over the battlements, and thus discharged their
contents without hurting the thrower.

He held long colloquies with Celadion, and was
shut up in a smoky chamber fitted up as a laboratory
for hours; but when questioned about his work by
venturesome strangers, he was grimly silent, and
to intimates he replied by a volley of maledictions,
in which the names of heathen gods and Christian
saints were strangely blended, directed on the head
of the Jew Reuben. It seemed that, either from
treacherous design or sheer devilry, his apprentice
had stolen some ingredient essential to the mixture

he was compounding, and though he worked through
long nights endeavouring to find a substitute, he
was not able to discover it. The majority of the
garrison knew nothing of the importance of these
researches; but Celadion, as we have seen, was fully
alive to it, and as the inventor came to him morning
after morning with a gloomy, baffled face, his own
spirits sank. Time was telling on the besieged.
The monotony and strain of the long imprisonment
within stone walls, the perpetual vigilance required,
above all, the gradual disappearance of the hope
of succour from Constantinople that had been
present in every soldier's breast, though unconfessed,
were breaking the spirits of all.

But there was another and a deadlier foe than
Amr and his zealots threatening the Christians, even
"the third of the daughters of War"—Famine. The
supply of food was failing. Every day the rations
given out were smaller in quantity. At sunset, when
the enemy were engaged in prayer and no attack was
likely to be made, a trumpet summoned the non-
combatants in the citadel fortress, and the soldiers
not on duty, to receive their allowance of meal, and
this was now scarcely sufficient to sustain life. The
Jew Eliezer and his brethren had bought up the

provision of grain, and were demanding exorbitant sums for the smallest measures of corn. The commander's supply of money or military chest was exhausted, and the food required for the troops was purchased by promissory notes bearing enormous interest. Rumours that the rich Jew was starving the people got abroad, and his life was menaced on more than one occasion when he showed himself abroad. Food had been brought across the Nile from Memphis at first; but the Arabs, who were reinforced by two thousand men from Syria, soon stopped this communication with the capital by their close investment of the place. Altogether the stronghold of Christian Egypt was sore beset, and her defenders were in evil case. Without, her enemies were gathering in numbers, and growing in confidence and courage. But her greatest danger was from within.

CHAPTER XXI.

A NEW SUITOR.

WHEN the gates were once closed and the fortress invested, George was allowed a greater appearance of liberty than was granted him in the interval between the Feast of the Nile Cutting and the approach of the Arab army, but he was really a prisoner. Celadion visited him and treated him with every outward mark of courtesy. He spoke of his close confinement after the scene in the square as a necessary measure to save him from the violence of his Melchite fanatics. Indeed in private it was the commander's habit to speak of the religious passions with the arched eyebrow and deprecating smile that was the fashion at Court, and he carefully avoided paying George so bad a compliment as to believe he took either of the

great parties seriously. Some few wrong - headed
ecclesiastics might probably think the doctrinal
questions of value; but amongst men of the world
they were only useful as party cries, to which at
certain seasons it was wise for policy's sake to
pretend to listen. Of course external and formal
marks of respect surrounded the Pagarch wherever
he went; but as in a state of war the control of
affairs passed naturally into military hands, he was
never consulted as formerly on general questions
of public security and administration. This supersession, though really owing to Celadion's distrust of
his colleague, was artfully assumed to arise only from
the altered circumstances of the case. Avowedly
George was deprived of authority because he was
a civilian,[1] really because he was a suspect. But
the Melchite dared not bring him to trial or in-
flict public disgrace on him. He was the highest
official in Egypt. A few months ago he had been
singled out by Heraclius for a special mark of
favour. His influence might still be large, and
to disgrace him publicly might be dangerous. He
contented himself with having George's movements

---

[1] The statement that the post of strategos was ever added to
that of Pagarch is not proved.

and correspondents watched, hoping that he would put himself in his power before long. The Jew visited George frequently; but as every one of mark in Memphis and Babylon had relations with the great dealer in money, this excited no attention. Still in this intercouse, which was considered of no importance, lay the real danger. Proposals of mysterious purport passed every week. Sometimes under the wings of carrier - pigeons, sometimes twisted round arrows, sometimes, during short truces, in the coffins of the dead. By emissaries and signal codes known only to the nation, Eliezer communicated to his brethren or confederates in the camp of Amr, and these men conveyed secret packets from George without themselves knowing their contents.

Thus the state of affairs within the walls was known to the besiegers with amazing precision. But Amr really gained little information of value. The situation of affairs was obvious. Given a crowded fortress beleaguered by a powerful and vigilant enemy, and the process of exhaustion felt by the besieged is a quantity easily estimated. The supplies of food were rapidly and surely diminishing. The tribesmen of Eliezer had bought up large

store of provisions, and were selling them at famine
prices to the garrison. The diseases always rife
in the Nile - land when the great river rises were
spreading amongst the soldiers, and the people
were waxing mutinous and discontented.

Armenosa saw little of her father. Her time
was spent in tending the sick and wounded. She
had gathered round her a little band of women
who, without religious vows, were in the truest
sense Sisters of Charity. They met every morning
in the Church of the Virgin for matins, and then
started on their several errands, returning for
vespers when their day's duties were done. Then
another body who had rested during the day under-
took the harder task of nursing through the night.
The name of the Pagarch's daughter was held in
honour over Egypt. Amidst rumours of cowardice,
treachery, and self-seeking, there stood out, bright
and unsullied by taint of detraction or breath of
calumny, the defender of Belbeis. The Melchite
Macrinus had talked of her heroism on the memorable day when she rallied her citizen soldiers, and
compared her to Deborah, Esther, and Judith.
Taking the hint, eloquent preachers had eulogised
her from their pulpits, until in the midst of one

florid comparison between the daughter of the
Pagarch and the wife of Heber the Kenite she
had risen and left the church. Now, however,
in less prominent places Armenosa's name was
cherished. Beside the pallets of fever - stricken
women and in vaults where wounded men tossed
in delirium, the lessons learned in the Convent
of the Holy Tree were practised with the sweet
sympathy and tenderness that Barbara's Sisterhood
had never attained unto. When not watching, she
slept in a chamber next to that assigned to her
father; but he was usually absent when she returned after vespers, and she seldom saw him.

Sometimes, but rarely, she knew by the light
glimmering through a small embrasure that he was
within; and if she was too tired to sleep, as often
happened, she heard his steps walking heavily to
and fro in his room, and occasionally voices, which
told her he was not alone.

One evening after mounting the first flight of
steep steps she found herself in unusual darkness,
and on looking up saw that the window on which
the staircase depended for light was blocked by
the figure of a man resting his arms on the ledge.
She at once recognised her father, and as she paused

for a moment to recover her breath she looked at
him without speaking. Since she had seen him
last he seemed to have grown much older. His
green robe hung loosely on his limbs, and his
hair was quite white. The contrast between the
Pagarch as he had looked in the days of his power
and the worn figure before her held her silent, but
the face he turned on her when she touched his
arm and called his name startled her yet more by
its strangeness. The eyes burned in their deep
hollowed sockets, the cheek - bones were almost
fleshless, the overgrowth of wiry beard could not
hide the nervous twitching of his jaws, and the
voice in which he spoke to her was more changed
than his expression.

"Armenosa, I have waited to see you. Come to
my chamber. I want your care as well as these
wretched cut - throats whose trade is bloodshed.
Forget them for a while and think of your father."

The words were unjust, but she did not feel the
sting of them. The speaker's tone and countenance
frightened her so much that she did not grasp the
meaning of what he said. She followed him up a
few more steps and entered his chamber. The room
was in the same tower in which he had been first

imprisoned, but was larger, and furnished with embroidered couches, a prayer-desk and crucifix, and a picture of St George. Some swords, arrows, and cross-bows stood in a corner. On the table was the day's ration of bread untasted, writing materials, and a dagger.

"I have not seen you for many days," he continued. "You have been doing work that you think meritorious, trying to save lives foredoomed to die. It has been painful and loathly drudgery. I do not blame you; but it will soon be over, and your future years will be as happy and splendid as I have always seen in the stars they must be. Years ago I studied . astronomy, the science of sciences. A Persian Fire-worshipper whose life I saved taught me the alphabet of the art, and Eliezer has drawn horoscopes of friends and enemies for me, not knowing whose they were. I have drawn yours, and I knew long ago you were to save Egypt by an alliance with its ruler. Hence the eagerness with which I welcomed the offer of Constantine."

"Father, in mercy forget all that. We have paid a bitter penalty for that dream. This is no time for marrying or giving in marriage. I love Marcus and no one else. For the supposed good of my

Church and nation I stifled that love and obeyed you. We were convicted of error and rebuked by a direct chastisement from God. Our private ambition, our plans and preparations, were overruled and turned against us. If ever God's voice spoke, it spoke when I was compelled to yield to Amr at Belbeis the gold that I was bearing as my dower to Constantine. All our devices failed, all our forecasts were foolishness. Forget these things, and let works of prayer and charity fill up the days— how few they may be God knows, they cannot be many—that have to pass before the night comes."

She laid her thin hand imploringly on his hand. He felt the beads of the rosary she held in her fingers touch his, and he drew it impatiently away.

"No, no. These are the dreams of convents and nunneries, not the thoughts of sane men and women of flesh and blood with brains to plan and hearts to aspire. I was wrong once, and, as you say, we have suffered for it, but tyros in all sciences make mistakes. It is written legibly so that a child may read it—HERE."

He drew from his breast a paper marked with astrological figures.

"This is the prophecy."

He opened another paper in Arabic characters rolled within the first.

"This is the fulfilment.

"It is no vanquished claimant of a throne he cannot hold who speaks, but the conqueror of Egypt, conquered by you after the siege of Belbeis. The moment this idle resistance to what is fated is ended—and I can hasten its end when I will— you may reign in Memphis."

She looked at him in absolute wonder. It seemed, as the bright eyes flashed and the nervous hands gesticulated in passion, that his misfortunes had driven him mad.

"Do I speak to a stone? Do you understand?"

"No, father. You are sorrow-wearied and brain-wearied. Rest a while."

She rose and tried with one of the loving gestures of old days to draw his head towards her, that she might clasp it in her arms. He thrust her aside.

"Am I father to an image? Have you ears to hear and brains to understand? I say you may be queen in Egypt, the wife of Amr."

Then it seemed as if the earth gave way under her feet. Not when the flame struck her from Reuben's arms at Heliopolis was she more utterly stunned; but then the thunderbolt saved, now it seemed to strike faith and hope out of her life for ever!

When he had bade her sacrifice Marcus, her belief in her father had been rudely shaken. But at that time, fresh from the disciplined and ordered life of the convent, and weak from the shock of the mysterious explosion, she had acquiesced after a struggle. Besides, her father had appealed as it were to the sacred picture of the Crucified, and the oracle that could not lie had spoken. Then she had Marcus's own handwriting, or what she believed to be his handwriting, releasing her from every promise to him and bidding her obey her father. Though the battle had been a hard one, she had conquered her love and gone forth on a mission that was to hasten the end Menas had taught her was worthy of every effort—the union of the Churches. Now she knew all this had been a pretext, and she had been deceived by her father. There could be no faith possible to her after that disclosure of treachery. When *he* had failed her, on whom could she depend? He was ready to betray the name of Christ—he was ready to betray anything for *self*.

All this was seen in a moment of time. It struck her speechless. If she had suddenly been shown that her father belonged to a different order of beings to herself, she could not have been more astounded.

But still he went on pouring out appeals. They sounded like the liturgy of some unknown religion to an unknown god.

"Think, my child, of the rage and shame of Celadion and his Melchites when the daughter of the man they imprisoned reigns in Memphis and they sue and supplicate to kiss her feet. Besides, the city of the Cæsars, their New Rome, is far off, and their throne is threatened by a hundred foes; but it is Egypt, our own Egypt, you shall rule."

Each sentence of base appeal seemed like a spell stripping off one veil after another and showing her the sordid material wherewithal her idol was composed. Then by some trick of association a picture of the Temptation seen years ago in some forgotten church rose before her, and she heard nothing he said, but only over and over again the text which was the legend of the picture, "All these things will I give thee, if thou wilt fall down and worship me."

As his words poured out she looked at him in
silence. The picture faded from her memory. The
text ceased to sound in her ears, but she felt herself
being ever removed farther and farther from him by
the black depths of a sundering gulf.

It happened that when the colloquy began they
had stood in the clear light of the moon. But a
cloud had passed over its face, and now between
father and daughter a shadow had indeed fallen.
The kind darkness hid him from her. It was easier
to speak when she could not see the face that she
had loved so well.

"Father, I beseech you, say no more. If you let
me go now, I will try to believe that all this is a
dream as fleeting as the shadow which now divides
us."

But his wild ambition had him in its clutch, and
he could listen to no other voice.

"Armenosa, stay, I command you. Honour, rank,
revenge, everything, hang upon your 'Yes.' It
is written in the stars, — you cannot fight against
it."

"It is written by Him who made the stars,
'Whoso loveth father or mother more than Me,
is not worthy of Me.' Do not hinder me. If I

hear no more, not one of those unhappy words which you have spoken to-night passes my lips; but if I hear more, I will not promise silence."

"Traitress, I see you have learned Melchite lessons well; would you betray your father?"

He reached out his hand to detain her, but she opened the door and sped down the stairs.

R

CHAPTER XXII.

THE CARRIER-PIGEON.

EARLY in the morning of the next day George was roused from the stupor in which he had passed the night by feeling the grasp of Eliezer on his shoulder.

"I have come for your daughter's answer to Amr's message. Have pity on a lover's impatience. The children of the Koreish are hot-blooded and are not used to coyness in their womankind." George looked him in the face with the preoccupied gaze of one who did not understand what was said to him. Eliezer continued.

"My messenger is waiting for his message," he said, drawing aside his robe and showing a carrier-pigeon nestling close to his breast. "There is no time to be lost. The hour just after dawn is the safest. Later there is danger from arrows and crossbow bolts."

George passed his hand across his face and seemed gradually to catch the speaker's meaning.

"There is no message to send," he said, in a strange dull voice. "The negotiations are broken off. I cannot treat with Amr."

"Cannot treat with Amr? Why, he has a score of your letters in his hands."

"He will receive no more."

"You refuse to give him Armenosa?"

"Armenosa herself refuses him."

"I expected as much. You Christians should learn how to rule your children from us."

"No, Eliezer. It is over, and I wish my tongue had been torn out by the roots ere I uttered the proposal. That is the only answer I can send," and he handed a slip of papyrus twisted in a quill to the Jew.

Eliezer unfolded it and glanced at the writing.

"That answer you will not send. Let Amr think the reply has gone astray. Give time, and Armenosa will change her mind. Women do not refuse thrones. She played the same game when you received Constantine's offer, but changed her mind

when she saw the bride's paraphernalia. Saving a
few Christian trinkets, she can wear it all as the
wife of the Moslem bridegroom."

The Jew held George so completely in his power
that he now threw aside his old air of deference;
but as he said these words he felt he had gone too
far, for there was a look in George's eyes and a
movement of the hand towards the dagger on the
table that warned Eliezer he had gone too far.

"Pardon me if I anger you. Let that pass. I
came to speak of a more pressing matter than
marriages or dowries. Babylon must fall. If the
siege lasts longer the Zobair party will remove Amr.
They have already sown suspicion of his loyalty in
the mind of Omar. At all events, we must hasten
the end; I cannot afford to wait. The fever has
begun to carry off the officers—all of whom are on
my books. Prefect Damien died yesterday. Twenty
men were put on the sick-list the day before. Celadion longs to end it, though he will never surrender
while he has a Spathar strong enough to hold a
spear. But his fierce courage will not let him
miss a chance of a fair fight. Urge him to call a
council, and then and there suggest a sally of the
garrison."

Hateful as the proposer was to him, at that moment the yearning to break out of the imprisoning walls was as strong on George as on the rest of the besieged, and he assented.

"The hour is come. There is nothing else to be done. I will do so."

"But you must not be seen too often with me; I am suspected. Propose a sally; that is all that is necessary. Only I must be certain that you have succeeded. If the council accepts your advice, throw your green chlamys over your right shoulder as you quit the conference. I will be on the watch. Leave the rest to me."

Assured by past experience that he would not be wise to press George further, Eliezer took his usual formal leave and left the tower. He turned down a narrow lane to avoid a party of soldiers who were relieving guard, and walked on for a few yards uninterrupted. Suddenly he found himself fronting a strange group. It was made up of half-starved men and boys seated in a circle. Most of them had sold all their possessions, save a few rags, for morsels of bread. They were diseased and filthy. Their hungry eyes glared from under mats of hair. Their limbs were stark and thin. Some were shivering and

chattering in ague fits, others coughing and spitting
blood, but all the wretched abjects laughing or trying
to laugh, and clapping their hands and wagging their
heads, in a spasm of mirthless merriment. The moving causes were a man and a dog. The man, one-eyed
and deformed ; the dog, a grotesque mongrel cur of
the breed that showmen teach to play conjuring tricks.
The animal's favourite performance was to pick up
rings one by one from a heap cast before him and to
return each to its proper owner ; but rings were scarce
among his present patrons, so he was attempting the
more popular act of character-telling. At the moment
Callinicus, for he it was, had achieved two successes.
First he had told the dog to point out a heretic, and
the cur had sniffed at the tattered robe of a little
Greek pedagogue. Next he had asked him to point
out a wine-bibber, and the beast had nosed a poor
fellow who had hidden a half - empty flask in his
tunic and had dragged him from a vault in which
he was skulking.

"Good dog, good dog," cried the philosopher.
"Now point out the cleverest man in the company."

The shaggy paws immediately rested on the
master's shoulder, and the pink tongue slobbered
his face.

"Good again! Now, Hylax, *attention*." He stopped
to emphasise his command. "Find the man who
starves the people!"

In an instant, with a low vicious growl, Hylax
sprang through the little circle and fastened his
white teeth in Eliezer's shoulder.

"A Jew! a Jew! Well done, dog! well done,
Hylax! Pull him down. See what he is hiding."

In the tussle the carrier-pigeon Eliezer was holding
fell fluttering to the ground. A dozen lean hands
clutched at it, and a scramble began among the
hungry wretches for the morsel. The attention of
the men was diverted from Eliezer and he darted off.

Callinicus took the opportunity to pick up his dog
and disappeared, while the mob vented their dis-
appointment at losing their sport by yells and
execrations against "Jews, Manicheans, and Samar-
itans!"

When they had shrieked themselves tired they
gradually melted away, and when the last of the
howling ragged crew had vanished, Callinicus, with
his dog under his arm, crept from his hiding-place,
and, shaking his fist fiercely in the direction the
Jew had taken, muttered, "I have found the father;
I shall be on the son's track soon."

CHAPTER XXIII.

THE SCAPEGOAT.

"DOWN with the accursed race! Death to those who keep the bread from the hungry! To the battle ments with him! Fetch a rope. No; hanging is too merciful. Starve him as he has starved us. Bring stones and mortar, and let him peak and pine inch by inch in the vaults below St Lazarus's Tower."

These cries, mingled with many less articulate, smote the ears of the captains as they stepped from the council-chamber into the street.

"What is this?" said the Pagarch, who wore the end of his chlamys over his right shoulder. "Is there a mutiny in the garrison?"

"No," said Marcus. "The people are shouting aloud what they have been muttering for a week past. Eliezer and his Jewish brethren have been raising the price of corn, until the people have taken the law in their own hands and broken open their storehouses. He has had warnings enough, but when could a Jew resist the glitter of an aureus? It must be stopped: the man is old, and the fright may be the death of him."

As he spoke the cries grew louder and shriller. The tramp of hurrying feet and the swaying and surging of a crowd pouring down one of the side-alleys mixed together in a babel of noises that sounded bestial rather than human.

"Draw the cord tight, or he will get his hand loose and cast a spell on us. Blindfold him, for his eye can strike you with paralysis. He touched the daughter of Cosmas lately, and she is dying of fever. To the platform of the Beacon! Hoop! We don't often get such a game as this afoot."

Then followed yells, shrieks, smacking of rhinoceros-hide whips, screams of agony, cries for mercy. And with a rush and sweep a crowd of men, women, and children confronted George and the captains.

They were haggard and hollow-eyed, their arms and legs fleshless, their nails like talons, their eyes bloodshot. Some of the men wore corselets a world too wide for their bodies, and sword-belts that hung loose about their waists. Others were non-combatants—half-naked wretches who had sold their garments for bread, and children emaciated with disease and hunger,—abjects who would have excited nothing but loathing, except that their ghastly intentness of purpose made them terrible; for in the eyes of all, from the eldest to the youngest, glared nothing but hate, and of this hate the victim was an old man weak and tottering on the grave's brink, whose steps those children should have propped and whose grey head those soldiers should have shielded. Absolutely different from the Eliezer who had shared the counsels of the Pagarch was the prisoner who confronted him now. George, though a master in the art of hiding his feelings, started back astonished. Was this blood-stained, dust-bedraggled bundle of yellow rags and streaming white hair the man whom he had so lately felt to be his master?

"Stop, for God's sake! This is too horrible," he said, raising his hand with his old gesture of authority.

The noisiest of the crowd, astonished at finding themselves in a presence that had still all the dignity of habitual command, paused. Menas seconded the appeal of George.

"Listen to the voice of Mercy. Have you no spark of humanity in your breasts? Let white hairs and seventy winters plead for him."

But the priest could not prevail over brutality blended with superstition; indeed his advocacy inflamed the mob, which was largely composed of Melchites.

"A Jacobite pleads for a Jew. Take care, or we may find a rope strong enough to swing both of them;" and with a yell that seemed the voice of the fiends of the pit, they began dragging Eliezer up the steps of the north tower. But only a few could mount the stairs at a time, and the main body of the ruffians, waiting to ascend in their turn, blocked the way.

Celadion, who had stayed a few moments behind the rest of the Council, now came up. He learned from the Pagarch the cause of the disturbance, which it was all-important to him to stop at once. His quick eye glanced along the straining line of hunger-bitten faces that fronted him, and tried to see any to whom an appeal could be made with likelihood of success. As things stood he dared not press his authority, though he was stronger than when he entered the council-chamber that morning.

There were Melchites all round him. He was
prepared, however, to make a strong effort to save
the Jew, and determined to use an argument which
would speak to Celadion with special force. He
knew that Eliezer held promissory notes the pay-
ment of which the Hebrew fraternity would demand
remorselessly if any evil befell their chief. Those
who had sought to escape the clutches of the Jewish
usurers by acts of violence had been over and
over again undeceived. They did not deal with
individuals ; their transactions were with a vast
secret organisation, and their bonds, in duplicate
and triplicate, were lodged in the hands of partners
in Constantinople, Alexandria, and Jerusalem. It
struck George as possible that Celadion had thought
that he would gain by letting the mob take their
course. He must be shown that it would not only
be cruel but ruinous to slacken his efforts to stay
violence.

"Celadion," he said, "stop these madmen. If
this Jew is injured, we make his nation our enemies.
They will destroy every barrel of meal rather than
give it us. They have begun throwing grain into
the Nile. If we conquer, we shall be bondsmen to
the usurers; if conquered, we shall have no money

to ransom ourselves. Stop them if you kill the ringleaders."

Celadion saw the truth of the words.

"Stop!" he thundered. "Prefect," to an officer who had been forced to a front place. The man struggled out of the ranks and came to him. "Fool," he whispered in his ear, "do you want to have every gentleman in Memphis summoned to pay up principal and interest at a week's notice? which we all shall be if this old scoundrel's weasand is cut."

The Prefect, and spendthrift whose acceptances filled several drawers in Eliezer's cabinet, started, drew his sword, and stood up to his chief with the instinct of discipline.

The yells ceased for a moment, and the crowd paused, not knowing what to expect.

"You may thank St Michael that you have come across me, you shouting fools, before you had gone too far to stop. Now stand aside and let the illustrious Pagarch, myself, and Prefect Theodore have a free passage to the staircase. And I may tell you that there is a caldron of hot water on the northern platform, which will be emptied on your heads if this street is not cleared by the time I have got there. Let no one follow us. I will cut down the first ruffian that puts foot on that step."

As he spoke Celadion passed beneath the arch and began to mount the steps slowly and haughtily; but directly he saw the cowering wretches turn away, and was sure he would not be followed, he quickened his pace and hurried up the tower stairs.

As it was, he was only just in time. While he had delayed to parley with the rioters the men who had Eliezer in their grasp had dragged the Jew up-stairs, stripped him of all his clothes save his under-garment, and pinioned his arms, unheeding his prayers and threats.

"For God's sake, have mercy! Pity an old man. I cannot live many years. I shall not be able to do any one harm long. Do not bring the guilt of blood on your hands for nothing. If I have done any evil, give me time to repent it. I am seventy years old, and would fain die in Jerusalem. Let me not die here and be buried like a dog. Let me die in mine own land and be buried in the sepulchre of my father Issachar and my grandfather Aaron."

"Don't pray to us, you hoary-headed robber," shouted the man who held him; "pray to God.

There may be mercy for you with Him; there is none with us."

"Who denied a crust to the widow of Chail? and let Marcian the deacon die though he had a medicine that would cure him as it cured thy kinsman Joseph?"

"Remember the jewels in his house, the gold goblets, the carpets of Persia, the ivory of India, and then think of the cellar which was all his usury left to the noble Callista to die in."

"Make haste! Will you never have that crossbeam fitted?"

The appeal was to another of the party who was busy extemporising a sort of gallows on the arm of a huge ballista that stood in a corner of the platform. The delay in getting a ladder and fastening the cordage exasperated the executioners, but gave time to Celadion. Just as the cries of the Jew were silenced by a blow on the mouth, and he grovelled on the ground uttering inarticulate cries of rage and pain, the crest of the commander appeared above the platform, and in a minute the man who was fitting a rope round the Jew's withered neck felt a gauntleted hand on his shoulder and heard a voice which compelled obedience in his ear.

"Who gave you the power of life and death? Untwist that rope and give the Jew his garments. Come down from the ladder. The use of that ballista is to hurl stones at Moslems, and not to form a gallows-beam for Jews. If Eliezer has offended, charge him before me to-morrow, and see that your charge is supported by witnesses."

"He denied my wife a handful of meal when our child was dying. A dog's death is too good for him. We should never have had the Moslem on us if we had put the sacred Emperor's laws in force against the Jews."

"And that we should have done if it had not been for the accursed Jacobite who had sold himself to the whole synagogue."

Charge followed charge thick and fast. The pent-up hate and contempt that had grown with the growth and strengthened with the strength of each speaker made themselves heard in each hissing, stinging accusation. Celadion almost repented of interfering. He had little doubt that Eliezer had committed every villany with which he was charged, and richly deserved hanging. At the same time, this was not the moment to provoke the wrath of the purse-holders of the East, and if one of such note as Eliezer were stricken the flood-gates of Hebrew vindictiveness would be opened, and who was strong enough to shut them? He tried a last appeal.

"Doubtless he hath deserved ill of us, but soil not your hands with his blood. Cast him out with a halter round his neck, and let him find his way to the camp of Amr."

"Is it safe? Will he not tell our secrets to the enemy?" whispered Theodore.

"He cannot tell what he does not know," returned Celadion in the same tone, adding aloud in a voice that silenced question, "Make haste, untie his hands. Open the door and let him run for it. If anybody likes to send a shaft after him to quicken his pace, he may; but not more than half-a-dozen, for we must husband our archery."

"Well said, gallant commander," shouted several voices. "Zobair's men stoned a Jew last Saturday, let Amr's men stone one to-day."

"Nay," said a single citizen. "Tie Jew and Jacobite together, and fling them both into the dead well yonder."

But the proposer had none to back him. The majority were glad to please their general, and the minority were disposed, half from fear and half from pity, to shift the doomsman's work to other hands.

Thus Celadion gained his point. In a moment they set about unbinding the Jew; but during the process of unfastening his manacles he contrived to exchange a look of intelligence, quick and furtive, but full of meaning, with the Pagarch. Then, amidst buffets and lashes, he fled down the stairs and through a small postern gate, like a scapegoat of his nation.

Two or three arrows and crossbow-bolts whizzed after him, and as one shaft buried itself in the sand near him he turned and threatened his enemies with a savage gesture. Then the bell announcing that the evening rations were to be doled out to the garrison called the famishing crowd away to their several stations. Hunger is stronger even than cruelty.

CHAPTER XXIV.

THE GUARDIAN OF THE TOMB.

SOMEWHAT to the north of the spot now occupied by
the mosque which bears his name Amr had pitched
his tent. The country presented a very different
appearance then from that which it does to-day.
Now we see little in any direction save the hills of
rubbish that have accumulated as one village has
been built on the ruins of its predecessor, all being
overgrowths on the ruins of Fostat, which was itself
to rise on the destruction of Babylon. Then the
space to the south between the fortress and the hills
was covered with country houses and villages em-
bosomed in vines. These were to disappear before
long; but the invader saw how useful would be the
shelter afforded by these leafy coverts, and prepared
to avail himself of their shade to mask a movement
which he had long contemplated.

There is one striking change in the geography of the scene which must be specially borne in mind, as, if it is forgotten, the Greek manœuvres are unintelligible. The Nile has altered its course, and there is now a much wider space of dry land between Babylon and the river than there was in the seventh century. If we examine the remains of the fortress carefully, we see that its west angle was cut off, and that the wall forming this blunted angle is furnished with two towers. This would lead us to conjecture, even if we had not information of the fact from other sources, that the Nile flowed near here, and that this was the head of the bridge of boats. Rhoda, the celebrated island, was thus nearly in mid-stream; for while we lessen the east bank, we allow for an increase of the west, which was then the more inhabited, and consequently the more conserved and protected bank, of the two.

Though the garrison would be compelled ultimately to yield by famine, the Arab commander was unwilling to wait for that end. His troops were growing impatient. His losses by the sword and by disease had been heavy. In spite of unmatched valour, the attempts against the fortress had been failures and had cost much blood. The two thousand men who had reinforced him were accustomed to be led by Kaled the "Sword of God," and to sweep the enemy before them in one glorious charge. They were growing impatient, and already the story-tellers and musicians were recalling the exploits and acts of gallantry which had made the besiegers of Damascus forget that it had taken twelve months.

The task before the armies of Islam involved sieges and siege operations, but let them be animated by combats and assaults. Anything was better than sitting down and watching while their enemies were starved to death. Accustomed in oriental fashion to wander about his camp in disguise, Amr learned the opinions of his soldiers, and felt sure that a longer delay must be perilous.

On the day that the Christian generals met in the Hall of the Picture, Amr, Zobair, and some other chiefs held their council. The invader's tent was pitched in an orchard of palms, and he and his advisers sat on carpets placed by the side of a small spring. The sun was setting over the Red Mountain, and the group were in deep shadow.

"You, O Zobair, art wont to listen to the voices of the people, and you know that they are discontented and weary, and desire to be led against the enemy.

Let us, then, not delay longer, but attack them the day after to-morrow, which is the holy day."

"Twice have we failed to draw them from their holes. They prefer to support their wretched bodies with the flesh of dogs, rats, and unclean beasts rather than to come out in open field and fight with sword and battle-axe. By what new device do you hope to induce them to come, out from behind their walls?"

"Once more we must attempt the hill which commands the city on the south-east. The force that holds it now has suffered much. I would make an attack on that hill, and, believe me, Celadion will be drawn to defend it. I shall engage him with my oldest soldiers. Meanwhile do you come under shelter of the palm-groves and vineyards, keeping close beneath the walls of the fortress; and as they fly before me to their gates, turn their flank, press upon them hotly, and drive them over the bridge of boats. Those in the castle will be too weak to hold out long. They are only now kept from surrendering by Celadion. He whom they call George aforetime treated with the Prophet, on whom be peace, and will be ready to make peace on our conditions."

"Your plan is good, if they can be forced to make

a sally. But the Nazarene captain is wary; and as
for the man George, I would sooner trust Abdallah-
Ibn-Obba the hypocrite, whom God confound, than
that Jacobite."

As he spoke there was a stir outside the tent, and
a clash of steel and a sentry's challenge were audible.
After a few moments' parley a soldier entered and
asked leave to speak.

"The men of the Koreish are bringing hither a
Jew who has escaped from Babylon, and who craves
permission to be shown into your presence."

Amr signified acquiescence, and Eliezer was
brought in, in the custody of two powerful Arabs.
He was bleeding from a recent wound in the forehead; his yellow robe was bedraggled and filthy; his
head was bare, and a rope still hung round his neck.

"Who is this abject? Do the Christians send as
envoys the refuse of the gallows?" said Zobair.

"No, noble Amr; no, valiant Zobair," replied the
Jew. "I come not on any ambassage from the
Christians, whom I hate and loathe as much as you
do. They would not employ *me*, neither would *I* do
their bidding. I come to tell you news which it
will profit Islam to hear; but it is for the ears of
chiefs and captains, not for soldiers and slaves."

"All the soldiers of Islam are brothers," said Amr, "and we have no secrets between us. We are not, like the Christians, a divided people plotting against each other. The humblest soldier would cut out his tongue rather than allow it to speak treason against his comrade or reveal that which should not be divulged."

"Be it known unto you then," said Eliezer, "that there has been a council held to-day at which George the Pagarch proposed that the day after to-morrow a sally will be made from the gate. The Christians are spent with hunger and disease. The common soldiers will rise against their officers and fling open the gates if they are kept longer on the defensive. They are clamouring to be led any-whither, and their word is as the word of the lepers of Samaria, 'If they kill us, we shall but die.'"

"We foresaw that the end would soon come, and the Nazarenes will find us ready when the time arrives."

He clapped his hands. "Give this Jew food and drink. Then take him without the lines of our encampment, and if he returns let him be hanged on the first tree. The traitor is abhorred by God and man. You have eaten the salt of the Christian, and yet betray him. You owe it to our clemency that the rope you bring with you is not now tightened round your neck."

And Eliezer was hurried out of the presence.

"These carrion taint the air. But these tidings consort well enough with our plans. We must draw them gradually towards the hill. Then I leave them to your mercies, O Zobair."

With these words the two chiefs of Islam parted.

Meanwhile the slaves hurried Eliezer through the encampment, sparing not buffets nor kicks, and answering his cries for mercy with blows upon the mouth. When the boundary was reached they thrust a water-bottle and some dried dates into his hand, and bidding him return on pain of death, set his face to the desert and left him.

For a while he lay on the ground stunned. Events had followed each other with such rapidity that he had had no time to think. The sudden outburst of popular rage, the violence, the cruelty, the blows, all had come on unexpectedly; then the access of passionate revenge, which weakened him if possible more than the struggle with the mob. The drunkenness of his wrath—for there was no other word for it—had left him faint and exhausted.

Again, the scorn with which Amr had treated his treachery was a new experience. The parties between whom he had been wont to intrigue had so little sense of loyalty or honour, that treason was current coin in their company : to find it flung back in his face as a worthless tender was something he could not comprehend. The personal insults, the blows, the wounds, cut him to the quick. His nation was accustomed to violence; but the terror that he inspired by his supposed mysterious knowledge, his enormous wealth, and the favour of the Pagarch, had saved him hitherto from the usage which his poorer brethren endured too frequently. Now he was spurned and trampled on by Moslem and Christian. Was there no place henceforth for the Jew ? Thrust from the gate of the Greek and the tent of the Arab, was there to be no foothold anywhere for him or his ? Into this new world that was to arise and supersede the Christian, as he devoutly believed, was the curse still to pursue him ? Eliezer went through a horror of darkness. Whither should he go ? Not back to George,—he was powerless to protect him. He must try and find his way to his house at Memphis. And Reuben —the thought of his son was if possible more poignant than any other, for it brought back the recollection of his baffled schemes to wed Armenosa to the Augustus and to Amr. Now she was in Babylon, might not Reuben's frantic passion bring the crowning disgrace on his house?

The thought of Armenosa suggested Menas, and the scenery around him was in some mysterious way connected with him. He was in the desert, not far from the spot where he had watched the priest and Marcus bury the treasure. The thought came to him like an inspiration. Here was something to gratify his vengeance and to satiate his greed. Here was a new reason for living, a quest for the unknown. Besides, was he not for the first time in his life poor? His loans to the Pagarch had stripped him of much of his hoarded wealth. The stores of jewels and money he had wrung from the famine-stricken populace were within the walls of Babylon, and were probably by this time broken open by his angry victims. At all events, in twenty-four hours they would be the property of the conqueror.

He rose from the sandy hollow into which he had thrown himself and looked round. The moon was not yet risen, and the desert stretched away as far as he could see. It seemed as if there were posi-

tively no landmarks in view. How had he been
persuaded that it was the place where the treasure
was hidden? One desert scene was like another.
It was not recognition of any definite place. It was
only the uncertain effect of association and resem-
blance. But he would not lose the only thread of
motive which tied him to life. He looked and
looked again at the scene. The first impression had
been right, after all. Gradually the familiar objects
came to his mind. There was a rising ground, and
on it the ruins of a hut of palm-trunks which some
hermit had put up to shield him from the *khamsín*
or sirocco-storms of the spring-time. A wind of unusual violence had blown all save a few of the
sturdier stems to pieces, and as a shelter it was
useless. This was the hut in which he had hidden
himself, and from it he expected to see the place
where the treasure was deposited. He went to his
old position. There in the sand opposite to him
was an aperture which in early times had admitted
the air to some ancient cave-dweller, the predecessor
of the Christian ascetic. It was too small for a man
to enter by it. This was not the place, then. The
sand had covered the entrance to the tomb which
Menas had opened. In the Egyptian desert sand-

storms periodically cover the excavator's work, and
if it is not constantly cleared away even spots lately
discovered are hardly recognisable.

The Jew was in despair. He put his hand before
his eyes and tried to picture the scene as it had
appeared. He was sure of the remains of the hut or
booth of palm-trunks. But the objects near it lay in
deep shadow. At last the moon rose, and a pale light
suffused with a slow rippling brightness the sand,
the palm-stems, and the cavity in the slope of the
little hill. Then it brought out clearly another
and larger opening, evidently that of a tomb. As
the light spread Eliezer seemed to be able to foresee
what would next be revealed : an ancient image of
the quaint treasure - guarding genius with hands
clasped on knees, carved in rose granite, showed
clear and sharp in the moonlight. This was the
mark which he had looked for. There could be no
mistake. He was on the very spot where Menas
had paused, and he must enter the tomb. He
shuddered for a moment. Used to act always by
himself and for himself, he rarely felt another's
presence anything save a hindrance ; but just now,
here in the solitude of the desert, with the yawning
tomb in front, he hesitated and longed for compan-

ionship. Even Reuben, strong of limb and lithe of movement, would have been helpful to him. But no! He could not trust him, though he was his own flesh and blood. He must work in age as he had worked in youth, now and always—*alone.*

And the aim and object of his life—the one act by which he had hoped to win the praise of men and to gain pardon for his sins, the repurchase of the tomb of Jeremiah from the conquerors of the Christians—was further off than ever. His hopes of aid from Amr, as we have seen, were gone. The rush of recent events and the terrible change they had wrought in his fate and fortunes were not at once realised. It took some time to grasp how completely all was altered: Even now that he had as an immediate object the seizure of the priest's supposed hoard, he could not move with his usual directness to his end. He must stop and think it all over. And he went through it again, beginning now a little further back. This time the yell of the mob when the dog fastened his teeth in him the day before rang in his ears. Then he felt the cord round his neck as they dragged him to the gallows. Then he saw the scornful face of Amr. . . .

At last by a strong effort he roused himself and

resolved to go on with the task before him. He
knelt down in order to enter the low door or hole
in the sand. His head and shoulders were inside
the arch, and he was dragging his limbs after him,
when he was sensible of a shock. There was a
rustling amongst the sticks, and a quick start as of
the hurrying away of some living creature. Then
he knew that he was bitten by a snake. He man-
aged to crawl back into the open air and waited.
For some time there was no pain, only he saw that
his leg below the knee was swollen. Then the
agony began. His forehead and hands were covered
with clammy sweat. His feet were icy cold, and his
breath came in quick short gasps. No words came to
his tongue. He could not call; and even if he could
have done so, he felt there was no one to hear his
plaint. He could not pray; and even if he could
have done so, was there any one to hear his prayer ?

Then it seemed as if Death, actual and palpable,
were close at hand, and under his wings was a
horror of darkness. The long hours crept by, but
Eliezer had lost all count of time. His eyes were
clouded. Then all his muscles were convulsed, and
he could only utter a low moaning.

It was mid-day. The deadly cobra-poison had
nearly done its work, when two men, making their
way across the desert, noticed something yellow
lying ‚on the little hillock near the wreck of the
hut. They drew near and hurried to the spot.
Eliezer's old servant Doeg, who lived amongst the
crowd of followers and sutlers on the verge of
Amr's camp, had heard of his master's expulsion, and
had brought Reuben to search for him. In spite of
the ghastly convulsions of his face they could not
fail to recognise Eliezer. But he was unable to
distinguish them, or to utter a single word. For
an hour they watched him in silence. Then he
passed away.

Directly he was dead Reuben bade Doeg search
the body, for he could not bring himself to touch the
corpse. The old man obeyed, and handed him a few
papers which he found in his vest. Reuben read
them eagerly. Then he cast one look of disgust
at the face as it lay staring at the sky, bade the
servant follow him, and hurried away.

But the old man was true to the traditions of his
race. He steadily refused to leave the dead unburied, and when Reuben was gone he slowly and
carefully dug a pit in the sand, and laid the body of

his master therein. For two days and two nights in fasting and prayer Doeg watched beside the narrow mound of sand. Then he returned to the deserted house in Memphis, and the cobra crept from his hiding-place and lay basking in the sun beside the grave.

CHAPTER XXV.

THE SON FOLLOWS THE FATHER.

DAYBREAK found all the garrison astir. Armenosa had passed the night in prayer and vigil, and as the early promise of the mounting sun whitened the sky she stepped out on the battlements, and strained her eyes to see if there was any unusual movement in the hostile camp. She hardly dared to hope the sally would be successful, and still less did she conceive it possible Amr could be surprised. So long had she been living in a world dominated by treachery and intrigue that it seemed impossible for any plan to remain long undiscovered. Whatever might be the issue, however, she had no doubt that the attempt to be made was the only possible one for her people to make, and braced herself to confront the perils it must involve as became the defender of Belbeis.

In a brief moment she compared her feelings *then* with her feelings *now*. It seemed that there was a difference. Then she gauged and measured accurately everything that could happen—the misery of her starved soldiers, the humiliation of her surrender, the peril from the passion of Amr. Now there was something besides all this—some sinister peril from an unknown source, some stab from an unknown hand — like the indefinite Something, the shape which has no shape, which frightens us in a nightmare. She tried to free herself from it by fixing her eyes on the brightening east and asking herself "what she feared?" Then behind her she heard the rustle of a robe and a voice speaking her name. That which she had dreaded had come. That which had been a formless fear was there in flesh and blood—the Jew Reuben.

"Armenosa," he said, "I know you hate me; but, loving or hating, mine you shall be body and soul. There is no time for words. I know your Nazarene devices. I know the plan on which you build your hopes. I know it as well as Amr knows it. You are prepared for that." . . .

"I could have believed it if any other lips had spoken it. When I hear it from you I know it must be a lie!"

" Foul words for a fair mouth to speak; but take
care. An obedient daughter should not thwart her
father's wishes."

" What do you mean ? "

" Plainly this. George has betrayed the garrison
to the Moslem. Of this I have written proof here.
Refuse me your love and I place this parchment in
Celadion's hands. The Greek has suspected him
from the day when Amr sent you back. He is eager
for proof, and when once he has it in his hand he
will be prompt to punish the traitor. In half an
hour the trumpets will give the signal for the sally.
Ahasuerus did not ask for longer time to hang
Haman. There is one way of saving the Pagarch.
You know it." . . .

He caught her by the arm and grasped her so
tightly that he drove a ruby in her bracelet into her
flesh. She felt his breath on her cheek. She could
not cry for help. The conviction that what Reuben
said was true held her dumb. Words of denial froze
on her tongue, but she could not confute the Jew's
charge; what, then, did anything else matter in this
world ? Truth had died out of it. She raised her
arms and staggered back against the parapet speechless with fear and shame. Then once more the same
voice that had brought her help on the road to Heli-

opolis rang in her ears. She heard steps, and was conscious of the presence of Marcus and another.

Her lover caught her as she was falling. His companion seized Reuben round the waist and threw him like a child to the ground.

" I have found you at last, thief and cheat! Prometheus paid for stealing the fire of Jove, and you shall pay for stealing the fire of Callinicus. Look to the maid, Marcus. My one eye can see to finish this circumcised coward, or my right hand has forgot the skill old Glycon taught me."

The two men closed in a death-grapple. Reuben endeavoured to unsheathe his knife, but the Greek's arm pinioned him, and his extraordinary strength held him as in a grip of steel. The Jew was not accustomed to physical exertion. His life was effeminate and self-indulgent, and he was wearied by his night's adventure in the desert and weakened by the violence of battling passions. But the energy of his hatred to Marcus, intensified to frenzy by seeing Armenosa in his arms, made up for lack of skill and training and inspired him with the strength of one possessed. The Greek was not struggling with an athlete, but with a demoniac whom he was holding back from assaulting another; for Reuben's hand was striving to seek his knife, that he might plunge it into the back of Marcus, not into the breast of the man with whom he was struggling. Frothing at the mouth, gnashing his teeth, and hissing out blasphemies, Reuben strove to force Callinicus to the parapet, as every inch he advanced towards Marcus and Armenosa seemed a gain. But the Greek saw something Reuben did not see. He saw that between the spot where they began the struggle and the stone step on which Armenosa had fallen the battlement had been levelled in order to work the pulley of a ballista. The war-engine itself had been removed elsewhere, but there was a space through which a man could be pushed with nothing to break his fall. Suddenly relaxing his hold, Callinicus saved himself from being dragged over the verge by catching tightly at an iron bar projecting from the wall. He then made a snatch at Reuben's knife. The Jew drew a step backward, and, suddenly freed from the other's clutch, staggered and fell over the unguarded edge of the parapet. He uttered a cry that rang in Armenosa's ears for months. Callinicus covered his eyes with his hand for a moment and paused before he looked down. When he did he saw nothing but a huddled mass in a yellow robe lying quite still on the bank of the moat.

CHAPTER XXVI.

THE SALLY.

With the first gleam of light in the east the call to prayer rang out. The troops of Amr were already under arms and waiting to be led against the enemy. After the prescribed forms were recited a grey-bearded imaum—the holiest of the holy—repeated the forty-eighth chapter of the Koran called " The Victory," the *sura* which was revealed to the prophet after the taking of the city of Mecca, and which contains in burning words the promises of God to the faithful and the valiant, and the denunciation of His wrath against the impious and the gainsayers. When it was finished Amr sprang from his horse, and facing his long line of turbaned warriors, spoke in a voice which reached in that clear morning air to the rear-most rank :—

"Comrades! you have heard the words of truth.
Whoso believeth not in God and His apostle, verily
we have prepared burning fire for the unbelievers.
We have been delayed too long before this city, and
your spirits have sunk, and you have been weary of
waiting. But now all will be well. We know that
Babylon is not as Damascus, a city to resist for many
months. It has held out as long as it can. The unbelievers have suffered a famine like that with which
the Meccans were afflicted, and have fed on carrion,
and dogs, and burnt bones. If they hold out any
longer they will suffer as the accursed Jews suffered
in the siege of Jerusalem, and eat the fruit of their
wombs. Who are these hunger-bitten wretches that
they should resist the warriors of the desert? Behind
the ramparts and towers they have defied us for a
moment, but to-day God has given them into our
hands, for they are about to issue from the gates.
Meet them with the cry which has struck terror to
the hearts of kings and emperors. Smite with the
sword which has stricken down already the armies
of Heraclius and Constantine. If you conquer, the
spoil shall be divided as after the battle of Bedr, and
every one shall be enriched; and if you fall, you will
be carried by the angels to the gardens watered by

the rivers of Paradise. Already Gabriel is setting in array the armies of heaven to fight on our side. Already the eyes of the Nazarenes are blinded with the light that flashes upon his falchion! Forward!"

He ended, and turning round signalled with his sword. The whole army followed in a close and compact formation in the direction of a hill where a considerable body of Christians were intrenched. The possession of this point of vantage had been often contested. It commanded Babylon, and if once in the hands of the Moslems the fortress would be at their mercy. It had been strongly garrisoned by Marianus at the beginning of the siege, but Amr had succeeded in investing it so closely that no provisions could reach the troops, who were famished and crazy for want of water. They had made a desperate sally a week before, and had broken through the Mohammedan lines and reopened their communications with the Nile. This and some success in small skirmishes had encouraged them, and it was fair to say that the Christian forces on the hill were for the moment in better spirits than any portion of the army. The courage of the hero of the standard was contagious, and Amr's desert chivalry were not more resolute or enthusiastic than the troops of Marianus. They had suspected some impending movement, and were on the alert when they heard the call to prayer and the sounds that followed in the direction of the enemy's camp.

The traveller who now stands on that hill, marked by one of the many windmills that Napoleon, another invader of Egypt, erected on every available rising ground, sees, as we noticed, a vast reach of fawn-coloured sand. He sees the pencil minarets and the dome of Mohammed Ali's mosque and the range of Mokattam. The City of Victory, Al Kahira, which was to merge the fortress of Babylon and the now extinct Fostat in its general name, stretches to the west. The stronghold which Celadion was defending so desperately lies beneath him ; but instead of the dull naked sand there were then vast orchards of palms and vineyards of luscious grapes. From these, in the direction of the desert, Amr's troops appeared, a dense mass of horsemen, making a wide detour and keeping free of the trees and vineyards that would encumber their cavalry. The object of the movement was clear. They were not going to attack the fortress, but were resolved to possess themselves of the hill and to sweep Marianus and his force into the Nile.

Behind the cavalry came a crowd· of slaves dragging a heavy ballista. This was moved very slowly, owing to its great weight. It was clearly the machine that Amr intended to place on the hill, in order to hurl stones into the town.

"But he has not got the hill yet," said the standard-bearer, as he watched the troops emerge from the vineyards and sweep away eastward almost as far as the quarried hills.

In truth no effort had been spared to fortify the position. A stockade had been made at the foot of the hill, behind which the archers could be placed, and again mid-way up the ascent. And on the summit a fence of palm-stems had been erected, so that the position was almost impregnable. The Moslem leader was far too wise to undervalue his enemies; and confident as had been the language of his battle-speech, he saw with uneasiness how judicious had been the Greek captain's precautions, and how his own lack of infantry would tell against him in the coming assault.

If the attempt was to be made at all, it must be made while the spirits of the men were aglow with religious enthusiasm. So, uttering his peculiar war-cry, Amr and a hundred of his chosen guards, protected by corselets of linked mail, dashed up the rising ground. But the Greeks were fully prepared for them, and as they came within bow-shot a flight of arrows from the archers behind the first stockade pierced their horses' eyes, stung their ungauntleted hands, penetrated every spot that the armour did not guard, and left a confused struggling mass of men and horses, stopped mid-way in their career, a target for another hailstorm poured from the higher plateau of the second stockade. Amr was untouched, but the steed of the chief who rode next him, wounded by an arrow in the nostril, reared with agony and threw his rider. Thus the front rank was in disorder. The men in very desperation put their horses at the stockade. But thicker and thicker flew the sharp steel points. Though the cavalry surrounded the hill and swarmed up it, they could not penetrate the wooden rings that girdled it round, nor touch the men who from behind those rings were raining blindness, torture, and death upon them in a fiery shower.

Foiled in his first attempt, Amr retired, and wheeling round with incredible swiftness, presented himself at the head of another squadron on the western side of the hill. So dense was the cloud of dust that his rapid movement raised that the defenders found the enemy upon them unawares, and as the ascent was less steep here than on the other side, two horsemen leapt the stockade and cut down half-a-dozen of the archers before they could draw their swords. But neither of the chiefs recrossed the wooden rampart. Marianus, who saw Amr's manœuvre before any one else, rushed to the place which the champion was endeavouring to force and launched a javelin at the foremost of the two horsemen, which pierced him to the heart. The horse of the second of the forlorn-hope was stabbed and rolled over its rider, who was brained by a blow from an iron mace. The task was impossible for cavalry, and Amr resolved to order up his Syrian levies—troops in every way inferior to his horse, but whom he could drive to attempt the assault on pain of death if they wavered. While these men were being hurried from the rear there was a pause. Both parties stopped, wellnigh exhausted, and as the dust and sand clouds cleared away the results of the first hour's fighting were visible. At the foot of the hill were strewn a heap of men and horses, some dead, some struggling in agony. On the little plateau at the foot of the first stockade there were piles of bodies in stark and ghastly attitudes, arrows sticking from their mouths, breasts, and eyeballs. Within the fence crouched the Greeks, counting with the miser's anxiety the few shafts that still remained in belt and quiver wherewithal to carry on the war. The store was nearly spent, and Marianus was issuing hurried orders to his bowmen not to waste a shot. The Arab chiefs, impatient at the delay, were extending their formation to leave room for the movement of the infantry. They had suffered severely in their various attempts to storm the hill. Their horses were caked in sand, and red with blood. Their chain-armour was hacked and broken. The first scene of the last act of the war drama was ended, and left victory with the soldiers of the Cross. . . .

Meanwhile within the fortress the preparations for the sally had been hurried on, but the Greeks were not ready so early as the Moslems. The various captains were jealous of each other. Discontent was rife. The troops were famished and almost desperate. The raid on the Jewish storehouses had given some of the men a meal, but they were in a condition little suited to meet the enemy. At last, however, the trumpets rang out clear and loud. The gates opened. The huge drawbridge was lowered, and the first files of the Christians began . to cross it.

The spearmen, a force in which the Greeks were strong, came first. They were the descendants of the well-greaved Achæans of the 'Iliad,' and were equipped with lances, shields, and short swords. Though exhausted and thin with privation, there was a flash of hope in their eyes, and the joy that is born of release from long inaction gave their march a pace and alertness that augured well for the result. Then came the archers in their leather jerkins and steel morions, and then the small body of cavalry with the ensign of the Cross flashing back the sunshine from its rubies and emeralds, the one radiant speck of brightness in the long war - worn array.

"How beautiful the banner shines!" cried Armenosa to Barbara, as they watched the array from the battlements. "Look at the glory of diamonds over the sacred Head. O God, who giveth victory, bless Thy soldiers and Thy standard this day!"

As she spoke, Celadion with Marcus by his side

passed over the bridge, and a body of cavalry armed with swords and heavy maces closed the array. It seemed as if the Arabs were in retreat, but they were really getting out of the reach of the archers from the hill, and drawing the Christians away from the fortress to ground where the cavalry would have space to manœuvre. Farther and farther they went, smaller and smaller seemed the cloud of dust that masked their numbers. Then a shrill cry, the word of command, rang out, and the host halted where they had presented themselves to the foe, in a long square of two deep and solid lines, the first of archers, the second of cavalry, a formation with which their enemies were so fatally acquainted.

Directly the moat was crossed the Christians formed also in two lines, and, with spearmen in the centre and cavalry on either wing, moved forward to the attack. The archers hurried on in front to begin the engagement iu loose order, like the skirmishers and sharpshooters of later days. The Christians were slightly inferior in numbers to the Moslems, but the armies were fairly matched. Amr, it is true, led six thousand men fired by a fanatic enthusiasm the like to which has only been seen once in the world's history.

The Puritan of the seventeenth century reproduced the Moslem of the seventh. At both epochs the soldiers were victorious because they were drunk, but not with wine. Fiery zeal supplied every other deficiency, and, in Bible words, ate them up. This feeling gave a new and strange character to their warfare, and made their charge irresistible as that of Azrael, the Angel of Death; but their enemies were not the superstitious and enfeebled folk that the historians of the last century have represented them to be. With certain writers the Byzantine of the Lower Empire has been a synonym for everything that was dastardly and effeminate; and certainly in the times of the Crusades the Greek emperors made guile take the place of brute valour. Yet at the time of which we are writing the defenders of Egypt were brave, disciplined, and capable of immense endurance. Many of them had fought under Heraclius in the campaign against the Persians. They had seen his valour on the banks of the Sarus and his skill and conduct at the siege of Dastagerd, and a few weeks later they were to take part in the retreat on Alexandria, which is one of the unpraised marvels of ancient warfare. Above all, though marred and weakened by religious

U

dissensions, there were soldiers like Marcus in the Greek army who anticipated the ardour which in a future century was to develop into the spirit of Christian chivalry.

The archers did little harm to the enemy at this stage of the battle. They did not get near enough to do more than send harmless volleys at the Arabs, and the Moslem host threw out no skirmishers or light horsemen. They were intent on forming their order of battle at the distance Amr considered sufficient to allow of the execution of his master stratagem, and were busy removing some of their wounded to a place of security. Celadion's suspicions were for a moment aroused by the distance to which the soldiers of Islam withdrew, but the evenness of the ground and the advantages it afforded for cavalry explained the movement. Weary with fighting behind stone walls, and seeing how desperate was the situation, he pushed on until he found a position that suited him not far from the present burial-ground of Imam Shafei.

There was no interchange of challenges, none of the picturesque courtesies of a later day. The Christians had hardly time to get into position when they saw a sudden dust-cloud hide the Arab army, then separate itself from them and storm down with thunder of hoofs and flash of swords on their centre. The few bowmen who had been thrown out in advance were ridden down and trampled out. It seemed as if the main body of the infantry must be broken in a few moments. But the old Macedonian pike, shortened to twelve feet, held by a kneeling rank in front and by a standing rank behind, opposed its usual formidable hedge of steel. Slingers and archers did their work, and the horsemen failed to break the bristling line.

Amr retired and held a hasty council with his chieftains. Though he had little doubt of ultimate victory, he could not afford to pay too high a price for it. The unity of Islam was at the moment rather nominal than real, and he more than any of the other leaders was surrounded by rivals and calumniators. Though he hardly dared to acknowledge it to himself, a suspicion rose in his mind that Zobair might not support him effectually unless his own part of the contract, so to speak, was performed with decisive success. Celadion's army must be beaten, and must be in full retreat towards the fortress, or Zobair might excuse himself and justify his non-co-operation on the plea that he should peril pre-

maturely the whole reserve force. The Greeks
without the fortress, once demoralised and on the
foot of fear, Zobair could cut them off from Babylon
and drive them to the river, while Amr summoned
the remnant of half-starved men and women to
capitulate and entered in triumph. But the Greeks
were *not* routed. They were standing their ground,
and successive charges of Moslem horsemen seemed
unable to shake them. Never during the whole of
his Egyptian campaign had the invader felt so keenly
the critical nature of his enterprise, never perhaps
before had he wished that he had read Omar's letter
on Syrian soil. There seemed one possibility and one
only. He might lead one charge against the front
and send a body of men simultaneously to attack
the left wing. The Greeks could hardly be expected
to sustain this double assault. In a few sentences
he gave the orders to Abadah and turned to his
crowd of horsemen, who were in a very different
plight from the band which had followed him an
hour ago. Most of them were dismounted, and were
hurriedly trying to repair their armour and to
breathe their horses. Some were tightening saddle-
girths, some plucking arrows out of their harness
or horse furniture, some stanching wounds, some

quenching their parched throats with draughts from the cups of the water - carriers, of whom Amr always caused a number to follow the army. He saw how sorely the men were in need of a few moments' pause, and dismounted to give a drink from his water-bottle to a wounded soldier whom his tribesmen had brought off the field.

"God forgive thy sins, O dispenser of the drink-offering," said the man, faintly, and the warriors caught it up, and repeated the grateful prayer.

Then after a space he remounted and spoke—

"Comrades, to our saddles! We must not let the first repulse dishearten us. God the most merciful, who at Medina sent a cold wind and destroyed the adversaries, will befriend us if we are of a good courage. Follow me, and let not an arrow leave a bow until I give the signal. Then, before the Nazarenes can recover, upon them with the sword. For him who first breaks the line, a horse of Yemen caparisoned with gold if he lives, and Paradise if he falls." . . .

Then once more the storm of cavalry burst on the Greeks. Amr's sword flashed like lightning through the dust, and the arrow-shower descended. In the midst of this, rather than after it, the horsemen began to ramp against the spears.

The Moslem tactics were only too successful.
Staunch as the Christians were, and firmly as their
line seemed to be preserved, Amr discerned, as the
dust-cloud rolled away, a gap in the front rank
caused by the fall of two or three spearmen pierced
by arrows aimed with a deadlier precision than the
rest. Swift as a falling star his horse leapt into the
gap, and his rider forced his way through the avenue
of flesh and steel that closed up round him as fast
as he drove his way into it. Afar off he saw the
sacred banner emblazoned with the figure of Christ
in diamonds and rubies, and he made for that and
that only. Though for a moment he seemed, like
the Egyptian hero of an earlier day, the Rameses of
Pentani's Iliad, to be absolutely *alone*, a file of six
of his chosen tribesmen who had never failed him
carved their way through the Greek phalanx, doing
as he did and seeing only what he saw. Yelling
rather than shouting the war-cry, red with the blood
of their enemies and their own, the men of the
Koreish dashed on until they were within bow-shot
of the standard. Amr was still ahead, and knowing
that the disappearance of the sacred banner would
be the same as its capture to the Christians, he un-
slung his iron mace from his saddle-bow and hurled

it in the face of the standard-bearer. Leo, for he it was, fell carrying the banner with him. Then rose a wail as of a host suddenly struck by an irrepressible horror. In an instant Marcus had seized the staff and held the banner aloft. But no cry of triumphant joy greeted the recovery of the ensign. Few indeed saw it, for all were overborne by the terror of a new discovery. Not only were the Arab horsemen breaking and bursting their embattled line in front, but their left wing was turned. White turbans, dark faces, shearing blades, and snorting horses encompassed them. The bows were returned to the cases and the arrows to the quivers. The time had come for the sword, and the sword alone. No longer confronting a serried line, but prancing and trampling in the midst of an orderless, panic-stricken crowd, Amr and Abadah met. With the single exception of Celadion's guard that still held together, the Christian host was a mob, the battle a rout. But the commander, Marcus, and the veterans of the Persian war—the bravest of the brave—retreated in a compact body towards the fortress gate.

Then came the last and most terrible surprise of that day of surprises. The enemy pressed them in front and in flank with the force and impetus with

which a conquering host always overbears a retreating foe, and foot by foot they fell back before
the horsemen. No Spartan phalanx or Roman
legion in the glorious wars of old ever showed a
firmer or steadier front than did the garrison of
Babylon as they fell back. So hateful had the
enclosure within the walls become to them, that
many probably preferred death under shield to a
return to the loathly companionship of disease
and death to which it seemed they were being
slowly driven. But from that fate at least they
were preserved.

Celadion, whose eyes seemed everywhere, detected
a movement amongst the troops of Abadah which
implied a wish to turn the flying army riverwards.
He looked back and saw the reason in an instant.
From the covert of the vines between him and the
fortress poured squadron on squadron. The long-
expected reserve had arrived at the last moment,
but in time. Between the garrison and the walls of
Babylon were long lines of horsemen, not wearied
with a long siege and a desperate battle, but fresh
and hungering for the war-feast.

"We are cut off," he said to Marcus. "Babylon
is lost. We must make for the bridge."

Had they wished to do otherwise it would have been impossible. The pressure of the enemy would have obliged them to move in that direction; but though panic was all around, Celadion's veterans could still keep a front to the enemy and cover the retreat. *They* were not a broken horde of fliers who could be thrust at spear-point into the Nile. Fortunately Zobair's fresh troops, in their eagerness to enter the fortress, interrupted and held back by a cross-stream the conquering force which was pressing the defeated Christians towards the river. The few moments of breathing-space thus secured gave the beaten men time to pause and rally, and the bridge was gained. Prescient of every contingency, and never so keenly alert as in the moment of desperate danger, Celadion, still facing the foe himself, sent Marcus to see that the troops did not overcrowd the bridge of boats, but cross slowly and in order. Grasping the banner as firmly as Marianus had done on his Syrian battle-field, Marcus kept back the over-eager who for a moment had lost the instinct of discipline, and contrived to get the flower of his men safely across the floating causeway to the island of Rhoda. It is doubtful if the result could have been won had Amr headed the pursuit, but when the end had seemed certain he had darted off towards the fortress lest Zobair should enter it before him.

Owing to the absence of their dreaded chief, and perhaps from sheer weariness, the Moslems slackened their pressure on the Christians, and Celadion and Marianus with the remnant of his archers were able to join Marcus. Babylon was lost. On the little island in mid-Nile gathered the only men who were hopeful enough and brave enough to uphold for a little space longer the cause of the Cross in Egypt.

CHAPTER XXVII.

RHODA ISLAND.

ON the island of Rhoda, in one of the many rose-
gardens to which in times of peace the citizens of
Memphis retired during the summer heats, Celadion
and Marcus flung themselves on a bank, and removing their helmets, bathed their faces in the shell-
shaped basin of a fountain. Celadion washed off
the dust and blood, then looked at himself in the
water, and gulping down his rage and mortification,
said with a shrug and a smile—

"This mirror shows me what I never hoped to
see—the portrait of Celadion after a sound beating.
We could not have held out a week longer, however,
and had we starved for another seven days behind
those walls, we should have been an army of
skeletons like those St Ezekiel saw in his vision.

The unbeliever has the honours of war. He has out-generalled the Christian and conquered him in fair fight. I could hate myself for not being prepared for that stale trick. You have brought off the banner, Marcus. Give me your hand," and in spite of himself a big tear stood in his eye. He rose and turned from his companion for a moment, then after a short pause conquered his passion and his shame and spoke in his natural voice.

"The men have been true as steel, and if ever the holy and orthodox Emperor can afford to give a donation to those who have served him well, my fellows should not be forgotten. But who knows? we may be food for the kites before sunset. There are four hours of daylight left to show those devils of archers the joints in our cuirasses. At all events we have brought off all we can. I am sorry Leo and Phocas had to be left behind, but 'tis the fortune of war. Hilloa! they are forming yonder, and we must move Memphiswards, and then cut half-a-dozen boats adrift and sink them."

Marcus looked in the direction of his commander's pointing finger, and saw that in truth one band of white-turbaned men were forming in order on the river's brink, while others were getting rid of the dead and wounded who lay heaped at the bridge-head by throwing them into the brown and brimming water.

"Up, Marcus. We must keep on the run now, and hope for the time when we shall be the chasers and not the chased."

Marcus hurried to a bank in the garden, once topped by a small summer - house now in ruins, whence he could get a view of the longer line of the bridge that stretched across the Nile towards Memphis. A few squadrons had resumed the crossing. The majority had thrown themselves on the ground, overwhelmed with heat and weariness. Many who had held up through the morning and noon had dropped down from the wounds they had bravely hidden. It seemed hopeless to attempt to get the men across before the enemy were upon them. For the first time on that terrible day Marcus lost heart. Already he heard the war-cries from the shore, for the Moslem knew the trade of war too well to give long respite to the Christians. Though Amr had hurried to the fortress and had ceased to head the pursuit, Abadah and other less known chieftains took his place. From the beginning the democratic element in Islam had been prominent, and though

Amr had a special commission from Omar, the other warriors had great liberty of action. It was plain that the signal victory must be followed up, and after a short rest and a shorter consultation the Arab chieftains mounted, and their horses' hoofs were already clattering on the planks of the boat bridge.

"We shall not get them off," Marcus said to Celadion. "The men have done all men can, and are wearied out."

It was the first and last despairing speech that the commander ever heard from his lieutenant, and before he could reply a rushing, tearing sound, the like to which Marcus had only heard once before, hissed in his ears, and a fire-ball whirled over his head and fell hissing and smoking into the river.[1]

"Callinicus, by all the saints!" cried Celadion.

Another and another flaming bolt screeched past them as they hurried up the slope to the spot where the engineer had placed his battery. And there, his half-naked body black with smoke, they found the Egyptian, wild with excitement, urging Hydrax and another slave as begrimed as himself to charge and recharge with cartridges an unwieldy catapult

[1] See Note G, Greek Fire.

which he had just pointed at a convenient angle
to send its contents amongst the enemy who were
crowding on the boats.

" Had it not been for that accursed Jew," he cried,
" who robbed me of half my tartar and Persian gum,
and hid the rest within reach of the rising Nile-
water, I could have saved Babylon; but as it is, I
can secure a free passage to Memphis. Steady. Let
the smoke clear. That last shot was wasted."

In blank astonishment the two men watched the
new engine, which, though clumsy in shape and uncertain in aim, was already producing results un-
attainable by any instrument of offence which then
existed in the armouries of the West. It was easy
to see that as long as the cartridges or shells held
out the Arabs would have no chance of crossing the
river, and that Celadion would be able to convey his
troops to Memphis, and then to destroy the bridge
and gain time to consider the next step to be taken.
The commander had already decided in his own mind
on the retreat to Alexandria. For the moment, however, he was silent, divided between wonder at the
results of the new invention and contempt of the
puny and deformed inventor.

" Where will be the use of stout arms and brave

hearts, of tempered blades, swift javelins, and armour
of proof against a foe that darts down on us like
Jove's own lightning or the fire that fell on Sodom
and Gomorrha?" he thought. "But, thank the
saints, the invention is in our hands first, and we
must try to keep it out of the hands of the enemy."

In truth it was impossible to imagine a figure less
like a controller of the destinies of nations than the
Egyptian appeared at that moment. He was, as
we have said, stripped to his waist, and his thin
dark body was stained a blue black with smoke and
chemicals. His bloodshot eye glared out from under
a fillet of coarse rope that tied up his inky hair.
One arm, injured by some fresh explosion, was
wrapped in bandages, and his legs were scarred with
old wounds from his thighs to the iron-soled sandals
that he wore to guard his feet from the burning
powder-flakes that strewed the ground. But mean
and hideous as was his body, there was something
awe-inspiring in the wild glee of the gestures and
shouts with which he directed the work of death his
genius had devised.

This war-frenzy, however, never disturbed the
concentrated attention which brain, hand, and eye
bestowed on his operations; and the two spectators

were so stupefied with surprise that they had no time for the joy of revenge or victory, so hard was it to understand that such a grotesque instrument could work out a deliverance for an Emperor's trusted champions.

But such a deliverance Callinicus effected on that day of rebuke and discomfiture. The great stake had been played for and lost. The citadel of Christian Egypt had fallen. The valour of Islam, helped by the machinations of the Jew and the fatal weakness of George, had won; but the honours of the day were with the so-called wizard of Heliopolis. His invention kept the enemy at bay through the precious hours of daylight, which gave time for rally and rest to the imperial army.

The Greek fire daunted and confounded the Moslem more than it is possible for us to understand. Steeped in strange and wild beliefs as to the magic productions of Egypt, which they believed to be a land of soothsayers, enchanters, and necromancers, they beheld in the mysterious death-dealing flame a confirmation of all their fears. Though they hardly dared to whisper it under their breaths, a secret dread that the Christians might have discovered the arts wherewith Moses afflicted

x

Pharaoh stole over them. Was this the plague of
fiery hail? And would the locusts, the darkness,
and the deaths of the first-born follow in horrible
succession?

Amr had heard through Reuben some hints as
to the studies of Callinicus, which the Jew had
thrown out when he thought he had discovered the
mystery and was speculating on the chance of selling the secret to the Arabs. The chief of the army
of Islam, therefore, had no supernatural terror; but
the imaums at evening prayer mixed with their
thanksgivings for the victory so many allusions to
the diabolic arts of the foe that the fears of the
more ignorant soldiery were aroused. All through
the afternoon, and still when sudden night
closed down, Callinicus and his assistants supplied
that terror with food. His combustibles set the
bridge of boats in a blaze, and scourged back with
fire troop after troop who tried to effect a crossing.
When the bridge was rendered useless the enemy
tried to get across in a flotilla of fishing-boats, but
in vain. Effort after effort failed. To the desert
Arabs Rhoda seemed an island inhabited by fiends,
and the attempt to land on it that night was aban-
doned as impossible.

While the Arabs were kept at bay the Greek captains made the best of their time. Their men were rested and then marched across, and the wounded were taken, with such scant care as the warfare of that age knew, to places of shelter.

At last when his ammunition was expended Callinicus joined Celadion and Marcus. To all it seemed hopeless to defend Memphis. As, however, they would be obliged to pass through the city, they resolved to collect such reinforcements as they could; but the best troops in the country had formed the garrison of Babylon, and they neither expected nor found any important accessions of strength. Before they had gone half a mile they met the citizens, Lampo and Batalan at their head, pouring out of the White Gate, carrying away their property in the wildest panic and confusion. It was clear that the enemy would either repair the bridge or cross in boats as soon as morning broke, and they found the Greek fire silenced, so there was nothing but to begin the retreat to Alexandria.

．　　．　　．　　．　　．　　．　　．

The three lingered in silence for a moment before the signal was given to march. They looked at the broad river, the island, on which a red fire was

still smouldering, and the dark outline of the
fortress they had defended so well. Then the
trumpet sounded, and they passed away in the
darkness. No chronicler has commemorated as it
deserves that wonderful march, which ranks with
the great retreats of history. The names of four
places [1] at which a gallant stand was made are
preserved, but the Arabs were usually victorious.
After fighting every inch of the way for three weeks,
the wearied army saw the sea.

The story of the defence of Alexandria has been
often told. The Christians held out as long as they
could, in the hope of being relieved by Heraclius;
but the Emperor died in the midst of his preparations to send them assistance, and the city surrendered to Amr.

[1] The four places were Teranat, Kom Sharik, Siltis, and Keriun.

CHAPTER XXVIII.

ON the same night in which Celadion and his army set out upon their march, a very different group moved slowly through the darkness in the direction of the ridge of hills that now bears the name of Mokattam. The moon was hidden by a dense black cloud shaped like an eagle's wing, which left only a patch of pallid green sky around its slender crescent. The desert stretched dark and mysterious before the wayfarers. The shapes of the mountains could not be discerned, but showed like a heavy cloud-bank on the horizon. The straining eye might discern a speck of light far off, which, as it was too low for a star, could only mark the existence of a monastery on a distant cliff. The silence could be felt. It seemed as if the terrible day had ex-

hausted all the voices of nature as well as those of
men. The dawn had broken to the roll and bray
of music, and ever since the shouts of combatants,
the trampling of horses, the clash and hurtle of
swords and arrows, and the crackle and roar of
fire, had tortured every ear through hideous hours.
Now all was over, and, as if in utter weariness,
the plain, the camp, the city lay at rest. In the
hours that had passed between the fall of the castle
and the sunset the dead had been hurriedly buried,
and the living were sleeping the sleep of blank exhaustion, as motionless and dreamless as death itself.

The figures who moved under the spectral sky
were mostly women in mourning weeds; but there
were some men in the party in the robes of priests,
and some servants carrying an old man in a litter.
The women were Armenosa, Barbara and her nuns;
the man the priest Menas.

After her rescue from Reuben that morning, Marcus had hurried the Pagarch's daughter from the
battlements and carried her to the house of Menas,
where the other women were busy tending the sick.
He had scarcely time to see her in safety when the
trumpet called him to his post beside Celadion.
Directly Armenosa recovered consciousness she had

busied herself with her usual work, learning of course the varying fortunes of the war from the watchers on the ramparts.

She had heard of the firm stand of the troops at the beginning of the day, the desperate charge of the Moslem leader, the struggle for the banner, the flank movement of Abadeh, and the sudden appearance of the new army which decided their fate. Armenosa heard first a murmur that fresh soldiers were coming through the vineyards; then the confirmation of their fears that the enemy had blocked all re-entry to the fortress, and that her countrymen were being driven to the Nile.

Then she knew by the rattle of chains and the creak of pulleys that the drawbridge had been lowered, and after a brief space the Arab music and the shouts of "Allah!" told her the enemy were in possession. It seemed that no ingredient could be added to embitter her cup until it was filled to the brim by the news that her father had given the order to open the gates.

Then one all-mastering dread possessed her, and that was the fear of Amr. Would George seek her out and strive to make his peace by sacrificing her to the Arab? All things were possible *now*. For

herself there was one course, and one only. At all
risks she must leave the fortress and take Menas
with her. This would have been difficult if Amr's
attention had not been diverted by the unexpected
defence of Rhoda. He had scarcely had time to
enter Babylon, and in a hurried interview with
George in the Hall of the Picture assure him and
all who were not in arms of safety and protection,
when the Greek fire began to scatter terror amongst
his soldiers, and his utmost efforts were needed to
stop a massacre. The panic called conquerors and
conquered to the battlements. The Arab leader was
busy first in restraining his men from putting the
Christians to the sword, and later, when the bridge
of boats was broken, in securing transport for his
troops on the morrow. The gates were not closed at
sundown, and men were hurrying in and out on
various errands long after dark. Menas, whose
faculties had been wonderfully alert, and who as
long as he could move had been comforting the
wounded, had at last sunk down exhausted. Barbara and her nuns were only too eager to escape;
and thus in the confusion Armenosa had contrived to
pass out, by a postern often used by Reuben in his
secret expeditions, and had carried off her little band.

'Far away across the desert, in a cleft between two masses of limestone rock, a little monastery dedicated to St Arsenius had hidden itself away, and thither she proposed to fly for shelter.

"Courage, mother," she said, as poor Barbara uttered a faint moan and seemed on the point of falling. "The light grows larger. Heaven be thanked that it is shining to-night, though it is the last night on which it will be safe to kindle it."

"Let me down and place the holy mother on the litter," said a trembling voice. "I am rested, and can walk easily."

"Never, O father, never," said the Mother Superior, in the bravest tone she could assume. "My feet did but sink in the sand. I have strength for another mile, and you are worn with illness."

"The holy mother is right. You are the weakest of us now, and must rest. We shall need you to give us spiritual food when the journey is finished. But the danger of pursuit is over, so the bearers can slacken their pace now and keep their strength for the steep part of the journey."

Thus simply and bravely Armenosa kept up the spirits of the band, and though her thoughts were often with the retreating army and her lover, she

set herself gallantly to the task before her, thanking
God that every step she took put a longer distance
between herself and her enemy.

The way was long and wearisome. Nothing but
the dread of what lay behind them could have
enabled weak women to traverse for so many hours
that uncertain trackless space. Slipping in the
shifty sand, stumbling over rocks, piercing their feet
with stones and thorns, the fugitives dragged on mile
after mile, until with the first quiver of dawn they
entered a sandy ravine, and began to mount a
twisting path that led to a plateau on which the
monastery was built.

It was a small square structure with a tower, in
which the light had been placed. When this was
not displayed, as the building was of the same colour
as the rocks, it was scarcely to be distinguished from
them. When it was first founded the occupants
and visitors were hoisted up in a basket, as is the
case with the monasteries in Thessaly and with the
Convent of the Pulley up the Nile. Later, however,
a few irregular steps had been hewn in the rock,
and a ladder with twenty-four rungs, which could
be drawn up at pleasure, was placed between the
narrow slit which formed the doorway and the

highest of the stone stairs. Directly the little
group appeared this ladder was pushed out, and a
monk showed himself, bidding them welcome.

The news they had to tell was received with
lamentation and tears; but these were soon suppressed, and the poor brotherhood set themselves
to provide for the refugees. The little refectory was
given up to Armenosa and the nuns, and the Abbot's
own chamber was assigned to Menas. A trusted
brother was sent out for food, and cautioned to buy
it at different villages lest the excess over the usual
rations should arouse suspicion.

After the strain and horrors of the siege the rest
in the little mountain monastery was inexpressibly
grateful. Armenosa and the nuns had been accustomed to poor fare and close confinement, and
this peaceful home in the clefts of the rocks, free
from the daily sight of bloodshed, seemed a haven
of happiness. Days added themselves to days,
and days lengthened into weeks. The routine of
religious duty was regularly gone through, and
Barbara, though she ever and anon contrasted the
bare walls of the chapel of Arsenius with the gild-
ing and painting of the Convent of the Holy Tree,
was kind and helpful, taking her turn in humble

services with the rest whenever they permitted her.

Though only a few miles from Memphis, tidings of what was going on in the world drifted in small fragments and at long intervals to the monastery, as the strictest caution in communicating with the capital was observed. Armenosa learned, however, that Amr had placed himself at the head of his army and followed the retreating Christians to Alexandria. Reports as to the condition of affairs in Memphis and Babylon were contradictory, but at last it seemed certain that a sufficient garrison had been left to hold the Greeks and Egyptians in check, and that the Arab commander was using victory moderately, and making sharp examples of those who committed outrages on the conquered.

She charged her messengers who went to and fro between the monastery and the city to avoid all communication with the Pagarch's household, as she dreaded lest her father should discover her retreat. An absolute dread of him possessed her, and often in the long nights she started in alarm when she dreamed that he had suddenly appeared to claim her. Menas was her true father, and she tended him with unflagging devotion.

Gradually, by piecing various facts together, she ascertained George's position. He was trusted by none, but maintained in his office to be the channel of communication with Constantinople. Amr had declared the Egyptians "a protected people," and announced the amount of tribute they were to pay for their safety. Many of the clergy were prepared to resist, but the authority of the exiled Patriarch Benjamin, whose name George had whispered in his memorable interview with Menas, was basely and without his knowledge used to enforce a compliance to which he would have been the last to submit.

Altogether the rule of the conquerors was milder than might have been expected. They felt perhaps that until they had possession of Alexandria the work was only half done, and that it would be folly to exasperate the men of Memphis by harshness, since, in case of a repulse at Alexandria, they might retaliate on the troops who now occupied the capital.

Thus time went on. The hopes of the little group rose and fell as the messengers brought tidings of the progress of the siege; but these soon became so conflicting and inconsistent that Armenosa resolved to trust no one, but to possess her soul in patience, to

employ herself in keeping up the courage of the nuns,
and to cherish with unsparing love and pains the
faint spark of life that burned in the worn and fragile
body of Menas.

.   .   .   .

It was a morning in early spring, fourteen months
after the fall of Babylon, when Armenosa sat on a
slab of rock which commanded a wide view of the
desert. A change had passed over her face. She
was unlike the spoiled playmate of Marcus. She
was different from the heroine of Belbeis. She had
none of the flush of joyous youth, and the harder
lines of resolve and determination were softened by
an expression for which there is no better word
than consecration. There were signs of endurance
in the face, but it was the endurance of the martyr,
not of the champion.

There was a small illuminated psalter in her
hand, and she had been reading the psalms over, as
was her custom, before singing them at morning
service. One verse, "Heaviness may endure for a
night, but joy cometh in the morning," she could
not help repeating over and over again.

It did not seem as if she had read it herself. It
was borne in upon her from outside. The water

that trickled from a little stream hard by seemed
to murmur it. The birds of the air seemed to sing
it. The night had been long and dark, she knew,
but it had not been starless. There had been the
priceless blessing of peace. There had been no
sights or sounds of agony and suffering; for the
slow decay of Menas had been painless and without
complaint, and the prayers of her devout companions
had come like flights of gentle doves to the darkened windows of her spirit. Still, though not un-
visited or unsoothed, the two years which had
passed since she left her father's house had been
so full of terrors and cruelties that she thought of
them with a shudder. Would this seclusion end?
And what would be the fashion of the world to
which she was to return? Would it be dark as the
days she had known in Belbeis and Babylon, or
would it be bright with hope—and love? Again, in
the singing of a bird mounting upward into the
pure air overhead, she heard an echo of the voice
her spirit was singing to herself, " Joy cometh in
the morning." Her eyes had been fixed on the
desert prospect before her, but she had seen nothing,
so full was her whole being of the old words and
the new message they were bringing her. And the

murmuring of the awakening life around taught her
to understand one sense of them truly. There was
joy in the quick pulsations of the dawn, and in the
light that was brimming over the saffron east and
overflowing land and river with colour and light.

But was there hope for the unit life in that great
recurring joy of the universe? She had felt the
gladness of the springing morn often, but never
did its freshness of delight touch her heart as
to-day. With one of those strange presentiments
which once or twice in a lifetime carry the sense
of certainty, she looked up and fixed her eyes on
the desert with its undulating swathes of sand, on
the rocks, and on the road winding between the
limestone cliffs: and there just beneath her was the
figure of a man. The visitors who mounted that hill
were wont to move with the slow steps of weariness
or age, but this traveller was strong of limb and
firm of tread. No grey pilgrim or slave-messenger,
but a youth and a soldier—her own Marcus!

.   .   .   .

She uttered his name, and in a few moments he
held her in his arms.

"I knew you were near," she said.   "You sent
me your message."

" No, dearest.   It was impossible."

" You did send it in the verse of to-day's psalm, 'Heaviness may endure for a night, but joy cometh in the morning.' "

The explanation of all was given in few words. Alexandria had surrendered. The long-expected succours had failed, and the death of the Emperor shut out all hope of immediate assistance from Constantinople. Celadion had fallen in the last sally, and Marianus earlier in the siege. Marcus had been treated by Amr with special favour, and had been allowed to visit Memphis on parole, with the alternative of taking service under Amr on his return or of quitting Egypt for ever. Had the two chief captains, named by their enemies " the Head and Arm of Heraclius," survived, it is probable they would have been executed publicly or murdered in prison ; but as they could do him no further harm, Amr declared that he deplored their loss, and to gain a character for clemency spared Marcus.   He set a heavy price on the head of Callinicus, but the Egyptian had disappeared.   He had not been able to employ his war-fire in the defence of Alexandria ; but he used it later with

Y

fatal effect, and delayed the conquest of the Byzantine empire for years.

The safe return of his son revived for some days the expiring strength of Menas. The old man's last prayer had been heard. He was vouchsafed strength to unite his two children in marriage. After this he was ready and eager to say his "Nunc Dimittis." During a portion of each day he was unconscious; but he followed the nuns singing the daily psalms in the little chapel, and he had many hours when he spoke feebly but with perfect clearness to his son and daughter.

At first he seemed to wish that Marcus should see George and convey to him a letter which he had carefully written before he was too weak to hold a pen; but later he consigned the charge of the document to a monk, dreading some attempt to seize Armenosa. He was nervously anxious to preserve the secret of their hiding-place, and forbade the letter to be sent to the Pagarch until it was certain that Marcus and Armenosa were out of his reach. The name of his old schoolfellow, however, occurred often in his prayers, and he never mentioned his name without tears.

One object was specially in his thoughts, and that was the precious Gospel of St Mark which he and Marcus had hidden in the desert tomb. For a time he hesitated; but at last, when it was evident that he was growing weaker and weaker every hour and that the end was near, he motioned that all should leave him but Marcus and Armenosa, and then he bade them stand one on either side of the bed, and bidding them clasp each other's hands, laid his hands upon them and spoke thus:—

"My children, I have been in much perplexity as to what I should do in regard to the Gospel of the holy evangelist St Mark, which has for ages been treasured by the priests of the Church of St Mary the pure lady in Babylon, and was intrusted to me by my predecessor Zacharias, who had it from the holy Molatius, who had received it from Sergius the Martyr. I asked God for light, and last night the blessed evangelist himself appeared to me in a dream and spake words of warning and comfort. He revealed to me that times of tribulation harder than those through which we are already passing are at hand, and that darkness shall cover the land of Egypt the like to which has not been felt since the days of Moses the man of God; and many grievous

plagues and terrible judgments, such as are foretold
by St John the Divine in the holy Apocalypse, shall
visit the nations, and this our land of Egypt shall
be desolate, and the holy Church shall be rent and
torn by factions; and men shall misrepresent the
words of our Saviour, and place Antichrist, of whom
the same St John spake, on the throne of the true
Lord. And in these days, if the very Gospel that
an evangelist wrote with his own hand were read in
their ears, men would not believe, but would corrupt
and distort it. Wherefore, said the vision, 'Let the
holy Gospel remain where it is, and in the fulness of
time, when men have eyes to see and ears to hear,
it shall be brought to light.'"

He paused for a while, closed his eyes, and sank
back in silence. Then after a time he spoke, and
his voice was strong as of a prophet of old, and his
face shining like that of an angel.

"But darkness shall not cover the earth, nor
gross darkness the people, for ever. At last men
shall learn the law of love and discern the mind of
Christ. Not by priests and bishops shall the unity
be restored, but by humble men of goodwill searching and recovering from tombs, and caverns, and
hiding-places the very words of the Lord Jesus.

Neither you nor your children nor your children's children shall see that day, but pray for it and it shall dawn in His good time."

The passion and pathos with which he had begun to speak failed not as he proceeded, and with the last words on his lips he sank into a stupor and remained speechless and as one in a lethargy for many hours.   But the life-lamp gave one last flicker before it went out for ever.   Early the next morning Menas was awakened from his sleep by the sisters singing their Easter hymns.   He caused them to carry him into the little chapel and to vest him in his robes.   Then lying on his bed, he celebrated the Holy Mysteries with unfaltering voice, and gave the sacred elements to Marcus and Armenosa, to Barbara and the sisters.   When the last benediction was spoken, he fell back on his couch.   For a while he remained, a smile of absolute peace on his face, his eyes fixed on the chalice set with onyxes he had guarded so well.

Then he entered into his rest.

.   .   .   .

On the deck of a tall galley bound for Constantinople stood Marcus and Armenosa.   Both were silent.   They had quitted the great harbour of

Alexandria, but the Pharos and the Diamond Island were visible. Henceforth wherever they were they would be exiles. They "sought a country" as really as did any patriarch of old, for the Egypt they had loved had passed away. The desert cemetery that contained the grave of Menas was the only spot which they were really sorry to leave. All was changed. Ruin had passed over the scenes where they had spent their childhood. The holy church in which they had worshipped, the gardens they had loved, the fortress in which they trusted,— all were lost to them for ever.

The outlook was as dark as dark could be, for no foe like unto Islam had lifted his hand against the Church since first she started, equipped with all the armour of the Spirit, on her war with ignorance and evil. She had opposed her patience to the fury of the persecutors. She had wounded the dragon, and the idols were shattered; but more to be feared than the rage of Nero and the subtlety of Julian was the Book which the new conqueror proffered to the nations. The warnings of his father came back to Marcus. He saw, as the towers of Alexandria grew dimmer and dimmer in the mists of distance, how all the woes which the Church had suffered and was destined to suffer were the penalties of her own disloyalty to the lessons of her Lord.

If half the zeal that had been shown in discovering the heresies and doctrinal errors of their brethren had been employed in deeds of mutual charity and love, the Church would have faced the foe with a united front. How useless now appeared the energy wasted on battles with rivals! How miserable the jealousies that had given the enemy such advantage! The demons of Envy and Malice and Hate had masked in holy vestments and called themselves by sacred titles, but they were now revealed to Marcus, bearing the names they would bear before the judgment-seat of God.

Menas the faithful priest had been right. His last words rang in his son's ears. The flash of insight vouchsafed to the dying man had lighted up the past for Marcus and was to brighten the future. Then as he was feeling after and trying to recall the words, the sunset pageants in the clouds took the form his thought impressed on them.

Now the clouds showed like the bastions of some huge castle with banners of crimson and gold glittering on the battlements. These vanished as their earthly Babylon had vanished, and above the rack a monster cloud-spirit seemed to bestride the sky with a shadowy balance in his outstretched hand.

Then one after another rose the forms of apocalyptic vision. The exiles saw in the burning skies the strong-winged angels, the outpoured vials, the mysterious horses John had seen in Patmos. Then the whole heaven was transfigured into the streets of a shining city; a pomp of clouds, amethyst, crimson, and purple, stretched in long vistas farther than the eye could reach, until they were lost in a piercing unapproachable brightness. It overspread the sky. It overflowed the sea, down to the very waters furrowed by their galley's oars,—all was blended and suffused in a world of glory and light.

Spellbound as if they beheld a veritable vision, Marcus and Armenosa watched each magic change. Then he said—

"He is speaking to us from the sky as He spoke to His evangelist of old. The oppressor crushes us under his horse's hoofs to-day, but the vintage of blood must be gathered in, the sickle must reap its harvest to the last shock. Then Christ shall triumph. See, it is written in the mystic characters with which God writes the destinies of nations in the heavens. The balance and the shadowy hand that grasps it vanish, and all is light and blessedness! See the holy city, new Jerusalem, descending from God out of heaven!"

The eye of Armenosa followed that of her husband, and his enthusiasm kindled hers.

"In that faith we will live," she said; "for it was the faith of Apostles, Martyrs, and Evangelists, of your father—yes, and, in his earlier and better days, of mine."

He clasped her closer to him, and both breathed the same prayer.

NOTES.

Note A (chap. i. p. 4).

THE PAGARCH.

We learn from the monograph on the Mokaukas by Karabacek, compiled after an examination of the papyrus documents in the collection of the Grand Duke Rainer, the following particulars as to this title and office.

At the close of the Byzantine dominion in Egypt the Nile land was divided into three provinces — Lower, Middle, and Upper Egypt. Each of these ἐπαρχίαι comprised several districts, νομοί. The administrative chiefs of these were the στρατηγοί. But the administration of the finances was intrusted to the Pagarchs. The powers of these officers increased as time went on. They had care of the public security; they were district sheriffs with police power. They superintended roads and ways, the navigation of the rivers and canals, the weights and measures, and latterly the coinage. It is remarkable that the Arab conquest changed all this very little. The conquerors had no skill in finance or internal administration, and for centuries the Christians had sole charge of the internal economy of the country. In a bilingual papyrus, dated the 22d year of the Hegira (A.D. 643), the equivalent for "Pagarch" is the Arabic word with which we are now so familiar, "Khalifa" or "substitute." The word "Mokaukas" is a title of honour equivalent to the Greek μεγαυχής, "The Illustrious." A similar word in Arabic means "a ring-dove," and is connected with the Pagarch's symbol of office referred to in the story.

NOTE B (chap. ii. p. 17).

THE ROMAN FORTRESS OF BABYLON.

In spite of much recent destruction, part of the old Roman fortress of Babylon may still be seen at Old Cairo. The existing walls were probably built by Trajan about A.D. 100, but a fortress of some kind had stood on or near the spot for quite six centuries previously. The name "Babylon" is said to have been given by a colony of Babylonians who revolted from Cambyses' army after the Persian conquest of Egypt; but it is curious that the Arab writers, who received the name from the Greek, retained it as "Bâbilûn," and never confuse it with "Bâbil," their name for the original city.

Mr Butler in his 'Ancient Coptic Churches of Egypt' gives a plan of the remains, and describes them fully, together with the very curious churches enclosed within the walls (vol. i. p. 155 *seq.*)   A few lines may be quoted :—

"There is plenty in Egypt to remind one of the period of Greek rule; but the traces of Roman conquest are rare and not striking.   One scarcely realises how firmly the power of Rome was planted on the Nile.   Yet the fortress of Babylon, with its massive walls and colossal bastions, is a type of the solid strength by which Rome won and kept her empire.   And beyond its value in the cause of Roman archæology, this ancient castle has a far wider interest; for it encloses no less than six churches of the Copts, some of which were certainly standing when the wave of Arab invasion dashed idly against their defences.   In this fortress too the fate of nations centred; for it was here that by their treacherous surrender the Jacobites sealed at once the triumph of Al Islâm and their own doom of perpetual subjection, well content to purchase at the price of their country's freedom a final victory over their religious adversaries the Melkites: it was here that the Greek empire over Egypt fell, and here that the Crescent rose above the Cross."

Note C (chap. iii. p. 26).

ARMENOSA.

The name of the heroine and the chief incidents in
the story are based on the following passage in M.
Etienne Quatremère's ' Mémoires Géographiques et His-
toriques sur l'Egypte,' vol. i. p. 54 :—

"Au rapport d'Al-Wakedy, le Makaukès ayant marié
sa fille à Constantin, fils d'Héraclius, l'avoit fait partir
avec ses trésors, ses esclaves, et toute sa suite afin qu'elle
se rendit à Césarée, ville maritime de Syrie, où les noces
devoient être célebrées. La Princesse ayant appris en
chemin que les Arabes étoient campés devant Césarée,
dont ils avoient formé le siège, retourna sur ses pas, et
s'arrêta à Belbeis. De cette ville elle envoya à Ferma
son grand chambellan, à la tête de deux mille cavaliers,
avec ordre de garder les passages et d'empêcher que
personne, Grec ou autre, ne pénétrât en Egypte. En
même temps le Makaukès dépêcha des courriers vers
les frontières de son Gouvernment du côté de la Syrie
pour défendre de laisser entrer personne en Egypte.
Car il craignoit que, si l'on venoit à y apprendre la
conquête de la Syrie par les Musulmans, le décourage-
ment ne s'emparât de ses troupes. Cependant Amrou-
ben-el-As étant entré en Egypte mit le siège devant
Belbeis, où se trouvoit renfermée Armanosah fille du
Makaukès. Il sé livra plusieurs combats dans lesquels
Amrou tua mille cavaliers de la garnison et fit trois mille

prisonniers. Le reste s'enfuit vers le Makaukes et la princesse fut prise avec ses trésors et tous les objets appartenants aux Coptes. Amrou voulant gagner l'amitié du Makaukes, lui envoya sa fille après l'avoir traitée avec la plus grande distinction. Il la fit accompagner par Kais al Sehmy, et rendit en même temps tout ce qui s'étoit trouvé dans Belbeis appartenant à la princesse et aux Coptes. Le Gouverneur fut charmé de l'arrivée de sa fille."

NOTE D (chap. v. p. 64).

THE JEWISH SYNAGOGUE AT OLD CAIRO.

In the middle of the nave of the Jewish synagogue at Kasr esh Shemma may still be seen a tomb, covered with silk wrappings, beneath which the body of Jeremiah the prophet is said to rest. The Jews of to-day have the strongest belief in the story, which runs as follows. When the prophet in the course of his missionary journey through Egypt came to the place which a few years later took the name of Babylon, the Jews of that place rose against him and stoned him to death. Too late they repented, and having buried him with all honour, they built his sepulchre and held it in the utmost veneration. As years rolled on most of the Jews turned Christians, and a Christian church was built over the tomb. But a small remnant preserved the memory of the prophet, and

their constant aim was to recover the holy place. At last
—in the ninth century of our era—they found their
opportunity, and bought the church from the Patriarch
Khail of evil repute. For a thousand years it has
remained as a synagogue.

Note E (chap. vi. p. 70).

CALLINICUS.

Heliopolis in Syria disputes with Heliopolis in Egypt
the honour of having given birth to Callinicus. He was
by profession an architect. It is not clear from the
words of the best authorities whether Romaic (Greek)
fire was actually used during the first siege of Alexandria,
but it was invented about this time and used in the
second siege. We read, " Having prepared marine fire
($\pi\hat{v}\rho$ $\theta a\lambda\acute{a}\varsigma\varsigma\iota o\nu$), he burned the ships of the Arabs and
their crews alive." The share of Callinicus in the defence
of Babylon—i.e., the Rhoda incident—is imaginary; but
if he was living at Heliopolis at the time, and employed
in his experiments, it is highly probable that he placed
at the disposal of the defenders his new though imperfect
invention.

NOTE F (chap. xiii. p. 162).

BELBEIS.

M. Etienne Quatremère says :—

"Il ne me reste plus maintenant qu'à examiner à quelle ancienne ville d'Egypte corresponde Belbeis. Guillaume·de Tyr est le premier qui ait confondu cette ville avec Péluse. Son erreur a été suivie par Sanuto,[1] qui pourtant dans un autre endroit distingue expressement ces deux villes, par Kircher, l'Abbé Renandot, Lequien, Reiske, et enfin M. Deguignes. Mais cette opinion a été solidement refutée par Golius, A. Schultens, et d'Anville, qui du reste son peu d'accord sur la ville dont Belbeis occupe l'emplacement."

Later he says Kircher's Coptic Lexicon translates φαρβαιτ by Belbeis. Makrizi the Arab historian says, "Farbit was given with Fakous, Barta, &c., to the Arab tribes who had taken part in the conquest of Egypt."

---

[1] "Postea rex intravit desertum inter Gazam et Egyptum indeque usque ad Belbeis processit. Inde Pelusium transiit et usque ad ripam fluminis pervenit."—From 'Gesta Dei per Francos,' by M. Sanuto.

Note G (chap. xxvii. p. 318).

GREEK FIRE.

The following recipe for manufacturing Greek fire is given by Marcus Græcus, a tenth century writer :—

"Take pure sulphur, tartar, sarcocolla [Persian gum], pitch, dissolved nitre, petroleum, *huile de gemme.* Boil these ingredients together. Saturate tow with the concoction and set fire to it. The conflagration will spread, and can only be extinguished by vinegar or sand."

Another compound closely resembled gunpowder. A pound of sulphur was pounded in a mortar with two pounds of charcoal and six pounds of nitre. The mixture was poured into long, narrow, and tight envelopes like cartridges, closed at the end with iron wire. These shells were ignited and hurled through the air, probably by catapults.

PRINTED BY WILLIAM BLACKWOOD AND SONS.

TWO BOOKS ON EGYPT.

UNDER CRESCENT AND STAR. By Lieut.-Col.
ANDREW HAGGARD, D.S.O., Author of 'Dodo and I,' 'Tempest
Torn,' &c. With a Portrait. Crown 8vo, 6s.

"A bright dashing narrative of military incident and adventure, written
throughout in an unflagging spirit of cheerfulness, by a typical British
officer of high distinction.......There is not a single 'chestnut' among the
scores of entertaining anecdotes scattered broadcast over the pages of a
book which is delightfully readable from commencement to finish."—
Daily Telegraph.

"A blithe picture of military life in the service of the Khedive. It
teems with anecdotes and stirring events, ranging from civilised life in
Cairo to a visit to the stronghold of a robber chief in the wilds of
Abyssinia."—*Daily News.*

"Written in a lively and amusing style.......The reminiscences have all
the force and freshness of the impressions of the hour, coupled with the
solid advantage of subsequent thought and information."—*Athenæum.*

"A lively account of military experiences in Egypt, and of life in camp
at Cairo.......Throws curious and detailed light on the incidents of the
Egyptian campaign."—*Speaker.*

RECOLLECTIONS OF AN EGYPTIAN PRINCESS. By
HER ENGLISH GOVERNESS (Miss E. CHENNELLS). Being
the Record of Five Years' Residence at the Court of Ismael Pasha,
Khédive. Second Edition. With Three Portraits. Post 8vo, 7s. 6d.

"Few books that have hitherto appeared have presented so vivid and
minute a picture of the domestic life of the court of a Mohammedan
sovereign."—*Daily News.*

"A book which, we may say at once, occupies quite a unique place
amongst accounts of modern Oriental travel.......A most startlingly vivid
conception of that cloistered life behind the lattice of the royal harem."—
Daily Chronicle.

"In these 'Recollections' will be found what is, perhaps, the most complete and vivid picture obtainable of Egyptian Society during Ismael's
régime. Especially minute is the account given of harem life in Egypt."
—*Globe.*

"Every page is Oriental in colour, and has something fresh and in-
teresting to tell of Egyptian scenes, customs, and, above all, private life
in the selectest order of society."—*Scotsman.*

WILLIAM BLACKWOOD & SONS, Edinburgh and London.

RECENT FICTION.

MIRIAM CROMWELL—ROYALIST: A ROMANCE OF THE GREAT REBELLION. BY DORA GREENWELL M'CHESNEY, Author of 'Kathleen Clare.' Crown 8vo, 6s.

THE PROVOST-MARSHAL: A ROMANCE OF THE MIDDLE SHIRES. By the HON. FREDERICK MONCREIFF, Author of 'The X Jewel.' Crown 8vo, 6s.

AMONG THE UNTRODDEN WAYS. By M. E. FRANCIS (Mrs FRANCIS BLUNDELL), Author of 'In a North Country Village,' 'A Daughter of the Soil,' 'Frieze and Fustian,' &c. Crown 8vo, 3s. 6d.

"She shows a grip of things in her new book that she has never shown hitherto.......Both touching and amusing."—*Sketch.*

FELLOW TRAVELLERS. By GRAHAM TRAVERS, Author of ' Mona Maclean.' Third Edition. Crown 8vo, 6s.

"This is a book, not a mere assemblage of unrelated matters.......Every worthy reader will feel that he has been brought into communion with a noble nature, with a mind that has estimated at their just value many of the conventionalities of life, and yet has maintained with unswerving fidelity its hold of the good and the true. Graham Travers must certainly be placed in the very front rank of living women authors. In many respects she is the first of them all."—*British Weekly.*

AN UNCROWNED KING: A ROMANCE OF HIGH POLITICS. By SYDNEY C. GRIER, Author of 'His Excellency's English Governess,' 'In Furthest Ind,' &c. Crown 8vo, 6s.

"Told in so graphic, vigorous, and entertaining a style that few readers will pause till they reach the end.......Thoroughly original. Any one who wishes to enjoy a novel of first-rate quality, brilliant and rapid as a drama, should read ' An Uncrowned King.' "—*British Weekly.*

IRAS: A MYSTERY. By THEO. DOUGLAS, Author of ' A Bride-Elect.' Crown 8vo, 3s. 6d.

"The story is singularly beautiful, and told in a refreshingly pure English style—a style, indeed, such as few of our present-day writers command." —*British Weekly.*

SOME UNCONVENTIONAL PEOPLE. By MRS GLADWYN JEBB, Author of 'Life and Adventures of J. G. Jebb.' With Illustrations. Crown 8vo, 3s. 6d.

" Delightfully refreshing in both subjects and style.......Mrs Jebb's light touch and keen appreciation of a humorous situation just suit the subjects she has handled, and we have found the book most enjoyable."—*Manchester Courier.*

WILLIAM BLACKWOOD & SONS, EDINBURGH AND LONDON.

Catalogue

of

Messrs Blackwood & Sons'

Publications

PHILOSOPHICAL CLASSICS FOR ENGLISH READERS.

EDITED BY WILLIAM KNIGHT, LL.D.,

Professor of Moral Philosophy in the University of St Andrews.

In crown 8vo Volumes, with Portraits, price 3s. 6d.

Contents of the Series.

DESCARTES, by Professor Mahaffy, Dublin.—BUTLER, by Rev. W. Lucas Collins, M.A.—BERKELEY, by Professor Campbell Fraser.—FICHTE, by Professor Adamson, Glasgow. — KANT, by Professor Wallace, Oxford.—HAMILTON, by Professor Veitch, Glasgow.—HEGEL, by the Master of Balliol. —LEIBNIZ, by J. Theodore Merz.—VICO, by Professor Flint, Edinburgh.—HOBBES, by Professor Croom Robertson.—HUME, by the Editor. — SPINOZA, by the Very Rev. Principal Caird, Glasgow.—BACON: Part I. The Life, by Professor Nichol.—BACON: Part II. Philosophy, by the same Author.—LOCKE, by Professor Campbell Fraser.

FOREIGN CLASSICS FOR ENGLISH READERS.

EDITED BY MRS OLIPHANT.

In crown 8vo, 2s. 6d.

Contents of the Series.

DANTE, by the Editor. — VOLTAIRE, by General Sir E. B. Hamley, K.C.B. —PASCAL, by Principal Tulloch. — PETRARCH, by Henry Reeve, C.B.—GOETHE, by A. Hayward, Q.C.—MOLIÈRE, by the Editor and F. Tarver, M.A.—MONTAIGNE, by Rev. W. L. Collins, M.A.—RABELAIS, by Sir Walter Besant. — CALDERON, by E. J. Hasell. — SAINT SIMON, by Clifton W. Collins, M.A. — CERVANTES, by the Editor. — CORNEILLE AND RACINE, by Henry M. Trollope. — MADAME DE SÉVIGNÉ, by Miss Thackeray.—LA FONTAINE, AND OTHER FRENCH FABULISTS, by Rev. W. Lucas Collins, M.A.—SCHILLER, by James Sime, M.A., Author of 'Lessing, his Life and Writings.'—TASSO, by E. J. Hasell. — ROUSSEAU, by Henry Grey Graham.—ALFRED DE MUSSET, by C. F. Oliphant.

ANCIENT CLASSICS FOR ENGLISH READERS.

EDITED BY THE REV. W. LUCAS COLLINS, M.A.

Complete in 28 Vols. crown 8vo, cloth, price 2s. 6d. each. And may also be had in 14 Volumes, strongly and neatly bound, with calf or vellum back, £3, 10s.

Contents of the Series.

HOMER: THE ILIAD, by the Editor.— HOMER: THE ODYSSEY, by the Editor.— HERODOTUS, by George C. Swayne, M.A.— XENOPHON, by Sir Alexander Grant, Bart., LL.D. — EURIPIDES, by W. B. Donne.— ARISTOPHANES, by the Editor.—PLATO, by Clifton W. Collins, M.A.—LUCIAN, by the Editor. — ÆSCHYLUS, by the Right Rev. the Bishop of Colombo.—SOPHOCLES, by Clifton W. Collins, M.A. — HESIOD AND THEOGNIS, by the Rev. J. Davies, M.A.— GREEK ANTHOLOGY, by Lord Neaves.— VIRGIL, by the Editor.—HORACE, by Sir Theodore Martin, K.C.B. — JUVENAL, by Edward Walford, M.A. — PLAUTUS AND TERENCE, by the Editor.—THE COMMENTARIES OF CÆSAR, by Anthony Trollope. —TACITUS, by W. B. Donne.—CICERO, by the Editor. — PLINY'S LETTERS, by the Rev. Alfred Church, M.A., and the Rev. W. J. Brodribb, M.A. — LIVY, by the Editor.—OVID, by the Rev. A. Church, M.A. — CATULLUS, TIBULLUS, AND PROPERTIUS, by the Rev. Jas. Davies, M.A. — DEMOSTHENES, by the Rev. W. J. Brodribb, M.A.—ARISTOTLE, by Sir Alexander Grant, Bart., LL.D.—THUCYDIDES, by the Editor. — LUCRETIUS, by W. H. Mallock, M.A.—PINDAR, by the Rev. F. D. Morice, M.A.

Saturday Review.—"It is difficult to estimate too highly the value of such a series as this in giving 'English readers' an insight, exact as far as it goes, into those olden times which are so remote, and yet to many of us so close."

CATALOGUE

OF

MESSRS BLACKWOOD & SONS'

PUBLICATIONS.

ALISON.
History of Europe. By Sir Archibald Alison, Bart., D.C.L.

1. From the Commencement of the French Revolution to
the Battle of Waterloo.
Library Edition, 14 vols., with Portraits. Demy 8vo, £10, 10s.
Another Edition, in 20 vols. crown 8vo, £6.
People's Edition, 13 vols. crown 8vo, £2, 11s.

2. Continuation to the Accession of Louis Napoleon.
Library Edition, 8 vols. 8vo, £6, 7s. 6d.
People's Edition, 8 vols. crown 8vo, 34s.

Epitome of Alison's History of Europe. Thirtieth Thousand, 7s. 6d.

Atlas to Alison's History of Europe. By A. Keith Johnston.
Library Edition, demy 4to, £3, 3s.
People's Edition, 31s. 6d.

Life of John Duke of Marlborough. With some Account of
his Contemporaries, and of the War of the Succession. Third Edition. 2 vols.
8vo. Portraits and Maps, 30s.

Essays : Historical, Political, and Miscellaneous. 3 vols.
demy 8vo, 45s.

ACROSS FRANCE IN A CARAVAN: Being some Account
of a Journey from Bordeaux to Genoa in the "Escargot," taken in the Winter
1889-90. By the Author of 'A Day of my Life at Eton.' With fifty Illustrations
by John Wallace, after Sketches by the Author, and a Map. Cheap Edition,
demy 8vo, 7s. 6d.

ACTA SANCTORUM HIBERNIÆ; Ex Codice Salmanticensi.
Nunc primum integre edita opera Caroli de Smedt et Josephi de Backer, e
Soc. Jesu, Hagiographorum Bollandianorum ; Auctore et Sumptus Largiente
Joanne Patricio Marchione Bothae. In One handsome 4to Volume, bound in
half roxburghe, £2, 2s.; in paper cover, 31s. 6d.

ADOLPHUS. Some Memories of Paris. By F. Adolphus.
Crown 8vo, 6s.

AIKMAN.
Manures and the Principles of Manuring. By C. M. Aikman,
D.Sc., F.R.S.E., &c., Professor of Chemistry, Glasgow Veterinary College ;
Examiner in Chemistry, University of Glasgow, &c. Crown 8vo, 6s. 6d.

Farmyard Manure : Its Nature, Composition, and Treatment.
Crown 8vo, 1s. 6d.

AIRD. Poetical Works of Thomas Aird. Fifth Edition, with
Memoir of the Author by the Rev. Jardine Wallace, and Portrait. Crown 8vo,
7s. 6d.

ALLARDYCE.
　The City of Sunshine. By ALEXANDER ALLARDYCE, Author of
　'Earlscourt,' &c. New Edition. Crown 8vo, 6s.
　Balmoral : A Romance of the Queen's Country. New Edition.
　Crown 8vo, 6s.
　Memoir of the Honourable George Keith Elphinstone, K.B.,
　Viscount Keith of Stonehaven, Marischal, Admiral of the Red. 8vo, with Por-
　trait, Illustrations, and Maps, 21s.

ALMOND. Sermons by a Lay Head-master. By HELY HUTCH-
　INSON ALMOND, M.A. Oxon., Head-Master of Loretto School. Crown 8vo, 5s.

ANCIENT CLASSICS FOR ENGLISH READERS. Edited
　by Rev. W. LUCAS COLLINS, M.A. Price 2s. 6d. each. *For List of Vols., see p. 2.*

ANDERSON. Daniel in the Critics' Den. A Reply to Dean
　Farrar's 'Book of Daniel.' By ROBERT ANDERSON, LL.D., Barrister-at-Law,
　Assistant Commissioner of Police of the Metropolis; Author of 'The Coming
　Prince,' 'Human Destiny,' &c. Post 8vo, 4s. 6d.

AYTOUN.
　Lays of the Scottish Cavaliers, and other Poems. By W.
　EDMONDSTOUNE AYTOUN, D.C.L., Professor of Rhetoric and Belles-Lettres in the
　University of Edinburgh. New Edition. Fcap. 8vo, 3s. 6d.
　　　ANOTHER EDITION. Fcap. 8vo, 7s. 6d.
　　　CHEAP EDITION. 1s. Cloth, 1s. 3d.
　An Illustrated Edition of the Lays of the Scottish Cavaliers.
　From designs by Sir NOEL PATON. Cheaper Edition. Small 4to, 10s. 6d.
　Bothwell : a Poem. Third Edition. Fcap., 7s. 6d.
　Poems and Ballads of Goethe. Translated by Professor
　AYTOUN and Sir THEODORE MARTIN, K.C.B. Third Edition. Fcap., 6s.
　The Ballads of Scotland. Edited by Professor AYTOUN.
　Fourth Edition. 2 vols. fcap. 8vo, 12s.
　Memoir of William E. Aytoun, D.C.L. By Sir THEODORE
　MARTIN, K.C.B. With Portrait. Post 8vo, 12s.

BACH.
　On Musical Education and Vocal Culture. By ALBERT B.
　BACH. Fourth Edition. 8vo, 7s. 6d.
　The Principles of Singing. A Practical Guide for Vocalists
　and Teachers. With Course of Vocal Exercises. Second Edition. With Portrait
　of the Author. Crown 8vo, 6s.
　The Art Ballad : Loewe and Schubert. With Musical Illus-
　trations. With a Portrait of LOEWE. Third Edition. Small 4to, 5s.

BEDFORD & COLLINS. Annals of the Free Foresters, from
　1856 to the Present Day. By W. K. R. BEDFORD, W. E. W. COLLINS, and other
　Contributors. With 55 Portraits and 59 other Illustrations. Demy 8vo, 21s. *net.*

BELLAIRS. Gossips with Girls and Maidens, Betrothed and
　Free. By LADY BELLAIRS. New Edition. Crown 8vo, 3s. 6d. Cloth, extra
　gilt edges, 5s.

BELLESHEIM. History of the Catholic Church of Scotland.
　From the Introduction of Christianity to the Present Day. By ALPHONS BEL-
　LESHEIM, D.D., Canon of Aix-la-Chapelle. Translated, with Notes and Additions,
　by D. OSWALD HUNTER BLAIR, O.S.B., Monk of Fort Augustus. Cheap Edition.
　Complete in 4 vols. demy 8vo, with Maps. Price 21s. net.

BENTINCK. Racing Life of Lord George Cavendish Bentinck,
　M.P., and other Reminiscences. By JOHN KENT, Private Trainer to the Good-
　wood Stable. Edited by the Hon. FRANCIS LAWLEY. With Twenty-three full-
　page Plates, and Facsimile Letter. Third Edition. Demy 8vo, 25s.

BESANT. The Revolt of Man. By Sir WALTER BESANT.
Tenth Edition. Crown 8vo, 8s. 6d.

BEVERIDGE.
Culross and Tulliallan ; or, Perthshire on Forth. Its History
and Antiquities. With Elucidations of Scottish Life and Character from the
Burgh and Kirk-Session Records of that District. By DAVID BEVERIDGE. 2 vols.
8vo, with Illustrations, 42s.
Between the Ochils and the Forth ; or, From Stirling Bridge
to Aberdour. Crown 8vo, 6s.

BICKERDYKE. A Banished Beauty. By JOHN BICKERDYKE,
Author of ' Days in Thule, with Rod, Gun, and Camera,' ' The Book of the All-
Round Angler,' ' Curiosities of Ale and Beer,' &c. With Illustrations. Crown
8vo, 6s.

BIRCH.
Examples of Stables, Hunting-Boxes, Kennels, Racing Estab-
lishments, &c. By JOHN BIRCH, Architect, Author of ' Country Architecture,'
&c. With 30 Plates. Royal 8vo, 7s.
Examples of Labourers' Cottages, &c. With Plans for Im-
proving the Dwellings of the Poor in Large Towns. With 34 Plates. Royal 8vo, 7s.
Picturesque Lodges. A Series of Designs for Gate Lodges,
Park Entrances, Keepers', Gardeners', Bailiffs', Grooms', Upper and Under Servants' Lodges, and other Rural Residences. With 16 Plates. 4to, 12s. 6d.

BLACK. Heligoland and the Islands of the North Sea. By
WILLIAM GEORGE BLACK. Crown 8vo, 4s.

BLACKIE.
Lays and Legends of Ancient Greece. By JOHN STUART
BLACKIE, Emeritus Professor of Greek in the University of Edinburgh. Second
Edition. Fcap. 8vo, 5s.
The Wisdom of Goethe. Fcap. 8vo. Cloth, extra gilt, 6s.
Scottish Song : Its Wealth, Wisdom, and Social Significance.
Crown 8vo. With Music. 7s. 6d.
A Song of Heroes. Crown 8vo, 6s.
John Stuart Blackie : A Biography. By ANNA M. STODDART.
With 3 Plates. Third Edition. 2 vols. demy 8vo, 21s.
POPULAR EDITION. With Portrait. Crown 8vo, 6s.

BLACKMORE. The Maid of Sker. By R. D. BLACKMORE,
Author of ' Lorna Doone,' &c. New Edition. Crown 8vo, 6s. Cheaper Edition. Crown 8vo, 3s. 6d.

BLACKWOOD.
Blackwood's Magazine, from Commencement in 1817 to August
1896. Nos. 1 to 970, forming 159 Volumes.
Index to Blackwood's Magazine. Vols. 1 to 50. 8vo, 15s.
Tales from Blackwood. First Series. Price One Shilling each,
in Paper Cover. Sold separately at all Railway Bookstalls.
They may also be had bound in 12 vols., cloth, 18s. Half calf, richly gilt, 30s.
Or the 12 vols. in 6, roxburghe, 21s. Half red morocco, 28s.
Tales from Blackwood. Second Series. Complete in Twenty-
four Shilling Parts. Handsomely bound in 12 vols., cloth, 30s. In leather back,
roxburghe style, 37s. 6d. Half calf, gilt, 52s. 6d. Half morocco, 55s.
Tales from Blackwood. Third Series. Complete in Twelve
Shilling Parts. Handsomely bound in 6 vols., cloth, 15s.; and in 12 vols., cloth,
18s. The 6 vols. in roxburghe, 21s. Half calf, 25s. Half morocco, 28s.
Travel, Adventure, and Sport. From ' Blackwood's Magazine.'
Uniform with ' Tales from Blackwood.' In Twelve Parts, each price 1s. Handsomely bound in 6 vols., cloth, 15s. And in half calf, 25s.

BLACKWOOD.

New Educational Series. *See separate Catalogue.*
New Uniform Series of Novels (Copyright).
Crown 8vo, cloth. Price 3s. 6d. each. Now ready:—

THE MAID OF SKER. By R. D. Blackmore.
WENDERHOLME. By P. G. Hamerton.
THE STORY OF MARGRÉDEL. By D. Storrar Meldrum.
MISS MARJORIBANKS. By Mrs Oliphant.
THE PERPETUAL CURATE, and THE RECTOR. By the Same.
SALEM CHAPEL, and THE DOCTOR's FAMILY. By the Same.
A SENSITIVE PLANT. By E. D. Gerard.
LADY LEE'S WIDOWHOOD. By General Sir E. B. Hamley.
KATIE STEWART, and other Stories. By Mrs Oliphant.
VALENTINE AND HIS BROTHER. By the Same.
SONS AND DAUGHTERS. By the Same.
MARMORNE. By P. G. Hamerton.

REATA. By E. D. Gerard.
BEGGAR MY NEIGHBOUR. By the Same.
THE WATERS OF HERCULES. By the Same.
FAIR TO SEE. By L. W. M. Lockhart.
MINE IS THINE. By the Same.
DOUBLES AND QUITS. By the Same.
ALTIORA PETO. By Laurence Oliphant.
PICCADILLY. By the Same. With Illustrations.
THE REVOLT OF MAN. By Walter Besant.
LADY BABY. By D. Gerard.
THE BLACKSMITH OF VOE. By Paul Cushing.
THE DILEMMA. By the Author of 'The Battle of Dorking.'
MY TRIVIAL LIFE AND MISFORTUNE. By A Plain Woman.
POOR NELLIE. By the Same.

Others in preparation.

Standard Novels. Uniform in size and binding. Each complete in one Volume.

FLORIN SERIES, Illustrated Boards. Bound in Cloth, 2s. 6d.

TOM CRINGLE'S LOG. By Michael Scott.
THE CRUISE OF THE MIDGE. By the Same.
CYRIL THORNTON. By Captain Hamilton.
ANNALS OF THE PARISH. By John Galt.
THE PROVOST, &c. By the Same.
SIR ANDREW WYLIE. By the Same.
THE ENTAIL. By the Same.
MISS MOLLY. By Beatrice May Butt.
REGINALD DALTON. By J. G. Lockhart.

PEN OWEN. By Dean Hook.
ADAM BLAIR. By J. G. Lockhart.
LADY LEE'S WIDOWHOOD. By General Sir E. B. Hamley.
SALEM CHAPEL. By Mrs Oliphant.
THE PERPETUAL CURATE. By the Same.
MISS MARJORIBANKS. By the Same.
JOHN: A Love Story. By the Same.

SHILLING SERIES, Illustrated Cover. Bound in Cloth, 1s. 6d.

THE RECTOR, and THE DOCTOR's FAMILY. By Mrs Oliphant.
THE LIFE OF MANSIE WAUCH. By D. M. Moir.
PENINSULAR SCENES AND SKETCHES. By F. Hardman.

SIR FRIZZLE PUMPKIN, NIGHTS AT MESS, &c.
THE SUBALTERN.
LIFE IN THE FAR WEST. By G. F. Ruxton.
VALERIUS: A Roman Story. By J. G. Lockhart.

BON GAULTIER'S BOOK OF BALLADS. Fifteenth Edi-
tion. With Illustrations by Doyle, Leech, and Crowquill. Fcap. 8vo, 5s.

BRADDON. Thirty Years of Shikar. By Sir EDWARD BRADDON,
K.C.M.G. With Illustrations by G. D. Giles, and Map of Oudh Forest Tracts and Nepal Terai. Demy 8vo, 18s.

BROUGHAM. Memoirs of the Life and Times of Henry Lord
Brougham. Written by HIMSELF. 3 vols. 8vo, £2, 8s. The Volumes are sold separately, price 16s. each.

BROWN. The Forester: A Practical Treatise on the Planting
and Tending of Forest-trees and the General Management of Woodlands. By JAMES BROWN, LL.D. Sixth Edition, Enlarged. Edited by JOHN NISBET, D.Œc., Author of 'British Forest Trees,' &c. In 2 vols. royal 8vo, with 350 Illustrations, 42s. net.

BROWN. Stray Sport. By J. MORAY BROWN, Author of 'Shikar
Sketches,' 'Powder, Spur, and Spear,' 'The Days when we went Hog-Hunting.' 2 vols. post 8vo, with Fifty Illustrations, 21s.

BROWN. A Manual of Botany, Anatomical and Physiological.
For the Use of Students. By ROBERT BROWN, M.A., Ph.D. Crown 8vo, with numerous Illustrations, 12s. 6d

BRUCE.
In Clover and Heather. Poems by WALLACE BRUCE. New and Enlarged Edition. Crown 8vo, 3s. 6d.
A limited number of Copies of the First Edition, on large hand-made paper, 12s. 6d.
Here's a Hand. Addresses and Poems. Crown 8vo, 5s.
Large Paper Edition, limited to 100 copies, price 21s.

BUCHAN. Introductory Text-Book of Meteorology. By ALEX-ANDER BUCHAN, LL.D., F.R.S.E., Secretary of the Scottish Meteorological Society, &c. New Edition. Crown 8vo, with Coloured Charts and Engravings.
[*In preparation.*

BURBIDGE.
Domestic Floriculture, Window Gardening, and Floral Decora-tions. Being Practical Directions for the Propagation, Culture, and Arrangement of Plants and Flowers as Domestic Ornaments. By F. W. BURBIDGE. Second Edition. Crown 8vo, with numerous Illustrations, 7s. 6d.
Cultivated Plants: Their Propagation and Improvement. Including Natural and Artificial Hybridisation, Raising from Seed, Cuttings, and Layers, Grafting and Budding, as applied to the Families and Genera in Cultivation. Crown 8vo, with numerous Illustrations, 12s. 6d.

BURGESS. The Viking Path: A Tale of the White Christ. By J. J. HALDANE BURGESS, Author of 'Rasmie's Büddie,' 'Shetland Sketches,' &c. Crown 8vo, 6s.

BURKE. The Flowering of the Almond Tree, and other Poems. By CHRISTIAN BURKE. Pott 4to, 5s.

BURROWS.
Commentaries on the History of England, from the Earliest Times to 1865. By MONTAGU BURROWS, Chichele Professor of Modern History in the University of Oxford; Captain R.N.; F.S.A., &c.; "Officier de l'In-struction Publique," France. Crown 8vo, 7s. 6d.
The History of the Foreign Policy of Great Britain. Demy 8vo, 12s.

BURTON.
The History of Scotland: From Agricola's Invasion to the Extinction of the last Jacobite Insurrection. By JOHN HILL BURTON, D.C.L., Historiographer-Royal for Scotland. New and Enlarged Edition, 8 vols., and Index. Crown 8vo, £3, 3s.
History of the British Empire during the Reign of Queen Anne. In 3 vols. 8vo. 36s.
The Scot Abroad. Third Edition. Crown 8vo, 10s. 6d.
The Book-Hunter. New Edition. With Portrait. Crown 8vo, 7s. 6d.

BUTCHER. The Fortunes of Armenosa. A Historical Romance of Memphis and Old Cairo. By the Very Rev. Dean BUTCHER, D.D., F.S.A., Chaplain at Cairo. Crown 8vo, 6s.

BUTE. The Altus of St Columba. With a Prose Paraphrase and Notes. In paper cover, 2s. 6d.

BUTT.
Theatricals: An Interlude. By BEATRICE MAY BUTT. Crown 8vo, 6s.
Miss Molly. Cheap Edition, 2s.
Eugenie. Crown 8vo, 6s. 6d.
Elizabeth, and other Sketches. Crown 8vo, 6s.
Delicia. New Edition. Crown 8vo, 2s. 6d.

CAIRD. Sermons. By JOHN CAIRD, D.D., Principal of the University of Glasgow. Seventeenth Thousand. Fcap. 8vo, 5s.

CALDWELL. Schopenhauer's System in its Philosophical Significance (the Shaw Fellowship Lectures, 1893). By WILLIAM CALDWELL, M.A., D.Sc., Professor of Moral and Social Philosophy, Northwestern University, U.S.A.; formerly Assistant to the Professor of Logic and Metaphysics, Edin., and Examiner in Philosophy in the University of St Andrews. Demy 8vo, 10s. 6d. net.

CALLWELL. The Effect of Maritime Command on Land Campaigns since Waterloo. By Major C. E. CALLWELL, R.A. With Plans. Post 8vo, 6s. *net.*

CAMPBELL. Sermons Preached before the Queen at Balmoral. By the Rev. A. A. CAMPBELL, Minister of Crathie. Published by Command of Her Majesty. Crown 8vo, 4s. 6d.

CAMPBELL. Records of Argyll. Legends, Traditions, and Recollections of Argyllshire Highlanders, collected chiefly from the Gaelic. With Notes on the Antiquity of the Dress, Clan Colours, or Tartans of the Highlanders. By Lord ARCHIBALD CAMPBELL. Illustrated with Nineteen full-page Etchings. 4to, printed on hand-made paper, £3, 3s.

CAMPBELL. Critical Studies in St Luke's Gospel : Its Demonology and Ebionitism. By COLIN CAMPBELL, D.D., Minister of the Parish of Dundee, formerly Scholar and Fellow of Glasgow University. Author of the 'Three First Gospels in Greek, arranged in parallel columns.' Post 8vo, 7s. 6d.

CANTON. A Lost Epic, and other Poems. By WILLIAM CANTON. Crown 8vo, 5s.

CARSTAIRS.
Human Nature in Rural India. By R. CARSTAIRS. Crown 8vo, 6s.
British Work in India. Crown 8vo, 6s.

CAUVIN. A Treasury of the English and German Languages. Compiled from the best Authors and Lexicographers in both Languages. By JOSEPH CAUVIN, LL.D. and Ph.D., of the University of Göttingen, &c. Crown 8vo, 7s. 6d.

CHARTERIS. Canonicity ; or, Early Testimonies to the Existence and Use of the Books of the New Testament. Based on Kirchhoffer's 'Quellensammlung.' Edited by A. H. CHARTERIS, D.D., Professor of Biblical Criticism in the University of Edinburgh. [*New Edition in preparation.*

CHENNELLS. Recollections of an Egyptian Princess. By her English Governess (Miss E. CHENNELLS). Being a Record of Five Years' Residence at the Court of Ismael Pasha, Khédive. Second Edition. With Three Portraits. Post 8vo, 7s. 6d.

CHESNEY. The Dilemma. By General Sir GEORGE CHESNEY, K.C.B., M.P., Author of 'The Battle of Dorking,' &c. New Edition. Crown 8vo, 3s. 6d.

CHRISTISON. Life of Sir Robert Christison, Bart., M.D., D.C.L. Oxon., Professor of Medical Jurisprudence in the University of Edinburgh. Edited by his SONS. In 2 vols. 8vo. Vol. I.—Autobiography. 16s. Vol. II.—Memoirs. 16s.

CHURCH. Chapters in an Adventurous Life. Sir Richard Church in Italy and Greece. By E. M. CHURCH. With Photogravure Portrait. Demy 8vo, 10s. 6d.

CHURCH SERVICE SOCIETY.
A Book of Common Order : being Forms of Worship issued by the Church Service Society. Seventh Edition, carefully revised. In 1 vol. crown 8vo, cloth, 3s. 6d. ; French morocco, 5s. Also in 2 vols. crown 8vo, cloth, 4s. ; French morocco, 6s. 6d.
Daily Offices for Morning and Evening Prayer throughout the Week. Crown 8vo, 3s. 6d.
Order of Divine Service for Children. Issued by the Church Service Society. With Scottish Hymnal. Cloth, 3d.

CLOUSTON. Popular Tales and Fictions: their Migrations and Transformations. By W. A. CLOUSTON, Editor of 'Arabian Poetry for English Readers,' &c. 2 vols. post 8vo, roxburghe binding, 25s.

COCHRAN. A Handy Text-Book of Military Law. Compiled chiefly to assist Officers preparing for Examination; also for all Officers of the Regular and Auxiliary Forces. Comprising also a Synopsis of part of the Army Act. By Major F. COCHRAN, Hampshire Regiment Garrison Instructor, North British District. Crown 8vo, 7s. 6d.

COLQUHOUN. The Moor and the Loch. Containing Minute Instructions in all Highland Sports, with Wanderings over Crag and Corrie, Flood and Fell. By JOHN COLQUHOUN. Cheap Edition. With Illustrations. Demy 8vo, 10s. 6d.

COLVILE. Round the Black Man's Garden. By Lady Z. COLVILE, F.R.G.S. With 2 Maps and 50 Illustrations from Drawings by the Author and from Photographs. Demy 8vo, 16s.

CONDER. The Bible and the East. By Lieut.-Col. C. R. CONDER, R.E., LL.D., D.C.L., M.R.A.S., Author of 'Tent Work in Palestine,' &c. With Illustrations and a Map. Crown 8vo, 5s.

CONSTITUTION AND LAW OF THE CHURCH OF SCOTLAND. With an Introductory Note by the late Principal Tulloch. New Edition, Revised and Enlarged. Crown 8vo, 3s. 6d.

COTTERILL. Suggested Reforms in Public Schools. By C. C. COTTERILL, M.A. Crown 8vo, 3s. 6d.

COUNTY HISTORIES OF SCOTLAND. In demy 8vo volumes of about 350 pp. each. With 2 Maps. Price 7s. 6d. net.

Fife and Kinross. By ÆNEAS J. G. MACKAY, LL.D., Sheriff of these Counties.

Dumfries and Galloway. By Sir HERBERT MAXWELL, Bart., M.P. [*Others in preparation.*

CRANSTOUN.

The Elegies of Albius Tibullus. Translated into English Verse, with Life of the Poet, and Illustrative Notes. By JAMES CRANSTOUN, LL.D., Author of a Translation of 'Catullus.' Crown 8vo, 6s. 6d.

The Elegies of Sextus Propertius. Translated into English Verse, with Life of the Poet, and Illustrative Notes. Crown 8vo, 7s. 6d.

CRAWFORD. Saracinesca. By F. MARION CRAWFORD, Author of 'Mr Isaacs,' &c., &c. Eighth Edition. Crown 8vo, 6s.

CRAWFORD.

The Doctrine of Holy Scripture respecting the Atonement. By the late THOMAS J. CRAWFORD, D.D., Professor of Divinity in the University of Edinburgh. Fifth Edition. 8vo, 12s.

The Fatherhood of God, Considered in its General and Special Aspects. Third Edition, Revised and Enlarged. 8vo, 9s.

The Preaching of the Cross, and other Sermons. 8vo, 7s. 6d.

The Mysteries of Christianity. Crown 8vo, 7s. 6d.

CROSS. Impressions of Dante, and of the New World; with a Few Words on Bimetallism. By J. W. CROSS, Editor of 'George Eliot's Life, as related in her Letters and Journals.' Post 8vo, 6s.

CUMBERLAND. Sport on the Pamirs and Turkistan Steppes. By Major C. S. CUMBERLAND. With Map and Frontispiece. Demy 8vo, 10s. 6d.

CURSE OF INTELLECT. Third Edition. Fcap. 8vo, 2s. 6d. net.

CUSHING. The Blacksmith of Voe. By PAUL CUSHING, Author of 'The Bull i' th' Thorn,' 'Cut with his own Diamond.' Cheap Edition. Crown 8vo, 3s. 6d.

DAVIES.

Norfolk Broads and Rivers; or, The Waterways, Lagoons, and Decoys of East Anglia. By G. CHRISTOPHER DAVIES. Illustrated with Seven full-page Plates. New and Cheaper Edition. Crown 8vo, 6s.

Our Home in Aveyron. Sketches of Peasant Life in Aveyron and the Lot. By G. CHRISTOPHER DAVIES and Mrs BROUGHALL. Illustrated with full-page Illustrations. 8vo, 15s. Cheap Edition, 7s. 6d.

DE LA WARR. An Eastern Cruise in the 'Edeline.' By the Countess DE LA WARR. In Illustrated Cover. 2s.

DESCARTES. The Method, Meditations, and Principles of Philosophy of Descartes. Translated from the Original French and Latin. With a New Introductory Essay, Historical and Critical, on the Cartesian Philosophy. By Professor VEITCH, LL.D., Glasgow University. Tenth Edition. 6s. 6d.

DOGS, OUR DOMESTICATED: Their Treatment in reference to Food, Diseases, Habits, Punishment, Accomplishments. By 'MAGENTA.' Crown 8vo, 2s. 6d.

DOUGLAS.

The Ethics of John Stuart Mill. By CHARLES DOUGLAS, M.A, D.Sc., Lecturer in Moral Philosophy, and Assistant to the Professor of Moral Philosophy in the University of Edinburgh. Crown 8vo, 7s. 6d. net.

John Stuart Mill: A Study of his Philosophy. Crown 8vo, 4s. 6d. net.

DOUGLAS. Chinese Stories. By ROBERT K. DOUGLAS. With numerous Illustrations by Parkinson, Forestier, and others. New and Cheaper Edition. Small demy 8vo, 5s.

DOUGLAS. Iras: A Mystery. By THEO. DOUGLAS, Author of 'A Bride Elect.' Crown 8vo, 3s. 6d.

DU CANE. The Odyssey of Homer, Books I.-XII. Translated into English Verse. By Sir CHARLES DU CANE, K.C.M.G. 8vo, 10s. 6d.

DUDGEON. History of the Edinburgh or Queen's Regiment Light Infantry Militia, now 3rd Battalion The Royal Scots; with an Account of the Origin and Progress of the Militia, and a Brief Sketch of the Old Royal Scots. By Major R. C. DUDGEON, Adjutant 3rd Battalion the Royal Scots. Post 8vo, with Illustrations, 10s. 6d.

DUNSMORE. Manual of the Law of Scotland as to the Relations between Agricultural Tenants and the Landlords, Servants, Merchants, and Bowers. By W. DUNSMORE. 8vo, 7s. 6d.

ELIOT.

George Eliot's Life, Related in Her Letters and Journals. Arranged and Edited by her husband, J. W. CROSS. With Portrait and other Illustrations. Third Edition. 3 vols. post 8vo, 42s.

George Eliot's Life. With Portrait and other Illustrations. New Edition, in one volume. Crown 8vo, 7s. 6d.

Works of George Eliot (Standard Edition). 21 volumes, crown 8vo. In buckram cloth, gilt top, 2s. 6d. per vol.; or in roxburghe binding, 3s. 6d. per vol.

ADAM BEDE. 2 vols.—THE MILL ON THE FLOSS. 2 vols.—FELIX HOLT, THE RADICAL. 2 vols.—ROMOLA. 2 vols.—SCENES OF CLERICAL LIFE. 2 vols.— MIDDLEMARCH. 3 vols.—DANIEL DERONDA. 3 vols.—SILAS MARNER. 1 vol. —JUBAL. 1 vol.—THE SPANISH GIPSY. 1 vol.—ESSAYS. 1 vol.—THEOPHRASTUS SUCH. 1 vol.

Life and Works of George Eliot (Cabinet Edition). 24 volumes, crown 8vo, price £6. Also to be had handsomely bound in half and full calf. The Volumes are sold separately, bound in cloth, price 5s. each.

ELIOT.
Novels by George Eliot. Cheap Edition.
Adam Bede. Illustrated. 3s. 6d., cloth.—The Mill on the Floss. Illustrated. 3s. 6d., cloth.—Scenes of Clerical Life. Illustrated. 3s., cloth.—Silas Marner: the Weaver of Raveloe. Illustrated. 2s. 6d., cloth.—Felix Holt, the Radical. Illustrated. 3s. 6d., cloth.—Romola. With Vignette. 3s. 6d., cloth.

Middlemarch. Crown 8vo, 7s. 6d.
Daniel Deronda. Crown 8vo, 7s. 6d.
Essays. New Edition. Crown 8vo, 5s.
Impressions of Theophrastus Such. New Edition. Crown 8vo, 5s.
The Spanish Gypsy. New Edition. Crown 8vo, 5s.
The Legend of Jubal, and other Poems, Old and New. New Edition. Crown 8vo, 5s.
Wise, Witty, and Tender Sayings, in Prose and Verse. Selected from the Works of GEORGE ELIOT. New Edition. Fcap. 8vo, 3s. 6d.

ENGLISH CHURCH AND THE ROMISH SCHISM. Crown 8vo, 2s. 6d.

ESSAYS ON SOCIAL SUBJECTS. Originally published in the 'Saturday Review.' New Edition. First and Second Series. 2 vols. crown 8vo, 6s. each.

FAITHS OF THE WORLD, The. A Concise History of the Great Religious Systems of the World. By various Authors. Crown 8vo, 5s.

FALKNER. The Lost Stradivarius. By J. MEADE FALKNER. Second Edition. Crown 8vo, 6s.

FERGUSON. Sir Samuel Ferguson in the Ireland of his Day. By LADY FERGUSON, Author of 'The Irish before the Conquest,' 'Life of William Reeves, D.D., Lord Bishop of Down, Connor, and Dromore,' &c., &c. With Two Portraits. 2 vols. post 8vo, 21s.

FERRIER.
Philosophical Works of the late James F. Ferrier, B.A. Oxon., Professor of Moral Philosophy and Political Economy, St Andrews. New Edition. Edited by Sir ALEXANDER GRANT, Bart., D.C.L., and Professor LUSHINGTON. 3 vols. crown 8vo, 34s. 6d.
Institutes of Metaphysic. Third Edition. 10s. 6d.
Lectures on the Early Greek Philosophy. 4th Edition. 10s. 6d.
Philosophical Remains, including the Lectures on Early Greek Philosophy. New Edition. 2 vols. 24s.

FLINT.
Historical Philosophy in France and French Belgium and Switzerland. By ROBERT FLINT, Corresponding Member of the Institute of France, Hon. Member of the Royal Society of Palermo, Professor in the University of Edinburgh, &c. 8vo, 21s.
Agnosticism. Being the Croall Lecture for 1887-88.
[*In the press.*]
Theism. Being the Baird Lecture for 1876. Ninth Edition, Revised. Crown 8vo, 7s. 6d
Anti-Theistic Theories. Being the Baird Lecture for 1877. Fifth Edition. Crown 8vo, 10s. 6d.

FOREIGN CLASSICS FOR ENGLISH READERS. Edited by Mrs OLIPHANT. Price 2s. 6d. *For List of Volumes, see page 2.*

FOSTER. The Fallen City, and other Poems. By WILL FOSTER. Crown 8vo, 6s.

FRANCILLON. Gods and Heroes; or, The Kingdom of Jupiter.
By R. E. FRANCILLON. With 8 Illustrations. Crown 8vo, 5s.

FRANCIS. Among the Untrodden Ways. By M. E. FRANCIS
(Mrs Francis Blundell), Author of 'In a North Country Village,' 'A Daughter of
the Soil,' 'Frieze and Fustian,' &c. Crown 8vo, 3s. 6d.

FRASER.
Philosophy of Theism. Being the Gifford Lectures delivered
before the University of Edinburgh in 1894-95. First Series. By ALEXANDER
CAMPBELL FRASER, D.C.L. Oxford; Emeritus Professor of Logic and Metaphysics in the University of Edinburgh. Post 8vo, 7s. 6d. net.

Philosophy of Theism. Being the Gifford Lectures delivered
before the University of Edinburgh in 1895-96. Second Series. Post 8vo,
7s. 6d. *net.*

FRASER. St Mary's of Old Montrose: A History of the Parish
of Maryton. By the Rev. WILLIAM RUXTON FRASER, M.A., F.S.A. Scot.,
Emeritus Minister of Maryton; Author of 'History of the Parish and Burgh of
Laurencekirk.' Crown 8vo, 3s. 6d.

FULLARTON.
Merlin: A Dramatic Poem. By RALPH MACLEOD FULLAR-
TON. Crown 8vo, 5s.

Tanhäuser. Crown 8vo, 6s.

Lallan Sangs and German Lyrics. Crown 8vo, 5s.

GALT.
Novels by JOHN GALT. With General Introduction and
Prefatory Notes by S. R. CROCKETT. The Text Revised and Edited by D.
STORRAR MELDRUM, Author of 'The Story of Margrédel.' With Photogravure
Illustrations from Drawings by John Wallace. Fcap. 8vo, 3s. net each vol.

ANNALS OF THE PARISH, and THE AYRSHIRE LEGATEES. 2 vols.—SIR ANDREW
WYLIE. 2 vols.—THE ENTAIL; or, The Lairds of Grippy. 2 vols.—THE PRO-
VOST, and THE LAST OF THE LAIRDS. 2 vols.

See also STANDARD NOVELS, *p. 6.*

GENERAL ASSEMBLY OF THE CHURCH OF SCOTLAND.
Scottish Hymnal, With Appendix Incorporated. Published
for use in Churches by Authority of the General Assembly. 1. Large type,
cloth, red edges, 2s. 6d.; French morocco, 4s. 2. Bourgeois type, limp cloth, 1s.;
French morocco, 2s. 3. Nonpareil type, cloth, red edges, 6d.; French morocco,
1s. 4d. 4. Paper covers, 3d. 5. Sunday-School Edition, paper covers, 1d.,
cloth, 2d. No. 1, bound with the Psalms and Paraphrases, French morocco, 8s.
No. 2, bound with the Psalms and Paraphrases, cloth, 2s.; French morocco, 3s.

Prayers for Social and Family Worship. Prepared by a
Special Committee of the General Assembly of the Church of Scotland. Entirely
New Edition, Revised and Enlarged. Fcap. 8vo, red edges, 2s.

Prayers for Family Worship. A Selection of Four Weeks'
Prayers. New Edition. Authorised by the General Assembly of the Church of
Scotland. Fcap. 8vo, red edges, 1s. 6d.

One Hundred Prayers. Prepared by the Committee on Aids
to Devotion. 16mo, cloth limp, 6d.

Morning and Evening Prayers for Affixing to Bibles. Prepared
by the Committee on Aids to Devotion. 1d. for 6, or 1s. per 100.

GERARD.
Reata: What's in a Name. By E. D. GERARD. Cheap
Edition. Crown 8vo, 3s. 6d.

Beggar my Neighbour. Cheap Edition. Crown 8vo, 3s. 6d.

The Waters of Hercules. Cheap Edition. Crown 8vo, 3s. 6d.

A Sensitive Plant. Crown 8vo, 3s. 6d.

GERARD.

A Foreigner. An Anglo-German Study. By E. GERARD.
Crown 8vo, 6s.

The Land beyond the Forest. Facts, Figures, and Fancies from Transylvania. With Maps and Illustrations. 2 vols. post 8vo, 25s.

Bis: Some Tales Retold. Crown 8vo, 6s.

A Secret Mission. 2 vols. crown 8vo, 17s.

GERARD.

The Wrong Man. By DOROTHEA GERARD. Second Edition. Crown 8vo, 6s.

Lady Baby. Cheap Edition. Crown 8vo, 3s. 6d.

Recha. Second Edition. Crown 8vo, 6s.

The Rich Miss Riddell. Second Edition. Crown 8vo, 6s.

GERARD. Stonyhurst Latin Grammar. By Rev. JOHN GERAED. Second Edition. Fcap. 8vo, 3s.

GILL.

Free Trade: an Inquiry into the Nature of its Operation. By RICHARD GILL. Crown 8vo, 7s. 6d.

Free Trade under Protection. Crown 8vo, 7s. 6d.

GORDON CUMMING.

At Home in Fiji. By C. F. GORDON CUMMING. Fourth Edition, post 8vo. With Illustrations and Map. 7s. 6d.

A Lady's Cruise in a French Man-of-War. New and Cheaper Edition. 8vo. With Illustrations and Map. 12s. 6d.

Fire-Fountains. The Kingdom of Hawaii: Its Volcanoes, and the History of its Missions. With Map and Illustrations. 2 vols. 8vo, 25s.

Wanderings in China. New and Cheaper Edition. 8vo, with Illustrations, 10s.

Granite Crags: The Yō-semité Region of California. Illustrated with 8 Engravings. New and Cheaper Edition. 8vo, 8s. 6d.

GRAHAM. Manual of the Elections (Scot.) (Corrupt and Illegal Practices) Act, 1890. With Analysis, Relative Act of Sederunt, Appendix containing the Corrupt Practices Acts of 1883 and 1885, and Copious Index. By J EDWARD GRAHAM, Advocate. 8vo, 4s. 6d.

GRAND.

A Domestic Experiment. By SARAH GRAND, Author of 'The Heavenly Twins,' 'Ideala: A Study from Life.' Crown 8vo, 6s.

Singularly Deluded. Crown 8vo, 6s.

GRANT. Bush-Life in Queensland. By A. C. GRANT. New Edition. Crown 8vo, 6s.

GRANT. Life of Sir Hope Grant. With Selections from his Correspondence. Edited by HENRY KNOLLYS, Colonel (H.P.) Royal Artillery, his former A.D.C., Editor of 'Incidents in the Sepoy War;' Author of 'Sketches of Life in Japan,' &c. With Portraits of Sir Hope Grant and other Illustrations. Maps and Plans. 2 vols. demy 8vo, 21s.

GRIER.

In Furthest Ind. The Narrative of Mr EDWARD CARLYON of Ellswether, in the County of Northampton, and late of the Honourable East India Company's Service, Gentleman. Wrote by his own hand in the year of grace 1697. Edited, with a few Explanatory Notes, by SYDNEY C. GRIER. Post 8vo, 6s.

His Excellency's English Governess. Crown 8vo, 6s.

An Uncrowned King: A Romance of High Politics. Crown 8vo, 6s.

GUTHRIE-SMITH. Crispus: A Drama. By H. GUTHRIE-SMITH. Fcap. 4to, 5s.

HAGGARD. Under Crescent and Star. By Lieut.-Col. ANDRI
HAGGARD, D.S.O., Author of 'Dodo and I,' 'Tempest Torn,' &c.   Wit
Portrait. Second Edition. Crown 8vo, 6s.

HALDANE. Subtropical Cultivations and Climates. A Han
Book for Planters, Colonists, and Settlers. By R. C. HALDANE. Post 8vo, 9:

HAMERTON.
Wenderholme : A Story of Lancashire and Yorkshire Li
By P. G. HAMERTON, Author of 'A Painter's Camp.' New Edition.   Crc
8vo, 3s. 6d.

Marmorne. New Edition. Crown 8vo, 3s. 6d.

HAMILTON.
Lectures on Metaphysics.   By Sir WILLIAM HAMILTO
Bart., Professor of Logic and Metaphysics in the University of Edinbur
Edited by the Rev. H. L. MANSEL, B.D., LL.D., Dean of St Paul's ; and Jc
VEITCH, M.A., LL.D., Professor of Logic and Rhetoric, Glasgow. Seve
Edition. 2 vols. 8vo, 24s.

Lectures on Logic. Edited by the SAME.   Third Editic
Revised. 2 vols., 24s.

Discussions on Philosophy and Literature, Education a
University Reform. Third Edition. 8vo, 21s.

Memoir of Sir William Hamilton, Bart., Professor of Loy
and Metaphysics in the University of Edinburgh. By Professor VEITCH, of
University of Glasgow. 8vo, with Portrait, 18s.

Sir William Hamilton : The Man and his Philosophy.   T
Lectures delivered before the Edinburgh Philosophical Institution, January
February 1883. By Professor VEITCH. Crown 8vo, 2s.

HAMLEY.
The Operations of War Explained and Illustrated.
General Sir EDWARD BRUCE HAMLEY, K.C.B., K.C.M.G. Fifth Edition, Rev.
throughout. 4to, with numerous Illustrations, 30s.

National Defence ; Articles and Speeches. Post 8vo, 6s.

Shakespeare's Funeral, and other Papers. Post 8vo, 7s. 6d.

Thomas Carlyle : An Essay. Second Edition. Crown 8
2s. 6d.

On Outposts. Second Edition. 8vo, 2s.

Wellington's Career ; A Military and Political Summa
Crown 8vo, 2s.

Lady Lee's Widowhood. New Edition. Crown 8vo, 3s.
Cheaper Edition, 2s. 6d.

Our Poor Relations. A Philozoic Essay. With Illustratio
chiefly by Ernest Griset. Crown 8vo, cloth gilt, 3s. 6d.

The Life of General Sir Edward Bruce Hamley, K.C.
K.C.M.G. By ALEXANDER INNES SHAND. With two Photogravure Portraits
other Illustrations.   Cheaper Edition. With a Statement by Mr EDW
HAMLEY. 2 vols. dcmy 8vo, 10s. 6d.

HARE. Down the Village Street : Scenes in a West Count
Hamlet. By CHRISTOPHER HARE. Second Edition. Crown 8vo, 6s.

HARRADEN. In Varying Moods : Short Stories.   By BEATR
HARRADEN, Author of 'Ships that Pass in the Night.' Twelfth Edition. Cr
8vo, 3s. 6d.

HARRIS.
From Batum to Baghdad, *viâ* Tiflis, Tabriz, and Persi
Kurdistan. By WALTER B. HARRIS, F.R.G.S., Author of 'The Land of
African Sultan ; Travels in Morocco,' &c. With numerous Illustrations at
Maps. Demy 8vo, 12s.

HARRIS.
Tafilet. The Narrative of a Journey of Exploration to the
Atlas Mountains and the Oases of the North-West Sahara. With Illustrations
by Maurice Romberg from Sketches and Photographs by the Author, and Two
Maps. Demy 8vo, 12s.

A Journey through the Yemen, and some General Remarks
upon that Country. With 3 Maps and numerous Illustrations by Forestier and
Wallace from Sketches and Photographs taken by the Author. Demy 8vo, 16s.

Danovitch, and other Stories. Crown 8vo, 6s.

HAWKER. The Prose Works of Rev. R. S. HAWKER, Vicar of
Morwenstow. Including ' Footprints of Former Men in Far Cornwall.' Re-edited,
with Sketches never before published. With a Frontispiece. Crown 8vo, 3s. 6d.

HAY. The Works of the Right Rev. Dr George Hay, Bishop of
Edinburgh. Edited under the Supervision of the Right Rev. Bishop STRAIN.
With Memoir and Portrait of the Author. 5 vols. crown 8vo, bound in extra
cloth, £1, 1s. The following Volumes may be had separately—viz.:
 The Devout Christian Instructed in the Law of Christ from the Written
 Word. 2 vols., 8s.—The Pious Christian Instructed in the Nature and Practice
 of the Principal Exercises of Piety. 1 vol., 3s.

HEATLEY.
The Horse-Owner's Safeguard. A Handy Medical Guide for
every Man who owns a Horse. By G. S. HEATLEY, M.R.C.V.S. Crown 8vo, 5s.

The Stock-Owner's Guide. A Handy Medical Treatise for
every Man who owns an Ox or a Cow. Crown 8vo, 4s. 6d.

HEDDERWICK. Lays of Middle Age ; and other Poems. By
JAMES HEDDERWICK, LL.D., Author of 'Backward Glances.' Price 3s. 6d.

HEMANS.
The Poetical Works of Mrs Hemans. Copyright Editions.
Royal 8vo, 5s. The Same with Engravings, cloth, gilt edges, 7s. 6d.

Select Poems of Mrs Hemans. Fcap., cloth, gilt edges, 3s.

HERKLESS. Cardinal Beaton: Priest and Politician. By
JOHN HERKLESS, Professor of Church History, St Andrews. With a Portrait.
Post 8vo, 7s. 6d.

HEWISON. The Isle of Bute in the Olden Time. With Illus-
trations, Maps, and Plans. By JAMES KING HEWISON, M.A., F.S.A. (Scot.)
Minister of Rothesay. Vol. I., Celtic Saints and Heroes. Crown 4to, 15s. net.
Vol. II., The Royal Stewards and the Brandanes. Crown 4to, 15s. net.

HIBBEN. Inductive Logic. By JOHN GRIER HIBBEN, Ph.D.,
Assistant Professor of Logic in Princeton University, U.S.A. Crown 8vo,
3s. 6d. net.

HOME PRAYERS. By Ministers of the Church of Scotland
and Members of the Church Service Society. Second Edition. Fcap. 8vo, 3s.

HORNBY. Admiral of the Fleet Sir Geoffrey Phipps Hornby,
G.C.B. A Biography. By Mrs FRED. EGERTON. With Three Portraits. Demy
8vo, 16s.

HUTCHINSON. Hints on the Game of Golf. By HORACE G.
HUTCHINSON. Ninth Edition, Enlarged. Fcap. 8vo. cloth, 1s.

HYSLOP. The Elements of Ethics. By JAMES H. HYSLOP,
Ph.D., Instructor in Ethics, Columbia College, New York, Author of 'The
Elements of Logic.' Post 8vo, 7s. 6d. net.

IDDESLEIGH.
Lectures and Essays. By the late EARL of IDDESLEIGH,
G.C.B., D.C.L., &c. 8vo, 16s.

Life, Letters, and Diaries of Sir Stafford Northcote, First
Earl of Iddesleigh. By ANDREW LANG. With Three Portraits and a View of
Pynes. Third Edition. 2 vols. post 8vo, 31s. 6d.
 POPULAR EDITION. With Portrait and View of Pynes. Post 8vo, 7s. 6d.

IGNOTUS. The Supremacy and Sufficiency of Jesus Christ, as set forth in the Epistle to the Hebrews. By IGNOTUS. Crown 8vo, 3s. 6d.

INDEX GEOGRAPHICUS: Being a List, alphabetically arranged, of the Principal Places on the Globe, with the Countries and Subdivisions of the Countries in which they are situated, and their Latitudes and Longitudes. Imperial 8vo, pp. 676, 21s.

JEAN JAMBON. Our Trip to Blunderland; or, Grand Excursion to Blundertown and Back. By JEAN JAMBON. With Sixty Illustrations designed by CHARLES DOYLE, engraved by DALZIEL. Fourth Thousand. Cloth, gilt edges, 6s. 6d. Cheap Edition, cloth, 3s. 6d. Boards, 2s. 6d.

JEBB. A Strange Career. The Life and Adventures of JOHN GLADWYN JEBB. By his Widow. With an Introduction by H. RIDER HAGGARD, and an Electrogravure Portrait of Mr Jebb. Third Edition. Demy 8vo, 10s. 6d. CHEAP EDITION. With Illustrations by John Wallace. Crown 8vo, 3s. 6d.
Some Unconventional People. By Mrs GLADWYN JEBB, Author of 'Life and Adventures of J. G. Jebb.' With Illustrations. Crown 8vo, 3s. 6d.

JENNINGS. Mr Gladstone: A Study. By LOUIS J. JENNINGS, M.P., Author of 'Republican Government in the United States,' 'The Croker Memoirs,' &c. Popular Edition. Crown 8vo, 1s.

JERNINGHAM.
Reminiscences of an Attaché. By HUBERT E. H. JERNINGHAM. Second Edition. Crown 8vo, 5s.
Diane de Breteuille. A Love Story. Crown 8vo, 2s. 6d.

JOHNSTON.
The Chemistry of Common Life. By Professor J. F. W. JOHNSTON. New Edition, Revised. By ARTHUR HERBERT CHURCH, M.A. Oxon.; Author of 'Food: its Sources, Constituents, and Uses,' &c. With Maps and 102 Engravings. Crown 8vo, 7s. 6d.
Elements of Agricultural Chemistry. An entirely New Edition from the Edition by Sir CHARLES A. CAMERON, M.D., F.R.C.S.I., &c. Revised and brought down to date by C. M. AIKMAN, M.A., B.Sc., F.R.S.E., Professor of Chemistry, Glasgow Veterinary College. 17th Edition. Crown 8vo, 6s. 6d.
Catechism of Agricultural Chemistry. An entirely New Edition from the Edition by Sir CHARLES A. CAMERON. Revised and Enlarged by C. M. AIKMAN, M.A., &c. 95th Thousand. With numerous Illustrations. Crown 8vo, 1s.

JOHNSTON. Agricultural Holdings (Scotland) Acts, 1883 and 1889; and the Ground Game Act, 1880. With Notes, and Summary of Procedure, &c. By CHRISTOPHER N. JOHNSTON, M.A., Advocate. Demy 8vo, 5s.

JOKAI. Timar's Two Worlds. By MAURUS JOKAI. Authorised Translation by Mrs HEGAN KENNARD. Cheap Edition. Crown 8vo, 6s.

KEBBEL. The Old and the New: English Country Life. By T. E. KEBBEL, M.A., Author of 'The Agricultural Labourers,' 'Essays in History and Politics,' 'Life of Lord Beaconsfield.' Crown 8vo, 5s.

KERR. St Andrews in 1645-46. By D. R. KERR. Crown 8vo, 2s. 6d.

KINGLAKE.
History of the Invasion of the Crimea. By A. W. KINGLAKE. New Edition, Abridged by Lt.-Colonel Sir GEORGE S. CLARKE, K.C.M.G., R.E. With Maps and Plans. [*In preparation.*
History of the Invasion of the Crimea. By A. W. KINGLAKE. Cabinet Edition, Revised. With an Index to the Complete Work. Illustrated with Maps and Plans. Complete in 9 vols., crown 8vo, at 6s. each.

KINGLAKE.
History of the Invasion of the Crimea. Demy 8vo. Vol. VI.
Winter Troubles. With a Map, 16s. Vols. VII. and VIII. From the Morrow of
Inkerman to the Death of Lord Raglan. With an Index to the Whole Work.
With Maps and Plans. 28s.
Eothen. A New Edition, uniform with the Cabinet Edition
of the 'History of the Invasion of the Crimea.' 6s.
CHEAPER EDITION. With Portrait and Biographical Sketch of the Author.
Crown 8vo, 3s. 6d.
KIRBY. In Haunts of Wild Game: A Hunter-Naturalist's
Wanderings from Kahlamba to Libombo. By FREDERICK VAUGHAN KIRBY,
F.Z.S. (Maqaqamba). With numerous Illustrations by Charles Whymper, and a
Map. Large demy 8vo, 25s.
KLEIN. Among the Gods. Scenes of India, with Legends by
the Way. By AUGUSTA KLEIN. With 22 Full-page Illustrations. Demy 8vo, 15s.
KNEIPP. My Water-Cure. As Tested through more than
Thirty Years, and Described for the Healing of Diseases and the Preservation of
Health. By SEBASTIAN KNEIPP, Parish Priest of Wörishofen (Bavaria). With a
Portrait and other Illustrations. Authorised English Translation from the
Thirtieth German Edition, by A. de F. Cheap Edition. With an Appendix, con-
taining the Latest Developments of Pfarrer Kneipp's System, and a Preface by
E. Gerard. Crown 8vo, 3s. 6d.
KNOLLYS. The Elements of Field-Artillery. Designed for
the Use of Infantry and Cavalry Officers. By HENRY KNOLLYS, Colonel Royal
Artillery; Author of 'From Sedan to Saarbrück,' Editor of 'Incidents in the
Sepoy War,' &c. With Engravings. Crown 8vo, 7s. 6d.
LANG. Life, Letters, and Diaries of Sir Stafford Northcote,
First Earl of Iddesleigh. By ANDREW LANG. With Three Portraits and a View
of Pynes. Third Edition. 2 vols. post 8vo, 31s. 6d.
POPULAR EDITION. With Portrait and View of Pynes. Post 8vo, 7s. 6d.
LEES. A Handbook of the Sheriff and Justice of Peace Small
Debt Courts. With Notes, References, and Forms. By J. M. LEES, Advocate,
Sheriff of Stirling, Dumbarton, and Clackmannan. 8vo, 7s. 6d.
LINDSAY.
Recent Advances in Theistic Philosophy of Religion. By Rev.
JAMES LINDSAY, M.A., B.D., B.Sc., F.R.S.E., F.G.S., Minister of the Parish of
St Andrew's, Kilmarnock. Demy 8vo, 9s.
The Progressiveness of Modern Christian Thought. Crown
8vo, 6s.
Essays, Literary and Philosophical. Crown 8vo, 3s. 6d.
LOCKHART.
Doubles and Quits. By LAURENCE W. M. LOCKHART. New
Edition. Crown 8vo, 3s. 6d.
Fair to See. New Edition. Crown 8vo, 3s. 6d.
Mine is Thine. New Edition. Crown 8vo, 3s. 6d.
LOCKHART.
The Church of Scotland in the Thirteenth Century. The
Life and Times of David de Bernham of St Andrews (Bishop), A.D. 1239 to 1253.
With List of Churches dedicated by him, and Dates. By WILLIAM LOCKHART,
A.M., D.D., F.S.A. Scot., Minister of Colinton Parish. 2d Edition. 8vo, 6s.
Dies Tristes: Sermons for Seasons of Sorrow. Crown 8vo, 6s.
LORIMER.
The Institutes of Law: A Treatise of the Principles of Juris-
prudence as determined by Nature. By the late JAMES LORIMER, Professor of
Public Law and of the Law of Nature and Nations in the University of Edin-
burgh. New Edition, Revised and much Enlarged. 8vo, 18s.
The Institutes of the Law of Nations. A Treatise of the
Jural Relation of Separate Political Communities. In 2 vols. 8vo. Volume I.,
price 16s. Volume II., price 20s.

LUGARD. The Rise of our East African Empire : Early Efforts
in Uganda and Nyassaland. By F. D. LUGARD, Captain Norfolk Regiment.
With 130 Illustrations from Drawings and Photographs under the personal
superintendence of the Author, and 14 specially prepared Maps. In 2 vols, large
demy 8vo, 42s.

M'CHESNEY.
Miriam Cromwell, Royalist : A Romance of the Great Rebel-
lion. By DORA GREENWELL M'CHESNEY. Crown 8vo, 6s.
Kathleen Clare : Her Book, 1637-41. Edited by DORA GREEN-
WELL M'CHESNEY. With Frontispiece, and five full-page Illustrations by James
A. Shearman. Crown 8vo, 6s.

M'COMBIE. Cattle and Cattle-Breeders. By WILLIAM M'COMBIE,
Tillyfour. New Edition, Enlarged, with Memoir of the Author by JAMES
MACDONALD, F.R.S.E., Secretary Highland and Agricultural Society of Scotland.
Crown 8vo, 3s. 6d.

M'CRIE.
Works of the Rev. Thomas M'Crie, D.D. Uniform Edition.
4 vols. crown 8vo, 24s.
Life of John Knox. Crown 8vo, 6s. Another Edition, 3s. 6d.
Life of Andrew Melville. Crown 8vo, 6s.
History of the Progress and Suppression of the Reformation
in Italy in the Sixteenth Century. Crown 8vo, 4s.
History of the Progress and Suppression of the Reformation
in Spain in the Sixteenth Century. Crown 8vo, 3s. 6d.

M'CRIE. The Public Worship of Presbyterian Scotland. Histori-
cally treated. With copious Notes, Appendices, and Index. The Fourteenth
Series of the Cunningham Lectures. By the REV. CHARLES G. M'CRIE, D.D.
Demy 8vo, 10s. 6d.

MACDONALD. A Manual of the Criminal Law (Scotland) Procedure Act, 1887. By NORMAN DORAN MACDONALD. Revised by the LORD
JUSTICE-CLERK. 8vo, 10s. 6d.

MACDONALD AND SINCLAIR. History of Polled Aberdeen
and Angus Cattle. Giving an Account of the Origin, Improvement, and Characteristics of the Breed. By JAMES MACDONALD and JAMES SINCLAIR. Illustrated
with numerous Animal Portraits. Post 8vo, 12s. 6d.

MACDOUGALL AND DODDS. A Manual of the Local Govern-
ment (Scotland) Act, 1894. With Introduction, Explanatory Notes, and Copious
Index. By J. PATTEN MACDOUGALL, Legal Secretary to the Lord Advocate, and
J. M. DODDS. Tenth Thousand, Revised. Crown 8vo, 2s. 6d. net.

MACINTYRE. Hindu - Koh : Wanderings and Wild Sports on
and beyond the Himalayas. By Major-General DONALD MACINTYRE, V.C., late
Prince of Wales' Own Goorkhas, F.R.G.S. *Dedicated to H.R.H. The Prince of
Wales.* New and Cheaper Edition, Revised, with numerous Illustrations. Post
8vo, 3s. 6d.

MACKAY.
A Manual of Modern Geography ; Mathematical, Physical,
and Political. By the Rev. ALEXANDER MACKAY, LL.D., F.R.G.S. 11th
Thousand, Revised to the present time. Crown 8vo, pp. 688, 7s. 6d.
Elements of Modern Geography. 55th Thousand, Revised to
the present time. Crown 8vo, pp. 300, 3s.
The Intermediate Geography. Intended as an Intermediate
Book between the Author's 'Outlines of Geography' and 'Elements of Geo-
graphy.' Eighteenth Edition, Revised. Fcap. 8vo, pp. 238, 2s.
Outlines of Modern Geography. 191st Thousand, Revised to
the present time. Fcap. 8vo, pp. 128, 1s.
Elements of Physiography. New Edition. Rewritten and
Enlarged. With numerous Illustrations. Crown 8vo. [*In the press.*

MACKENZIE. Studies in Roman Law. With Comparative
Views of the Laws of France, England, and Scotland. By Lord MACKENZIE,
one of the Judges of the Court of Session in Scotland. Sixth Edition, Edited
by JOHN KIRKPATRICK, M.A., LL.B., Advocate, Professor of History in the
University of Edinburgh. 8vo, 12s.

MACPHERSON. Glimpses of Church and Social Life in the
Highlands in Olden Times. By ALEXANDER MACPHERSON, F.S.A. Scot. With
6 Photogravure Portraits and other full-page Illustrations. Small 4to, 25s.

M'PHERSON. Golf and Golfers. Past and Present. By J.
GORDON M'PHERSON, Ph.D., F.R.S.E. With an Introduction by the Right Hon.
A. J. BALFOUR, and a Portrait of the Author. Fcap. 8vo, 1s. 6d.

MACRAE. A Handbook of Deer-Stalking. By ALEXANDER
MACRAE, late Forester to Lord Henry Bentinck. With Introduction by Horatio
Ross, Esq. Fcap. 8vo, with 2 Photographs from Life. 3s. 6d.

MAIN. Three Hundred English Sonnets. Chosen and Edited
by DAVID M. MAIN. New Edition. Fcap. 8vo, 3s. 6d.

MAIR. A Digest of Laws and Decisions, Ecclesiastical and
Civil, relating to the Constitution, Practice, and Affairs of the Church of Scot-
land. With Notes and Forms of Procedure. By the Rev. WILLIAM MAIR, D.D.,
Minister of the Parish of Earlston. New Edition, Revised. Crown 8vo, 9s. net.

MARCHMONT AND THE HUMES OF POLWARTH. By
One of their Descendants. With numerous Portraits and other Illustrations.
Crown 4to, 21s. net.

MARSHMAN. History of India. From the Earliest Period to
the present time. By JOHN CLARK MARSHMAN, C.S.I. Third and Cheaper
Edition. Post 8vo, with Map, 6s.

MARTIN.
The Æneid of Virgil. Books I.-VI. Translated by Sir THEO-
DORE MARTIN, K.C.B. Post 8vo, 6s.
Goethe's Faust. Part I. Translated into English Verse.
Second Edition, crown 8vo, 6s. Ninth Edition, fcap. 8vo, 3s. 6d.
Goethe's Faust. Part II. Translated into English Verse.
Second Edition, Revised. Fcap. 8vo, 6s.
The Works of Horace. Translated into English Verse, with
Life and Notes. 2 vols. New Edition. Crown 8vo, 21s.
Poems and Ballads of Heinrich Heine. Done into English
Verse. Third Edition. Small crown 8vo, 5s.
The Song of the Bell, and other Translations from Schiller,
Goethe, Uhland, and Others. Crown 8vo, 7s. 6d.
Madonna Pia: A Tragedy; and Three Other Dramas. Crown
8vo, 7s. 6d.
Catullus. With Life and Notes. Second Edition, Revised
and Corrected. Post 8vo, 7s. 6d.
The 'Vita Nuova' of Dante. Translated, with an Introduction
and Notes. Third Edition. Small crown 8vo, 5s.
Aladdin: A Dramatic Poem. By ADAM OEHLENSCHLAEGER.
Fcap. 8vo, 5s.
Correggio: A Tragedy. By OEHLENSCHLAEGER. With Notes.
Fcap. 8vo, 3s.

MARTIN. On some of Shakespeare's Female Characters. By
HELENA FAUCIT, Lady MARTIN. Dedicated by permission to Her Most Gracious
Majesty the Queen. Fifth Edition. With a Portrait by Lehmann. Demy
8vo, 7s. 6d.

MARWICK. Observations on the Law and Practice in regard
to Municipal Elections and the Conduct of the Business of Town Councils and
Commissioners of Police in Scotland. By Sir JAMES D. MARWICK, LL.D.,
Town-Clerk of Glasgow. Royal 8vo, 30s.

MATHESON.
Can the Old Faith Live with the New ? or, The Problem of Evolution and Revelation. By the Rev. GEORGE MATHESON, D.D. Third Edition. Crown 8vo, 7s. 6d.
The Psalmist and the Scientist ; or, Modern Value of the Reli- gious Sentiment. Third Edition. Crown 8vo, 5s.
Spiritual Development of St Paul. Third Edition. Cr. 8vo, 5s.
The Distinctive Messages of the Old Religions. Second Edition. Crown 8vo, 5s.
Sacred Songs. New and Cheaper Edition. Crown 8vo, 2s. 6d.
MAURICE. The Balance of Military Power in Europe. An Examination of the War Resources of Great Britain and the Continental States. By Colonel MAURICE, R.A., Professor of Military Art and History at the Royal Staff College. Crown 8vo, with a Map, 6s.
MAXWELL.
A Duke of Britain. A Romance of the Fourth Century. By Sir HERBERT MAXWELL, Bart., M.P., F.S.A., &c., Author of 'Passages in the Life of Sir Lucian Elphin.' Fourth Edition. Crown 8vo, 6s.
Life and Times of the Rt. Hon. William Henry Smith, M.P. With Portraits and numerous Illustrations by Herbert Railton, G. L. Seymour, and Others. 2 vols. demy 8vo, 25s.
POPULAR EDITION. With a Portrait and other Illustrations. Crown 8vo, 3s. 6d.
Scottish Land-Names : Their Origin and Meaning. Being the Rhind Lectures in Archæology for 1893. Post 8vo, 6s.
Meridiana : Noontide Essays. Post 8vo, 7s. 6d.
Post Meridiana : Afternoon Essays. Post 8vo, 6s.
Dumfries and Galloway. Being one of the Volumes of the County Histories of Scotland. With Two Maps. Demy 8vo, 7s. 6d. *net.*
MELDRUM.
The Story of Margrédel : Being a Fireside History of a Fife- shire Family. By D. STORRAR MELDRUM. Cheap Edition. Crown 8vo, 3s. 6d.
Grey Mantle and Gold Fringe. Crown 8vo, 6s.
MERZ. A History of European Thought in the Nineteenth Cen- tury. By JOHN THEODORE MERZ. Vol. I., post 8vo. [*Immediately.*
MICHEL. A Critical Inquiry into the Scottish Language. With the view of Illustrating the Rise and Progress of Civilisation in Scotland. By FRANCISQUE-MICHEL, F.S.A. Lond. and Scot., Correspondant de l'Institut de France, &c. 4to, printed on hand-made paper, and bound in roxburghe, 66s.
MICHIE.
The Larch : Being a Practical Treatise on its Culture and General Management. By CHRISTOPHER Y. MICHIE, Forester, Cullen House. Crown 8vo, with Illustrations. New and Cheaper Edition, Enlarged, 5s.
The Practice of Forestry. Crown 8vo, with Illustrations. 6s.
MIDDLETON. The Story of Alastair Bhan Comyn ; or, The Tragedy of Dunphail. A Tale of Tradition and Romance. By the Lady MIDDLETON. Square 8vo, 10s. Cheaper Edition, 5s.
MILLER. The Dream of Mr H——, the Herbalist. By HUGH MILLER, F.R.S.E., late H.M. Geological Survey, Author of 'Landscape Geology.' With a Photogravure Frontispiece. Crown 8vo, 2s. 6d.
MINTO.
A Manual of English Prose Literature, Biographical and Critical : designed mainly to show Characteristics of Style. By W. MINTO, M.A., Hon. LL.D. of St Andrews ; Professor of Logic in the University of Aberdeen. Third Edition, Revised. Crown 8vo, 7s. 6d.
Characteristics of English Poets, from Chaucer to Shirley. New Edition, Revised. Crown 8vo, 7s. 6d.
Plain Principles of Prose Composition. Crown 8vo, 1s. 6d.

MINTO.
The Literature of the Georgian Era. Edited, with a Biographical Introduction, by Professor KNIGHT, St Andrews. Post 8vo, 6s.
MOIR. Life of Mansie Wauch, Tailor in Dalkeith. By D. M. MOIR. With CRUIKSHANK'S Illustrations. Cheaper Edition. Crown 8vo, 2s. 6d. Another Edition, without Illustrations, fcap. 8vo, 1s. 6d.
MOLE. For the Sake of a Slandered Woman. By MARION MOLE. Fcap. 8vo, 2s. 6d. net.
MOMERIE.
Defects of Modern Christianity, and other Sermons. By ALFRED WILLIAMS MOMERIE, M.A., D.Sc., LL.D. Fifth Edition. Crown 8vo, 5s.
The Basis of Religion. Being an Examination of Natural Religion. Third Edition. Crown 8vo, 2s. 6d.
The Origin of Evil, and other Sermons. Eighth Edition, Enlarged. Crown 8vo, 5s.
Personality. The Beginning and End of Metaphysics, and a Necessary Assumption in all Positive Philosophy. Fifth Edition, Revised. Crown 8vo, 3s.
Agnosticism. Fourth Edition, Revised. Crown 8vo, 5s.
Preaching and Hearing ; and other Sermons. Fourth Edition, Enlarged. Crown 8vo, 5s.
Belief in God. Third Edition. Crown 8vo, 3s.
Inspiration ; and other Sermons. Second Edition, Enlarged. Crown 8vo, 5s.
Church and Creed. Third Edition. Crown 8vo, 4s. 6d.
The Future of Religion, and other Essays. Second Edition. Crown 8vo, 3s. 6d.
MONCREIFF.
The Provost-Marshal. A Romance of the Middle Shires. By the Hon. FREDERICK MONCREIFF. Crown 8vo, 6s.
The X Jewel. A Romance of the Days of James VI. Crown 8vo, 6s.
MONTAGUE. Military Topography. Illustrated by Practical Examples of a Practical Subject. By Major-General W. E. MONTAGUE, C.B., P.S.C., late Garrison Instructor Intelligence Department, Author of 'Campaigning in South Africa.' With Forty-one Diagrams. Crown 8vo, 5s.
MONTALEMBERT. Memoir of Count de Montalembert. A Chapter of Recent French History. By Mrs OLIPHANT, Author of the 'Life of Edward Irving,' &c. 2 vols. crown 8vo, £1, 4s.
MORISON.
Doorside Ditties. By JEANIE MORISON. With a Frontispiece. Crown 8vo, 3s. 6d.
Æolus. A Romance in Lyrics. Crown 8vo, 3s.
There as Here. Crown 8vo, 3s.
₊ *A limited impression on hand-made paper, bound in vellum, 7s. 6d.*
Selections from Poems. Crown 8vo, 4s. 6d.
Sordello. An Outline Analysis of Mr Browning's Poem. Crown 8vo, 3s.
Of "Fifine at the Fair," "Christmas Eve and Easter Day,' and other of Mr Browning's Poems. Crown 8vo, 3s.
The Purpose of the Ages. Crown 8vo, 9s.
Gordon : An Our-day Idyll. Crown 8vo, 3s.
Saint Isadora, and other Poems. Crown 8vo, 1s. 6d.
Snatches of Song. Paper, 1s. 6d. ; cloth, 3s.
Pontius Pilate. Paper, 1s. 6d. ; cloth, 3s.

MORISON.
Mill o' Forres. Crown 8vo, 1s.
Ane Booke of Ballades. Fcap. 4to, 1s.

MOZLEY. Essays from 'Blackwood.' By the late ANNE
MOZLEY, Author of 'Essays on Social Subjects'; Editor of 'The Letters and
Correspondence of Cardinal Newman,' 'Letters of the Rev. J. B. Mozley,' &c.
With a Memoir by her Sister, FANNY MOZLEY. Post 8vo, 7s. 6d.

MUNRO. The Lost Pibroch, and other Sheiling Stories. By
NEIL MUNRO. Crown 8vo, 6s.

MUNRO. Rambles and Studies in Bosnia - Herzegovina and
Dalmatia. With an Account of the Proceedings of the Congress of Archæolo-
gists and Anthropologists held at Sarajevo in 1894. By ROBERT MUNRO, M.A.,
M.D., F.R.S.E., Author of 'The Lake-Dwellings of Europe,' &c. With numerous
Illustrations. Demy 8vo, 12s. 6d. net.

MUNRO. On Valuation of Property. By WILLIAM MUNRO,
M.A., Her Majesty's Assessor of Railways and Canals for Scotland. Second
Edition, Revised and Enlarged. 8vo, 3s. 6d.

MURDOCH. Manual of the Law of Insolvency and Bankruptcy:
Comprehending a Summary of the Law of Insolvency, Notour Bankruptcy,
Composition - Contracts, Trust - Deeds, Cessios, and Sequestrations; and the
Winding-up of Joint-Stock Companies in Scotland; with Annotations on the
various Insolvency and Bankruptcy Statutes; and with Forms of Procedure
applicable to these Subjects. By JAMES MURDOCH, Member of the Faculty of
Procurators in Glasgow. Fifth Edition, Revised and Enlarged. 8vo, 12s. net.

MY TRIVIAL LIFE AND MISFORTUNE: A Gossip with
no Plot in Particular. By A PLAIN WOMAN. Cheap Edition. Crown 8vo, 3s. 6d.
By the SAME AUTHOR.

POOR NELLIE. Cheap Edition. Crown 8vo, 3s. 6d.

MY WEATHER - WISE COMPANION. Presented by B. T.
Fcap. 8vo, 1s. net.

NAPIER. The Construction of the Wonderful Canon of Loga-
rithms. By JOHN NAPIER of Merchiston. Translated, with Notes, and a
Catalogue of Napier's Works, by WILLIAM RAE MACDONALD. Small 4to, 15s.
A few large-paper copies on Whatman paper, 30s.

NEAVES. Songs and Verses, Social and Scientific. By An Old
Contributor to 'Maga.' By the Hon. Lord NEAVES. Fifth Edition. Fcap.
8vo, 4s.

NICHOLSON.
A Manual of Zoology, for the Use of Students. With a
General Introduction on the Principles of Zoology. By HENRY ALLEYNE
NICHOLSON, M.D., D.Sc., F.L.S., F.G.S., Regius Professor of Natural History in
the University of Aberdeen. Seventh Edition, Rewritten and Enlarged. Post
8vo, pp. 956, with 555 Engravings on Wood, 18s.

Text-Book of Zoology, for Junior Students. Fifth Edition,
Rewritten and Enlarged. Crown 8vo, with 358 Engravings on Wood, 10s. 6d.

Introductory Text-Book of Zoology, for the Use of Junior
Classes. Sixth Edition, Revised and Enlarged, with 166 Engravings, 3s.

Outlines of Natural History, for Beginners: being Descriptions of a Progressive Series of Zoological Types. Third Edition, with
Engravings, 1s. 6d.

A Manual of Palæontology, for the Use of Students. With a
General Introduction on the Principles of Palæontology. By Professor H.
ALLEYNE NICHOLSON and RICHARD LYDEKKER, B.A. Third Edition, entirely
Rewritten and greatly Enlarged. 2 vols. 8vo, £3, 3s.

The Ancient Life-History of the Earth. An Outline of the
Principles and Leading Facts of Palæontological Science. Crown 8vo, with 276
Engravings, 10s. 6d.

NICHOLSON.
On the "Tabulate Corals" of the Palæozoic Period, with Critical Descriptions of Illustrative Species. Illustrated with 15 Lithographed Plates and numerous Engravings. Super-royal 8vo, 21s.
Synopsis of the Classification of the Animal Kingdom. 8vo, with 106 Illustrations, 6s.
On the Structure and Affinities of the Genus Monticulipora and its Sub-Genera, with Critical Descriptions of Illustrative Species. Illustrated with numerous Engravings on Wood and Lithographed Plates. Super-royal 8vo, 18s.

NICHOLSON.
Thoth. A Romance. By JOSEPH SHIELD NICHOLSON, M.A., D.Sc., Professor of Commercial and Political Economy and Mercantile Law in the University of Edinburgh. Third Edition. Crown 8vo, 4s. 6d.
A Dreamer of Dreams. A Modern Romance. Second Edition. Crown 8vo, 6s.

NICOLSON AND MURE. A Handbook to the Local Government (Scotland) Act, 1889. With Introduction, Explanatory Notes, and Index. By J. BADENACH NICOLSON, Advocate, Counsel to the Scotch Education Department, and W. J. MURE, Advocate, Legal Secretary to the Lord Advocate for Scotland. Ninth Reprint. 8vo, 5s.

OLIPHANT.
Masollam : A Problem of the Period. A Novel. By LAURENCE OLIPHANT. 3 vols. post 8vo, 25s. 6d.
Scientific Religion; or, Higher Possibilities of Life and Practice through the Operation of Natural Forces. Second Edition. 8vo, 16s.
Altiora Peto. Cheap Edition. Crown 8vo, boards, 2s. 6d. ; cloth, 3s. 6d. Illustrated Edition. Crown 8vo, cloth, 6s.
Piccadilly. With Illustrations by Richard Doyle. New Edition, 3s. 6d. Cheap Edition, boards, 2s. 6d.
Traits and Travesties ; Social and Political. Post 8vo, 10s. 6d.
Episodes in a Life of Adventure ; or, Moss from a Rolling Stone. Cheaper Edition. Post 8vo, 3s. 6d.
Haifa : Life in Modern Palestine. Second Edition. 8vo, 7s. 6d.
The Land of Gilead. With Excursions in the Lebanon. With Illustrations and Maps. Demy 8vo, 21s.
Memoir of the Life of Laurence Oliphant, and of Alice Oliphant, his Wife. By Mrs M. O. W. OLIPHANT. Seventh Edition. 2 vols. post 8vo, with Portraits. 21s.
POPULAR EDITION. With a New Preface. Post 8vo, with Portraits. 7s. 6d.

OLIPHANT.
Who was Lost and is Found. By Mrs OLIPHANT. Second Edition. Crown 8vo, 6s.
Miss Marjoribanks. New Edition. Crown 8vo, 3s. 6d.
The Perpetual Curate, and The Rector. New Edition. Crown 8vo, 3s. 6d.
Salem Chapel, and The Doctor's Family. New Edition. Crown 8vo, 3s. 6d.
Katie Stewart, and other Stories. New Edition. Crown 8vo, cloth, 3s. 6d.
Katie Stewart. Illustrated boards, 2s. 6d.
Valentine and his Brother. New Edition. Crown 8vo, 3s. 6d.
Sons and Daughters. Crown 8vo, 3s. 6d.
Two Stories of the Seen and the Unseen. The Open Door —Old Lady Mary. Paper covers, 1s.

OLIPHANT.   Notes of a Pilgrimage to Jerusalem and the Holy
Land.   By F. R. OLIPHANT.   Crown 8vo, 3s. 6d.

OSWALD.   By Fell and Fjord ; or, Scenes and Studies in Ice-
land.   By E. J. OSWALD.   Post 8vo, with Illustrations.   7s. 6d.

PAGE.
Introductory Text-Book of Geology.   By DAVID PAGE, LL.D.,
Professor of Geology in the Durham University of Physical Science, Newcastle.
With Engravings and Glossarial Index.   New Edition.   Revised by Professor
LAPWORTH of Mason Science College, Birmingham.   [*In preparation.*

Advanced Text-Book of Geology, Descriptive and Industrial.
With Engravings, and Glossary of Scientific Terms.   New Edition.   Revised by
Professor LAPWORTH.   [*In preparation.*

Introductory Text-Book of Physical Geography.   With Sketch-
Maps and Illustrations.   Edited by Professor LAPWORTH, LL.D., F.G.S., &c.,
Mason Science College, Birmingham.   Thirteenth Edition, Revised and Enlarged.
2s. 6d.

Advanced Text-Book of Physical Geography.   Third Edition.
Revised and Enlarged by Professor LAPWORTH.   With Engravings.   5s.

PATON.
Spindrift.   By Sir J. NOEL PATON.   Fcap., cloth, 5s.

Poems by a Painter.   Fcap., cloth, 5s.

PATON.   Body and Soul.   A Romance in Transcendental Path-
ology.   By FREDERICK NOEL PATON.   Third Edition.   Crown 8vo, 1s.

PATRICK.   The Apology of Origen in Reply to Celsus.   A
Chapter in the History of Apologetics.   By the Rev. J. PATRICK, D.D.   Post 8vo,
7s. 6d.

PAUL.   History of the Royal Company of Archers, the Queen's
Body-Guard for Scotland.   By JAMES BALFOUR PAUL, Advocate of the Scottish
Bar.   Crown 4to, with Portraits and other Illustrations.   £2, 2s.

PEILE.   Lawn Tennis as a Game of Skill.   By Lieut.-Col. S. C.
F. PEILE, B.S.C.   Revised Edition, with new Scoring Rules.   Fcap. 8vo, cloth, 1s.

PETTIGREW.   The Handy Book of Bees, and their Profitable
Management.   By A. PETTIGREW.   Fifth Edition, Enlarged, with Engravings.
Crown 8vo, 3s. 6d.

PFLEIDERER.   Philosophy and Development of Religion.
Being the Edinburgh Gifford Lectures for 1894.   By OTTO PFLEIDERER, D.D.
Professor of Theology at Berlin University.   In 2 vols. post 8vo, 15s. net.

PHILOSOPHICAL CLASSICS FOR ENGLISH READERS.
Edited by WILLIAM KNIGHT, LL.D., Professor of Moral Philosophy, University
of St Andrews.   In crown 8vo volumes, with Portraits, price 3s. 6d.
[*For List of Volumes, see page 2.*

POLLARD.   A Study in Municipal Government : The Corpora-
tion of Berlin.   By JAMES POLLARD, C.A., Chairman of the Edinburgh Public
Health Committee, and Secretary of the Edinburgh Chamber of Commerce.
Second Edition, Revised.   Crown 8vo, 3s. 6d.

POLLOK.   The Course of Time : A Poem.   By ROBERT POLLOK,
A.M.   Cottage Edition, 32mo, 8d.   The Same, cloth, gilt edges, 1s. 6d.   Another
Edition, with Illustrations by Birket Foster and others, fcap., cloth, 3s. 6d., or
with edges gilt, 4s.

PORT ROYAL LOGIC.   Translated from the French ; with
Introduction, Notes, and Appendix.   By THOMAS SPENCER BAYNES, LL.D., Professor in the University of St Andrews.   Tenth Edition, 12mo, 4s.

POTTS AND DARNELL.
Aditus Faciliores : An Easy Latin Construing Book, with
Complete Vocabulary   By A. W. POTTS, M.A., LL.D., and the Rev. C. DARNELL,
M.A., Head-Master of Cargilfield Preparatory School Edinburgh.   Tenth Edition,
fcap. 8vo, 3s. 6d.

POTTS AND DARNELL.
Aditus Faciliores Graeci. An Easy Greek Construing Book,
with Complete Vocabulary. Fifth Edition, Revised. Fcap. 8vo, 3s.

POTTS. School Sermons. By the late ALEXANDER WM. POTTS,
LL.D., First Head-Master of Fettes College. With a Memoir and Portrait.
Crown 8vo, 7s. 6d.

PRINGLE. The Live Stock of the Farm. By ROBERT O.
PRINGLE. Third Edition. Revised and Edited by JAMES MACDONALD. Crown
8vo, 7s. 6d.

PRYDE. Pleasant Memories of a Busy Life. By DAVID PRYDE,
M.A., LL.D., Author of 'Highways of Literature,' 'Great Men in European History,' 'Biographical Outlines of English Literature,' &c. With a Mezzotint Portrait. Post 8vo, 6s.

PUBLIC GENERAL STATUTES AFFECTING SCOTLAND
from 1707 to 1847, with Chronological Table and Index. 3 vols. large 8vo, £3, 3s.

PUBLIC GENERAL STATUTES AFFECTING SCOTLAND,
COLLECTION OF. Published Annually, with General Index.

RAE. The Syrian Church in India. By GEORGE MILNE RAE,
M.A., D.D., Fellow of the University of Madras; late Professor in the Madras
Christian College. With 6 full-page Illustrations. Post 8vo, 10s. 6d.

RAMSAY. Scotland and Scotsmen in the Eighteenth Century.
Edited from the MSS. of JOHN RAMSAY, Esq. of Ochtertyre, by ALEXANDER
ALLARDYCE, Author of 'Memoir of Admiral Lord Keith, K.B.,' &c. 2 vols.
8vo, 31s. 6d.

RANKIN.
A Handbook of the Church of Scotland. By JAMES RANKIN,
D.D., Minister of Muthill; Author of 'Character Studies in the Old Testament,'
&c. An entirely New and much Enlarged Edition. Crown 8vo, with 2 Maps,
7s. 6d.

The First Saints. Post 8vo, 7s. 6d.

The Creed in Scotland. An Exposition of the Apostles
Creed. With Extracts from Archbishop Hamilton's Catechism of 1552, John
Calvin's Catechism of 1556, and a Catena of Ancient Latin and other Hymns.
Post 8vo, 7s. 6d.

The Worthy Communicant. A Guide to the Devout Obser-
vance of the Lord's Supper. Limp cloth, 1s. 3d.

The Young Churchman. Lessons on the Creed, the Com-
mandments, the Means of Grace, and the Church. Limp cloth, 1s. 3d.

First Communion Lessons. 25th Edition. Paper Cover, 2d.

RANKINE. A Hero of the Dark Continent. Memoir of Rev.
Wm. Affleck Scott, M.A., M.B., C.M., Church of Scotland Missionary at Blantyre,
British Central Africa. By W. HENRY RANKINE, B.D., Minister at St Boswells.
With a Portrait and other Illustrations. Crown 8vo, 5s.

RECORDS OF THE TERCENTENARY FESTIVAL OF THE
UNIVERSITY OF EDINBURGH. Celebrated in April 1884. Published under
the Sanction of the Senatus Academicus. Large 4to, £2, 12s. 6d.

ROBERTSON. The Early Religion of Israel. As set forth by
Biblical Writers and Modern Critical Historians. Being the Baird Lecture for
1888-89. By JAMES ROBERTSON, D.D., Professor of Oriental Languages in the
University of Glasgow. Fourth Edition. Crown 8vo, 10s. 6d.

ROBERTSON.
Orellana, and other Poems. By J. LOGIE ROBERTSON,
M.A. Fcap. 8vo. Printed on hand-made paper. 6s.

A History of English Literature. For Secondary Schools.
With an Introduction by Professor MASSON, Edinburgh University. Cr. 8vo, 3s.

ROBERTSON.
English Verse for Junior Classes. In Two Parts. Part I.—
Chaucer to Coleridge. Part II.—Nineteenth Century Poets. Crown 8vo, each
1s. 6d. net.

ROBERTSON. Our Holiday among the Hills. By JAMES and
JANET LOGIE ROBERTSON. Fcap. 8vo, 3s. 6d.

ROBERTSON. Essays and Sermons. By the late W. ROBERT-
SON, B.D., Minister of the Parish of Sprouston. With a Memoir and Portrait.
Crown 8vo, 5s. 6d.

RODGER. Aberdeen Doctors at Home and Abroad. The Story
of a Medical School. By ELLA HILL BURTON RODGER. Demy 8vo, 10s. 6d.

ROSCOE. Rambles with a Fishing-Rod. By E. S. ROSCOE.
Crown 8vo, 4s. 6d.

ROSS AND SOMERVILLE. Beggars on Horseback : A Riding
Tour in North Wales. By MARTIN ROSS and E. Œ. SOMERVILLE. With Illustrations by E. Œ. SOMERVILLE. Crown 8vo, 3s. 6d.

RUTLAND.
Notes of an Irish Tour in 1846. By the DUKE OF RUTLAND,
G.C.B. (Lord JOHN MANNERS). New Edition. Crown 8vo, 2s. 6d.

Correspondence between the Right Honble. William Pitt
and Charles Duke of Rutland, Lord-Lieutenant of Ireland, 1781-1787. With
Introductory Note by JOHN DUKE OF RUTLAND. 8vo, 7s. 6d.

RUTLAND.
Gems of German Poetry. Translated by the DUCHESS OF
RUTLAND (Lady JOHN MANNERS). [*New Edition in preparation.*

Impressions of Bad-Homburg. Comprising a Short Account
of the Women's Associations of Germany under the Red Cross. Crown 8vo, 1s. 6d.

Some Personal Recollections of the Later Years of the Earl
of Beaconsfield, K.G. Sixth Edition. 6d.

Employment of Women in the Public Service. 6d.

Some of the Advantages of Easily Accessible Reading and
Recreation Rooms and Free Libraries. With Remarks on Starting and Maintaining them. Second Edition. Crown 8vo, 1s.

A Sequel to Rich Men's Dwellings, and other Occasional
Papers. Crown 8vo, 2s. 6d.

Encouraging Experiences of Reading and Recreation Rooms,
Aims of Guilds, Nottingham Social Guide, Existing Institutions, &c., &c.
Crown 8vo, 1s.

SAINTSBURY. The Flourishing of Romance and the Rise of
Allegory (12th and 13th Centuries). By GEORGE SAINTSBURY, M.A., Professor of
Rhetoric and English Literature in Edinburgh University. Being the first vol-
ume issued of "PERIODS OF EUROPEAN LITERATURE." Edited by Professor
SAINTSBURY. Crown 8vo, 3s. 6d.

SALMON. Songs of a Heart's Surrender, and other Verse.
By ARTHUR L. SALMON. Fcap. 8vo, 2s.

SCHEFFEL. The Trumpeter. A Romance of the Rhine. By
JOSEPH VICTOR VON SCHEFFEL. Translated from the Two Hundredth German
Edition by JESSIE BECK and LOUISA LORIMER. With an Introduction by Sir
THEODORE MARTIN, K.C.B. Long 8vo, 3s. 6d.

SCHILLER. Wallenstein. A Dramatic Poem. By FRIEDRICH
VON SCHILLER. Translated by C. G. N. LOCKHART. Fcap. 8vo, 7s. 6d.

SCOTT. Tom Cringle's Log. By MICHAEL SCOTT. New Edition.
With 19 Full-page Illustrations. Crown 8vo, 3s. 6d.

SCOUGAL. Prisons and their Inmates ; or, Scenes from a
Silent World. By FRANCIS SCOUGAL. Crown 8vo, boards, 2s.

SELKIRK. Poems. By J. B. SELKIRK, Author of 'Ethics and
Æsthetics of Modern Poetry,' 'Bible Truths with Shakespearian Parallels,' &c.
Crown 8vo, printed on antique paper, 6s.

SELLAR'S Manual of the Acts relating to Education in Scotland. By J. EDWARD GRAHAM, B.A. Oxon., Advocate. Ninth Edition. Demy
8vo, 12s. 6d.

SETH.
Scottish Philosophy. A Comparison of the Scottish and
German Answers to Hume. Balfour Philosophical Lectures, University of
Edinburgh. By ANDREW SETH, LL.D., Professor of Logic and Metaphysics in
Edinburgh University. Second Edition. Crown 8vo, 5s.

Hegelianism and Personality. Balfour Philosophical Lectures.
Second Series. Second Edition. Crown 8vo, 5s.

SETH. A Study of Ethical Principles. By JAMES SETH, M.A.,
Professor of Philosophy in Cornell University, U.S.A. Second Edition, Revised.
Post 8vo, 10s. 6d. net.

SHADWELL. The Life of Colin Campbell, Lord Clyde. Illustrated by Extracts from his Diary and Correspondence. By Lieutenant-General
SHADWELL, C.B. With Portrait, Maps, and Plans. 2 vols. 8vo, 36s.

SHAND.
The Life of General Sir Edward Bruce Hamley, K.C.B.,
K.C.M.G. By ALEX. INNES SHAND, Author of 'Kilcarra,' 'Against Time,' &c.
With two Photogravure Portraits and other Illustrations. Cheaper Edition, with
a Statement by Mr Edward Hamley. 2 vols. demy 8vo, 10s. 6d.

Half a Century; or, Changes in Men and Manners. Second
Edition. 8vo, 12s. 6d.

Letters from the West of Ireland. Reprinted from the
'Times.' Crown 8vo, 5s.

SHARPE. Letters from and to Charles Kirkpatrick Sharpe.
Edited by ALEXANDER ALLARDYCE, Author of 'Memoir of Admiral Lord Keith,
K.B.,' &c. With a Memoir by the Rev. W. K. R. BEDFORD. In 2 vols. 8vo.
Illustrated with Etchings and other Engravings. £2, 12s. 6d.

SIM. Margaret Sim's Cookery. With an Introduction by L. B.
WALFORD, Author of 'Mr Smith: A Part of his Life,' &c. Crown 8vo, 5s.

SIMPSON. The Wild Rabbit in a New Aspect; or, Rabbit-
Warrens that Pay. A book for Landowners, Sportsmen, Land Agents, Farmers,
Gamekeepers, and Allotment Holders. A Record of Recent Experiments con-
ducted on the Estate of the Right Hon. the Earl of Wharncliffe at Wortley Hall.
By J. SIMPSON. Second Edition, Enlarged. Small crown 8vo, 5s.

SKELTON.
The Table-Talk of Shirley. By JOHN SKELTON, Advocate,
C.B., LL.D., Author of 'The Essays of Shirley.' With a Frontispiece. Sixth
Edition, Revised and Enlarged. Post 8vo, 7s. 6d.

The Table-Talk of Shirley. Second Series. Summers and
Winters at Balmawhapple. With Illustrations. Two Volumes. Post 8vo, 10s.
net.

Maitland of Lethington; and the Scotland of Mary Stuart.
A History. Limited Edition, with Portraits. Demy 8vo, 2 vols., 28s. net.

The Handbook of Public Health. A Complete Edition of the
Public Health and other Sanitary Acts relating to Scotland. Annotated, and
with the Rules, Instructions, and Decisions of the Board of Supervision brought
up to date with relative forms. Second Edition. With Introduction, containing
the Administration of the Public Health Act in Counties. 8vo, 8s. 6d.

The Local Government (Scotland) Act in Relation to Public
Health. A Handy Guide for County and District Councillors, Medical Officers,
Sanitary Inspectors, and Members of Parochial Boards. Second Edition. With
a new Preface on appointment of Sanitary Officers. Crown 8vo, 2s.

SKRINE. Columba: A Drama. By JOHN HUNTLEY SKRINE,
Warden of Glenalmond; Author of 'A Memory of Edward Thring.' Fcap. 4to, 6s.

SMITH.
Thorndale; or, The Conflict of Opinions. By WILLIAM SMITH,
Author of 'A Discourse on Ethics,' &c. New Edition. Crown 8vo, 10s. 6d.

Gravenhurst; or, Thoughts on Good and Evil. Second Edition. With Memoir and Portrait of the Author. Crown 8vo, 8s.

The Story of William and Lucy Smith. Edited by GEORGE
MERRIAM. Large post 8vo, 12s. 6d.

SMITH. Memoir of the Families of M'Combie and Thoms,
originally M'Intosh and M'Thomas. Compiled from History and Tradition. By
WILLIAM M'COMBIE SMITH. With Illustrations. 8vo, 7s. 6d.

SMITH. Greek Testament Lessons for Colleges, Schools, and
Private Students, consisting chiefly of the Sermon on the Mount and the Parables
of our Lord. With Notes and Essays. By the Rev. J. HUNTER SMITH, M.A.,
King Edward's School, Birmingham. Crown 8vo, 6s.

SMITH. The Secretary for Scotland. Being a Statement of the
Powers and Duties of the new Scottish Office. With a Short Historical Intro-
duction, and numerous references to important Administrative Documents. By
W. C. SMITH, LL.B., Advocate. 8vo, 6s.

"SON OF THE MARSHES, A."
From Spring to Fall; or, When Life Stirs. By "A SON OF
THE MARSHES." Cheap Uniform Edition. Crown 8vo, 3s. 6d.

Within an Hour of London Town: Among Wild Birds and
their Haunts. Edited by J. A. OWEN. Cheap Uniform Edition. Crown 8vo,
3s. 6d.

With the Woodlanders and by the Tide. Cheap Uniform
Edition. Crown 8vo, 3s. 6d.

On Surrey Hills. Cheap Uniform Edition. Crown 8vo, 3s. 6d.

Annals of a Fishing Village. Cheap Uniform Edition. Crown
8vo, 3s. 6d.

SORLEY. The Ethics of Naturalism. Being the Shaw Fellowship Lectures, 1884. By W. R. SORLEY, M.A., Fellow of Trinity College, Cambridge, Professor of Moral Philosophy in the University of Aberdeen. Crown
8vo, 6s.

SPEEDY. Sport in the Highlands and Lowlands of Scotland
with Rod and Gun. By TOM SPEEDY. Second Edition, Revised and Enlarged.
With Illustrations by Lieut.-General Hope Crealocke, C.B., C.M.G., and others.
8vo, 15s.

SPROTT. The Worship and Offices of the Church of Scotland.
By GEORGE W. SPROTT, D.D., Minister of North Berwick. Crown 8vo, 6s.

STATISTICAL ACCOUNT OF SCOTLAND. Complete, with
Index. 15 vols. 8vo, £16, 16s.

STEPHENS.
The Book of the Farm; detailing the Labours of the Farmer,
Farm-Steward, Ploughman, Shepherd, Hedger, Farm-Labourer, Field-Worker,
and Cattle-man. Illustrated with numerous Portraits of Animals and Engravings
of Implements, and Plans of Farm Buildings. Fourth Edition. Revised, and
in great part Rewritten by JAMES MACDONALD, F.R.S.E., Secretary Highland
and Agricultural Society of Scotland. Complete in Six Divisional Volumes,
bound in cloth, each 10s. 6d., or handsomely bound, in 3 volumes, with leather
back and gilt top, £3, 3s.

Catechism of Practical Agriculture. 22d Thousand. Revised
by JAMES MACDONALD, F.R.S.E. With numerous Illustrations. Crown 8vo, 1s.

The Book of Farm Implements and Machines. By J. SLIGHT
and R. SCOTT BURN, Engineers. Edited by HENRY STEPHENS. Large 8vo, £2, 2s.

STEVENSON. British Fungi. (Hymenomycetes.) By Rev. JOHN STEVENSON, Author of 'Mycologia Scotica,' Hon. Sec. Cryptogamic Society of Scotland. Vols. I. and II., post 8vo, with Illustrations, price 12s. 6d. net each.

STEWART. Advice to Purchasers of Horses. By JOHN STEWART, V.S. New Edition. 2s. 6d.

STEWART. Boethius: An Essay. By HUGH FRASER STEWART, M.A., Trinity College, Cambridge. Crown 8vo, 7s. 6d.

STODDART. Angling Songs. By THOMAS TOD STODDART. New Edition, with a Memoir by ANNA M. STODDART. Crown 8vo, 7s. 6d.

STODDART.
John Stuart Blackie: A Biography. By ANNA M. STODDART. With 3 Plates. Third Edition. 2 vols. demy 8vo, 21s.
POPULAR EDITION, with Portrait. Crown 8vo, 6s.
Sir Philip Sidney: Servant of God. Illustrated by MARGARET L. HUGGINS. With a New Portrait of Sir Philip Sidney. Small 4to, with a specially designed Cover. 5s.

STORMONTH.
Dictionary of the English Language, Pronouncing, Etymological, and Explanatory. By the Rev. JAMES STORMONTH. Revised by the Rev. P. H. PHELP. Library Edition. New and Cheaper Edition, with Supplement. Imperial 8vo, handsomely bound in half morocco, 18s. net.
Etymological and Pronouncing Dictionary of the English Language. Including a very Copious Selection of Scientific Terms. For use in Schools and Colleges, and as a Book of General Reference. The Pronunciation carefully revised by the Rev. P. H. PHELP, M.A. Cantab. Thirteenth Edition, with Supplement. Crown 8vo, pp. 800. 7s. 6d.
The School Etymological Dictionary and Word-Book. New Edition, Revised. [*In preparation.*]

STORY.
Nero; A Historical Play. By W. W. STORY, Author of 'Roba di Roma.' Fcap. 8vo, 6s.
Vallombrosa. Post 8vo, 5s.
Poems. 2 vols., 7s. 6d.
Fiammetta. A Summer Idyl. Crown 8vo, 7s. 6d.
Conversations in a Studio. 2 vols. crown 8vo, 12s. 6d.
Excursions in Art and Letters. Crown 8vo, 7s. 6d.
A Poet's Portfolio: Later Readings. 18mo, 3s. 6d.

STRACHEY. Talk at a Country House. Fact and Fiction. By Sir EDWARD STRACHEY, Bart. With a Portrait of the Author. Crown 8vo, 4s. 6d. net.

STURGIS. Little Comedies, Old and New. By JULIAN STURGIS. Crown 8vo, 7s. 6d.

SUTHERLAND. Handbook of Hardy Herbaceous and Alpine Flowers, for General Garden Decoration. Containing Descriptions of upwards of 1000 Species of Ornamental Hardy Perennial and Alpine Plants; along with Concise and Plain Instructions for their Propagation and Culture. By WILLIAM SUTHERLAND, Landscape Gardener; formerly Manager of the Herbaceous Department at Kew. Crown 8vo, 7s. 6d.

TAYLOR. The Story of my Life. By the late Colonel MEADOWS TAYLOR, Author of 'The Confessions of a Thug,' &c., &c. Edited by his Daughter. New and Cheaper Edition, being the Fourth. Crown 8vo, 6s.

THOMSON.
The Diversions of a Prime Minister. By Basil Thomson.
With a Map, numerous Illustrations by. J. W. Cawston and others, and Repro-
ductions of Rare Plates from Early Voyages of Sixteenth and Seventeenth Centuries. Small demy 8vo, 15s.

South Sea Yarns. With 10 Full-page Illustrations. Cheaper
Edition. Crown 8vo, 3s. 6d.

THOMSON.
Handy Book of the Flower-Garden: Being Practical Direc-
tions for the Propagation, Culture, and Arrangement of Plants in Flower-
Gardens all the year round. With Engraved Plans. By DAVID THOMSON,
Gardener to his Grace the Duke of Buccleuch, K.T., at Drumlanrig. Fourth
and Cheaper Edition. Crown 8vo, 5s.

The Handy Book of Fruit-Culture under Glass: Being a
series of Elaborate Practical Treatises on the Cultivation and Forcing of Pines,
Vines, Peaches, Figs, Melons, Strawberries, and Cucumbers. With Engravings
of Hothouses, &c. Second Edition, Revised and Enlarged. Crown 8vo, 7s. 6d.

THOMSON. A Practical Treatise on the Cultivation of the
Grape Vine. By WILLIAM THOMSON, Tweed Vineyards. Tenth Edition. 8vo, 5s.

THOMSON. Cookery for the Sick and Convalescent. With
Directions for the Preparation of Poultices, Fomentations, &c. By BARBARA
THOMSON. Fcap. 8vo, 1s. 6d.

THORBURN. Asiatic Neighbours. By S. S. THORBURN, Bengal
Civil Service, Author of 'Bannú; or, Our Afghan Frontier,' 'David Leslie:
A Story of the Afghan Frontier,' 'Musalmans and Money-Lenders in the Pan-
jab.' With Two Maps. Demy 8vo, 10s. 6d. net.

THORNTON. Opposites. A Series of Essays on the Unpopular
Sides of Popular Questions. By LEWIS THORNTON. 8vo, 12s. 6d.

TRANSACTIONS OF THE HIGHLAND AND AGRICUL-
TURAL SOCIETY OF SCOTLAND. Published annually, price 5s.

TRAVERS.
Mona Maclean, Medical Student. A Novel. By GRAHAM
TRAVERS. Eleventh Edition. Crown 8vo, 6s.

Fellow Travellers. Third Edition. Crown 8vo, 6s.

TRYON. Life of Admiral Sir George Tryon. By Rear-Admiral
C. C. PENROSE FITZGERALD. With Portrait and numerous Illustrations. Demy
8vo, 18s.

TULLOCH.
Rational Theology and Christian Philosophy in England in
the Seventeenth Century. By JOHN TULLOCH, D.D., Principal of St Mary's College in the University of St Andrews, and one of her Majesty's Chaplains in
Ordinary in Scotland. Second Edition. 2 vols. 8vo, 16s.

Modern Theories in Philosophy and Religion. 8vo, 15s.

Luther, and other Leaders of the Reformation. Third Edition, Enlarged. Crown 8vo, 3s. 6d.

Memoir of Principal Tulloch, D.D., LL.D. By Mrs OLIPHANT,
Author of 'Life of Edward Irving.' Third and Cheaper Edition. 8vo, with
Portrait, 7s. 6d.

TWEEDIE. The Arabian Horse: His Country and People.
By Major-General W. TWEEDIE, C.S.I., Bengal Staff Corps; for many years
H.B.M.'s Consul-General, Baghdad, and Political Resident for the Government
of India in Turkish Arabia. In one vol. royal 4to, with Seven Coloured Plates
and other Illustrations, and a Map of the Country. Price £3, 3s. nat.

TYLER. The Whence and the Whither of Man. A Brief History of his Origin and Development through Conformity to Environment. The Morse Lectures of 1895. By John M. Tyler, Professor of Biology, Amherst College, U.S.A. Post 8vo, 6s. net.

VEITCH.
Memoir of John Veitch, LL.D., Professor of Logic and Rhetoric, University of Glasgow. By Mary R. L. Bryce. With Portrait and 3 Photogravure Plates. Demy 8vo, 7s. 6d.
Border Essays. By John Veitch, LL.D., Professor of Logic and Rhetoric, University of Glasgow. Crown 8vo, 4s. 6d. *net.*
The History and Poetry of the Scottish Border : their Main Features and Relations. New and Enlarged Edition. 2 vols. demy 8vo, 16s.
Institutes of Logic. Post 8vo, 12s. 6d.
The Feeling for Nature in Scottish Poetry. From the Earliest Times to the Present Day. 2 vols. fcap. 8vo, in roxburghe binding, 15s.
Merlin and other Poems. Fcap. 8vo, 4s. 6d.
Knowing and Being. Essays in Philosophy. First Series. Crown 8vo, 5s.
Dualism and Monism ; and other Essays. Essays in Philosophy. Second Series. With an Introduction by R. M. Wenley. Crown 8vo, 4s. 6d. net.

VIRGIL. The Æneid of Virgil. Translated in English Blank Verse by G. K. Rickards, M.A., and Lord Ravensworth. 2 vols. fcap. 8vo, 10s.

WACE. Christianity and Agnosticism. Reviews of some Recent Attacks on the Christian Faith. By Henry Wace, D.D., Principal of King's College, London ; Preacher of Lincoln's Inn ; Chaplain to the Queen. Second Edition. Post 8vo, 10s. 6d. net.

WADDELL. An Old Kirk Chronicle : Being a History of Auldhame, Tyninghame, and Whitekirk, in East Lothian. From Session Records, 1615 to 1850. By Rev. P. Hately Waddell, B.D., Minister of the United Parish. Small Paper Edition, 200 Copies. Price £1. Large Paper Edition, 50 Copies. Price £1, 10s.

WALFORD. Four Biographies from 'Blackwood' : Jane Taylor, Hannah More, Elizabeth Fry, Mary Somerville. By L. B. Walford. Crown 8vo, 5s.

WARREN'S (SAMUEL) WORKS :—
Diary of a Late Physician. Cloth, 2s. 6d. ; boards, 2s.
Ten Thousand A-Year. Cloth, 3s. 6d. ; boards, 2s. 6d.
Now and Then. The Lily and the Bee. Intellectual and Moral Development of the Present Age. 4s. 6d.
Essays : Critical, Imaginative, and Juridical. 5s.

WENLEY.
Socrates and Christ : A Study in the Philosophy of Religion. By R. M. Wenley, M.A., D.Sc., D.Phil., Professor of Philosophy in the University of Michigan, U.S.A. Crown 8vo, 6s.
Aspects of Pessimism. Crown 8vo, 6s.

WHITE.
The Eighteen Christian Centuries. By the Rev. James White. Seventh Edition. Post 8vo, with Index, 6s.
History of France, from the Earliest Times. Sixth Thousand. Post 8vo, with Index, 6s.

WHITE.
Archæological Sketches in Scotland—Kintyre and Knapdale.
By Colonel T. P. WHITE, R.E., of the Ordnance Survey. With numerous Illustrations. 2 vols. folio, £4, 4s. Vol. I., Kintyre, sold separately, £2, 2s.

The Ordnance Survey of the United Kingdom. A Popular
Account. Crown 8vo, 5s.

WILLIAMSON. The Horticultural Handbook and Exhibitor's
Guide. A Treatise on Cultivating, Exhibiting, and Judging Plants, Flowers, Fruits, and Vegetables. By W. WILLIAMSON, Gardener. Revised by MALCOLM DUNN, Gardener to his Grace the Duke of Buccleuch and Queensberry, Dalkeith Park. New and Cheaper Edition, enlarged. Crown 8vo, paper cover, 2s.; cloth, 2s. 6d.

WILLIAMSON. Poems of Nature and Life. By DAVID R.
WILLIAMSON, Minister of Kirkmaiden. Fcap. 8vo, 3s.

WILLS. Behind an Eastern Veil. A Plain Tale of Events
occurring in the Experience of a Lady who had a unique opportunity of observing the Inner Life of Ladies of the Upper Class in Persia. By C. J. WILLS, Author of 'In the Land of the Lion and Sun,' 'Persia as it is,' &c., &c. Cheaper Edition. Demy 8vo, 5s.

WILSON.
Works of Professor Wilson. Edited by his Son-in-Law,
Professor FERRIER. 12 vols. crown 8vo, £2, 8s.

Christopher in his Sporting-Jacket. 2 vols., 8s.

Isle of Palms, City of the Plague, and other Poems. 4s.

Lights and Shadows of Scottish Life, and other Tales. 4s.

Essays, Critical and Imaginative. 4 vols., 16s.

The Noctes Ambrosianæ. 4 vols., 16s.

Homer and his Translators, and the Greek Drama. Crown
8vo, 4s.

WORSLEY.
Poems and Translations. By PHILIP STANHOPE WORSLEY,
M.A. Edited by EDWARD WORSLEY. Second Edition, Enlarged. Fcap. 8vo, 6s.

Homer's Odyssey. Translated into English Verse in the
Spenserian Stanza. By P. S. Worsley. New and Cheaper Edition. Post 8vo, 7s. 6d. net.

Homer's Iliad. Translated by P. S. Worsley and Prof. Con-
ington. 2 vols. crown 8vo, 21s.

YATE. England and Russia Face to Face in Asia. A Record of
Travel with the Afghan Boundary Commission. By Captain A. C. YATE, Bombay Staff Corps. 8vo, with Maps and Illustrations, 21s.

YATE. Northern Afghanistan; or, Letters from the Afghan
Boundary Commission. By Major C. E. YATE, C.S.I., C.M.G., Bombay Staff Corps, F.R.G.S. 8vo, with Maps, 18s.

YULE. Fortification : For the use of Officers in the Army, and
Readers of Military History. By Colonel YULE, Bengal Engineers. 8vo, with Numerous Illustrations, 10s.

www.ingramcontent.com/pod-product-compliance
Lightning Source LLC
Chambersburg PA
CBHW032339280326
41935CB00008B/387